INTRODUCTION TO EXEGESIS

Robert L. Thomas

To Simon,
On our 6th wedding anniversary,
Love you always,
Lorna
x

1st June 2019

Tyndale Seminary Press

Introduction to Exegesis
By Robert L. Thomas
© 2017, Tyndale Seminary Press
Hurst, TX

ISBN-10: 1981277315
ISBN-13: 978-1981277315

Greek Bible text from: The Greek New Testament, Fourth revised edition, Edited by Barbara Aland and others, © 1993 Deutsche Bibelgesellschaft, Stuttgart.

TABLE OF CONTENTS

4

8

INTRODUCTION TO EXEGESIS

I. The Meaning of Exegesis

A. Derivation.

The word *exegesis* finds its ultimate source in the Greek verb ἐξηγέομαι. This Greek word is made up of two components, the combination of which means "lead out." The literal sense of the verb found in Greek lexicons includes such meanings as "lead" and "show the way." The metaphorical senses listed by various sources include "unfold," "narrate," "declare," "interpret," "tell," "report," and "describe." These latter meanings conceive of an intellectual type of leading or a leading of the understanding.

A noun corresponding to this Greek verb is ἐξήγησις. This noun, though not found in the New Testament, has meanings that are relevant to this discussion. They fall into two categories, both of which are metaphorical: "narrative" or "description" and "exploration" or "interpretation."

The New Testament occurrences of the verb are in the follow places (its NASB and NIV renderings respectively, are given in parenthesis after each reference): Luke 24:35 ("relate," "told"); John 1:18 ("explained," "made known"); Acts 10:8 ("explained," "told,"); 15:12 ("relating," "telling"), 14 ("related," "described"), 21:19 ("relate," "reported"). In summary, New Testament usages include only metaphorical meanings of the word such as "tell," "make known," "relate," "report," "describe," and "explain."

The English word *exegesis* also bears a relationship to the Latin verb *sagire* which means "perceive quickly." This Latin word is also the source of the English words *seek* and *sage*.

B. Usage

The dominant usage of "exegesis" has been in relation to the Bible. It names a field of investigation that has been and is very prominent in theological studies. It is therefore quite beneficial to discuss the word's usage as it designates a segment of theological discipline.

The phases of theological investigation as currently construed are multiple, yet they are integrally related to each other. The mode of their relationships to one another may be presented in various ways, of which the following discussion in Chare #1 is only one. Level one of the following scheme is the foundational stage or starting point for theological study and level four is the goal toward which it aims.

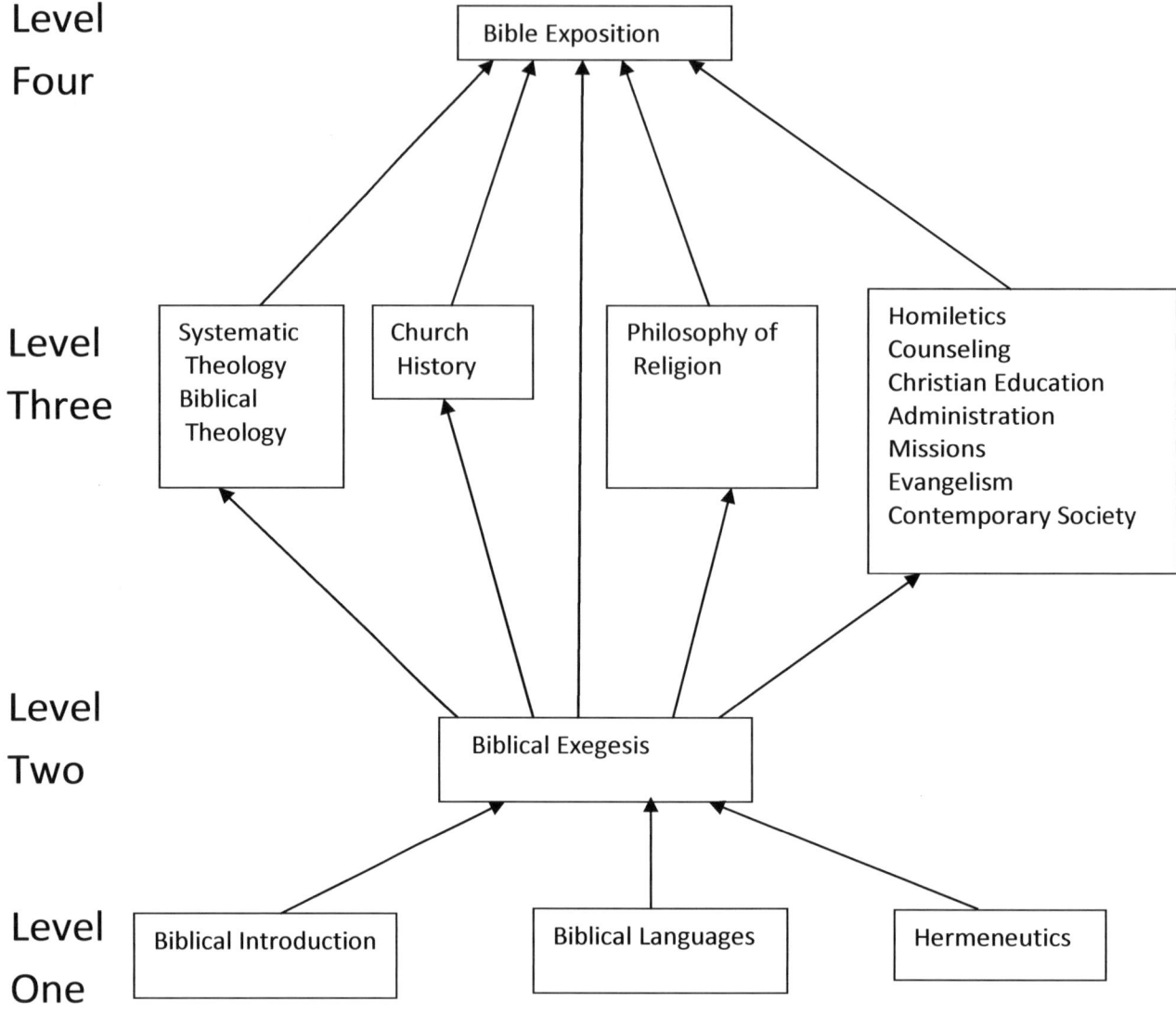

Schema of Relationships Between Fields of Theological Study

A somewhat detailed discussion of these areas of study is prerequisite to a thorough comprehension of the role filled by exegesis in the total field of theological studies.

Level One. The disciplines included at Level One are basic, and no orderly progress "up the ladder" is possible without a reasonable mastery of these. *Biblical Introduction* deals with many issues related to each book of the Bible. Where was it written? Was it originally written as a unit; or was it done in several parts and later put together? Along with answering these and other questions like them, Biblical Introduction supplies information about the historical backgrounds of writers, readers, locations, cultures, philosophies, viewpoints, and an almost endless list of other matters that are necessary to any attempt to grasp the meaning of the Bible. Also a very vital part of Biblical Introduction is Textual Criticism. This is the process of study whereby one establishes the exact words that were written by the original author, based on the thousands of documents resulting from the copyings of the originals.

That *Biblical Languages* must be learned to a reasonable degree is obvious. One cannot be conversant with what an author said without an ability to read his words in the language in which he wrote them. A translation is inadequate as are a plurality of translations. Languages differ from one another sufficiently so as to guarantee the loss of indispensable nuances of meaning in the translation from one to another. A good grasp of the biblical languages leads to a greatly heightened sensitivity to the message of the biblical writers.

Hermeneutics is the science of interpretation. It is "that branch of theology which defines the laws applied by exegesis." It determines the rules which are legitimate in the interpretive process and those which are not. Considerable confusion has been introduced into modern-day discussions of hermeneutics. Any effort to incorporate anything of a subjective nature or to insist that objective interpretation is impossible must be soundly repudiated. One example of such confusion is the ill-founded concept that contemporary application of a passage is integral to an understanding of what the passage meant in its original setting. Another example of corruption in hermeneutics is the policy allowing for reading into a passage a meaning that is derived from another passage. More attention will be given to these aberrations below. It is sufficient to note here the extreme importance of hermeneutics at the foundational level of theological investigation.

Level Two. Biblical Exegesis, and Biblical Exegesis alone, is based directly on the disciplines of Level One. This field of study consists of taking Biblical Introduction, the Biblical Languages, and Hermeneutics and investigating what is their combined impact upon a given passage of Scripture. In other words, Exegesis is the step in which the biblical text is interpreted. The meaning is discerned by utilizing valid principles of Hermeneutics in connection with data supplied by Biblical Introduction and the Biblical Languages. The cruciality of Exegesis is apparent. No one can with propriety move directly from Level One to Levels Three and Four. Level Two cannot be ignored or deleted without serious consequences. Standing alone as the intermediate step between what is foundational and the topical and practical disciplines which lie beyond it, Exegesis is irreplaceable. More of its importance will be shown in later observations.

Level Three. Systematic Theology is a very prominent representative of Level Three disciplines. *Biblical Theology* is closely associated with it. One cannot derive an accurate understanding of theology apart from a correct interpretation of the Bible. Hence, Systematic Theology must be based on Biblical Exegesis. The reverse cannot be true. Reversing the order can only result in a Systematic Theology tainted with subjective preferences and a Biblical Exegesis distorted by human prejudices. Neither can Systematic Theology use human philosophical reasoning as a basis, because the latter is punctuated with ill-founded logic.

One's interpretation of *Church History* is also deeply dependent on Biblical Exegesis. For example, the orthodox can be distinguished from the heretical only by measurement alongside biblical teaching. Church History also offers an almost unlimited supply of illustrations of biblical truth and of lessons to be learned in using Scripture.

Various fields of practical ministry are also placed at Level Three. One of these, *Homiletics* or sermon preparation, organizes the products of exegetical study into a form suitable for public presentation. Considerations of sermon delivery cannot be determinative in reaching exegetical decisions, but must instead be based on decisions already reached in regard to the meaning of the text. This is the only acceptable sequence.

Christian Counseling is nothing more than an application of the correct interpretation of Scripture to the situation of the counselee. If the application is not based on a sound interpretation, the counseling is secular rather than Christian. The same is true if the counselor reads some preconceived meaning into a passage so as to give secular advice an appearance of being Christian. All too often considerations of pragmatism have forced wrong meanings on portions of Scripture. Biblical Exegesis, on the other hand, yields advice worthy of heeding.

Christian Education that is truly Christian will likewise find its foundation in Biblical Exegesis. It is bad practice to assume that educational practice assumed to be profitable in a secular framework is automatically a legitimate Christian approach. It may have no biblical basis and even be unbiblical. One needs to be very wary of using the Bible to justify something that it does not support. This amounts to basing exegesis on educational philosophy. This, of course, is the opposite of the correct sequence. The correct order, basing Christian Education on Biblical Exegesis, has much of value to offer and is the only valid approach to Christian Education procedures.

Administration in a local church and other Christian organizations also must adopt guidelines that find a solid basis in biblical teaching. Secular administrative practices are not necessarily acceptable in a Christian setting. They may not be acceptable ethically. Or they may not succeed in Christian work because of a difference in objectives. The only administrative methods and procedures appropriate to Christian work are the ones that firmly rest on a correct interpretation of Scripture.

The same may be said about methodologies employed in *Missions*. A strategy and philosophy of Missions cannot be founded on pragmatism if it is to accomplish any worthwhile objectives for Christ. Missiological principles which foist upon the Scripture wrong meanings abound in the present day. Much more long-range benefit accrues as the result of those approaches that adhere closely to a right understanding of the biblical mandate, the one derived from a valid Biblical Exegesis.

Evangelism needs such a foundation too. The Bible is quite straightforward in telling what is to be done and how it is to be done in spreading the good news of the gospel. But if one is not careful to discern accurately what the Bible says, he may easily fall into the trap of reading man's ideas into some passage. So Biblical Exegesis is the only adequate foundation for evangelistic methodology.

How is a Christian to relate to *Contemporary Society*? What standard of ethics should be followed? Answers to these and similar questions show once again the critical importance of Biblical Exegesis. One can respond properly to current issues only in light of a correct interpretation of passages touching on these issues. To use a preconceived response as a basis for arriving at an interpretation is the reverse of right procedure. Following the steps in the orderly sequence inevitably leads to sound biblical decisions.

True philosophical approaches to Christianity also belong at Level Three, because only here can they be freed from antibiblical human presuppositions and approaches. These include disciplines like *Philosophy of Religion* and *Apologetics*. Arguments to prove the existence of God, explanations of the origin of evil, and the like need the safeguards of a thorough biblical foundation. These are possible only when a system is based solidly on well-done exegesis.

Level Four. The climax toward which all other areas of endeavor are geared is *Bible Exposition*. This is the setting forth of the teaching of a passage in a more popular form. Such a popular presentation draws upon all the other parts of theological study with a view to presenting the meaning of and lessons to be derived from a portion of Scripture in the most effective way. Clearly the heart of the presentation is taken from the exegetical step, but the other disciplines can be used to very good advantage in enhancing an exposition. This is the climax of Levels One, Two, and Three, because it is here that one "preaches the Word."

C. Definition.

The above survey helps to clarify the usage of the word "exegesis" in the theological realm by showing its relationships to other disciplines. A closer comparison with two of these disciplines is particularly beneficial, since these two have often been confused with Exegesis. The two are Hermeneutics and Exposition. As indicated above, Hermeneutics sets down principles which govern the understanding of literature. These are rules by which a game is played. Rules do not constitute the action entailed in playing the game, but rather govern the way the game is played. It is the same when comparing Hermeneutics and Exegesis. The former discipline is theoretical in nature and has the latter as its practical counterpart. The relationship between the two is, then, that Hermeneutics sets forth the rules of interpretation and Exegesis applies them to the text.

The relationship of Exegesis to Exposition is also especially significant. Exegesis is narrower and more technical than Exposition. It normally deals directly with the original languages of Scripture, while Exposition sets forth its explanation of a passage from a translation. It is more critically oriented, while Exposition cannot be because it must cater to the interests of a more popular audience. The distinction between the two is quite pronounced and important. Nevertheless, the link between the two is just as vital. All meaningful Exposition must be based on Exegesis. If it is not, it does not represent biblical truth fairly. It should expand upon, apply, and illustrate the interpretation derived from Exegesis, but it cannot exist independently. It must be solidly founded upon Exegesis.

Comparison of Exegesis with Hermeneutics and Exposition furnishes a convenient opportunity for drawing up a definition of Exegesis. It is "the critical or technical application of hermeneutical principles to a biblical text in the original languages with a view to the exposition or declaration of its meaning." This definition reflects

(1) the dependence of Exegesis on Hermeneutics,
(2) the practical nature of Exegesis compared to Hermeneutics,
(3) the critical nature of Exegesis compared to Exposition,
(4) the dependence of Exposition on Exegesis, and
(5) the attention of Exegesis to the original languages.

D. Significance.

Almost limitless elaborations on the usage and definition of Exegesis are possible. For instance, the importance of valid principles of Hermeneutics could be underscored, because without these Exegesis has nothing to rest upon. For the sake of placing some limit on the discussion of significance, however, only two observations about maintaining a correct sequence in theological study will be presented:

Observation #1: It is of utmost importance to remember that Exegesis precedes and is the basis of Systematic Theology, and not vice versa. This sequence must be adhered to rigidly. If not, a door is opened to read into a passage meanings that are foreign to what the Holy Spirit and the human author intended. One's theological prejudices become the eye-gate through which he interprets Scripture, and the true meaning is lost.

Doctrinal persuasions should not be a factor in settling exegetical issues. Confusion is widespread regarding this point. Some accept the need to base Systematic Theology upon Exegesis as a general rule, but want to reserve the right to reverse the order whenever a passage does not fit their systems. To make such an exception is devastating to an orderly exegetical approach.

Dana has described this wrong practice in relation to the past: "Formerly the Bible was viewed as a collection of doctrinal proof texts. Theological conceptions were formed by speculative reasoning and the Bible was appealed to for support. When this is the case, Scripture becomes a slave of doctrine rather than doctrine being the product of Scripture. The fallacy in this reasoning must be seen before exegetical theology can become a reality. . . . The dialectical approach is a name which could be given to the former method. This method is characterized in two ways: (1) dominant interest is to determine the relation of a given passage to a preconceived doctrinal position and (2) Formulate the interpretation which most easily harmonizes the passage under consideration with the doctrinal views of the interpreter" (H. E. Dana, *Searching the Scriptures* [New Orleans: Bible Institute Memorial Press, 1936], 162–63).

If, then, it is wrong for doctrinal considerations to influence exegetical matters, where does the well known "analogy of faith" principle fit in? Many assume it to be a principle of interpretation to be used along with other hermeneutical principles. But this cannot be done with propriety, as a careful reading of standard textbooks on hermeneutics will reveal. A knowledge of the Bible's teaching as a whole on a given subject presupposes a completed exegesis of *all* the individual passages related to that subject. This being the case, it is impossible to know what details of doctrine the Bible supports until the exegetical task on every related passage is finished. Hence, it is preferable to relegate the "analogy of faith" to a point subsequent to the exegetical procedure and use it as more or less of a "double check" on the results of one's exegetical investigation. If a conclusion about one passage seems to run counter to conclusions reached in other passages, the interpreter needs to return for further study and weighing of exegetical evidence to the passage which stands alone as contradictory.

The only accurate approach is Exegesis *before* Systematic Theology.

Observation #2: It is vital also to keep Exegesis before Exposition, as the basis of Exposition, and not vice versa. To shift any aspect of Exposition to a stage before Exegesis can only result in misinterpretation. Such a shift comes when a subjectively preconceived meaning finds its way into the interpretation.

This trend has arisen even in learned circles, among some who have suggested a new approach to interpretation. Smart furnishes an example of this: "Has the exegete any access to the original meaning of the text *except by way of the present meaning of the text for him*?" (James D. Smart, *The Interpretation of Scripture*, [LCM Press, 1961], 42). The words "by the way of the present meaning of the text for him" are another way of saying "a present application of the text in his own experience." "Application" is an aspect of Exposition, and there is no way to make an intelligent application until after thorough Exegesis has been accomplished. This approach to Exegesis, i.e. through the eyes of Exposition, represents the influence of existential thought on exegetical methodology. Existential thinking has thoroughly permeated this last part of the twentieth century. In theological studies it is seen in such areas as neo-orthodoxy, demythologizing the gospels, the new hermeneutic, and even in a number of treatments of Hermeneutics. Recent attention given to the matter of "contextualization" in missiological circles is most cases is more of the same. In Exegesis this mold of thought consists of the license of an interpreter to impose his own subjective opinions on the text. This is wrong because it places Exposition before Exegesis. It decides what the meaning can be and must be before letting the text speak for itself.

Another form of this same basic error can be found in many conservative evangelical circles. It springs up in private or group Bible study where there is inadequate guidance provided by a leader of the group. "This is what the verse means to me" is not a safe approach to Bible study. To be sure, the Holy Spirit applies Scripture to individual lives in various ways, but without a reliable interpretation as a foundation for applications, there is no safeguard to assure the legitimacy of such applications. What often happens is a person comes up with an application for a passage, whether from the Holy Spirit or not is uncertain, that appears to help him in his Christian life. Because of the application's apparent helpfulness, he automatically assumes the correctness of an interpretation of the passage which is necessarily demanded by the application. Yet this interpretation may be clearly opposed to the principles of grammar and the facts of history as they relate to that passage. Where did the error arise? It arose when considerations from personal experience were made the criteria for deciding the text's meaning. Or, in other words, Exposition was put into the driver's seat in reaching exegetical decisions.

Personal Bible study by every Christian is highly desirable, even a "must" for consistent Christian living, but there are limits to the degree of understanding attainable by a person without a knowledge of Biblical Introduction, the Biblical Languages, or Hermeneutics. He needs guidance. He needs the help of teachers whom Christ has given to the church to explain correct interpretations to him. Then, based on these, he can make valid applications of various portions of Scripture to his own life.

II. Erroneous Methods of Exegesis

Knowing correct procedure and carrying it out are often matters quite separate from each other. It is possible to know something quite well, but to have difficulty putting it into practice. This is especially true in Exegesis where procedures and information become so complex.

Valuable assistance in implementation has been found in surveying various erroneous methods of exegesis, because knowing what not to do can serve as a valuable reminder of what the correct procedure is. To know the mistakes made in the past is of great assistance in enabling the interpreter to reach a good balance in his exegetical method.

In each of the erroneous methods to be described there is value by way of attention to a positive feature of Exegesis, but in each case the positive feature has been pushed to an extreme. The result of not keeping various parts of the procedure in balance is a distortion of the text's meaning. This extremism or imbalance is related in most cases to not following a correct sequence in theological study (see discussion of "Usage" under IB above).

A. The Rationalistic Method

The prime consideration in the rationalistic method is human reason. Of course, human reason must be used in any adequate exegetical approach. It is when human reason becomes so dominant that it overrules other legitimate considerations, that the method becomes erroneous. For example, the miraculous elements of Scripture are unacceptable according to standards of human rationalism. The feeding of the five thousand with only five loaves and two fish is impossible, humanly speaking. So this humanistic method finds a purely natural explanation for how the feat was accomplished. They explain that the lad's generosity was contagious, and when he offered his own lunch to Jesus, it prompted others in the crowd to bring out their lunches that they had hidden and offer them to the rest of the people. According to this scheme, the alleged miracle of feeding so many people with so little has a purely naturalistic explanation.

The God-given reasoning faculty must be used in exegesis, but allowance must be made for its finiteness. Some parts of Scripture are supernatural and transcend the ability of the human mind to comprehend. At times natural laws are not adequate to explain its phenomena. Merely human philosophical reasoning (Level Three) must be postponed until Exegesis (Level Two) has been completed. It must not influence exegetical decisions, but must rather be guided by them.

B. The Mythological Method.

The mythological method puts the spotlight on the spiritual application of the text, but it does so to such an extent that the objective historical facts are written off as unnecessary. The historical aspect of the Bible is treated as myth which is comparable to the shell of a walnut. The shell is removed to get at the meat inside and is of no further use once the meat has been obtained. For example, the physical resurrection of Jesus Christ is the shell which, when broken away, is seen to contain the truth of Christ's ongoing spiritual life within the believer. Once this spiritual truth is grasped, the teaching of His physical resurrection may be discarded. It was not a real historical event, but only a myth.

The spiritual lessons of Scripture are vital, to be sure, but this does not necessitate relegating to a status of inconsequential, the historical framework in which they are found. On the contrary, the historical aspect is vital too. The end does not justify the means, i.e., the spiritual lesson cannot be a ground for saying it does not matter if the vehicle used to teach the lesson is deceptive. If the vehicle is not what it appears to be, historical, then the lesson has no factual foundation. But the spiritual lesson derives its validity from the factuality of its historical framework. For instance, believers cannot be motivated to seek the things which are above, if in fact Christ was not raised physically from the dead (Col 3:1–4). In seeking to make such an application of the text (Level Four), if one incorporates his preconception of the impossibility of physical resurrection (human philosophy, Level Three), he cannot help coming up with a tainted Exegesis (Level Two).

C. The Purely Historical Method.

The purely historical method is a type of extremism opposite to the mythological method. No place is allowed for spiritual lessons, while historical interests receive all the attention. This method fails to take into account that history is only a means to an end. The process of Exegesis cannot be limited to the means only. The biblical writers incorporated spiritual implications along with their historical treatments, and these cannot be ignored without doing violence to the meaning of the text. For example, John expressly states that his gospel has a spiritual purpose (John 20:3031).

This sample of extremism, however, serves as a reminder of the validity of basing Exegesis on history. History is an important anchor to sound interpretive procedure. But if it occupies the exclusive attention of the exegete, historical background (i.e. Biblical Introduction,

Level One) has become the end of theological study rather than a foundation for Exegesis (Level Two).

D. The Extreme Literal Method.

The extreme literal method makes insufficient allowance for figures of speech in Scripture. To the extreme literalist, to interpret a statement figuratively is tantamount to making it unhistorical. This is confusion, however, because history may very well be described in figurative language. It does not amount to a dilution of scriptural truth when one allows for figurative language. If the writer chose to use figurative language, the interpreter must likewise follow a figurative approach.

This extreme literal method is often associated with ultra-dispensational tendencies. This particular system is unwilling to allow "bride" and "body" as figurative descriptions of the same company of believers, the church. Or, it disallows "sleep" as a figurative representation of death, insisting that it apply literally to the immaterial part of man as well as to his body.

Recognition of figures of speech is an important part of Exegesis. Common sense, a knowledge of common figures of speech, and the context of a passage are the three primary means of recognizing figures of speech. A passage should be assumed to be literal unless one or more of these indicates otherwise. "When the plain sense of Scripture makes common sense, seek no other sense" (David L. Cooper).

By and large, the Bible is to be interpreted literally, and the extreme literal method is a reminder of this. But this literal framework does not rule out instances of figurative language.

E. The Allegorical Method

The allegorical method does injustice to the literal framework of the Bible by seeing too many figures of speech. Figures of speech are imagined where the author never intended them to be. Non-dispensational interpreters err in this respect by failure to allow that literal fulfillment of promises to Israel excludes their fulfillment by the church. All kinds of interpreters, including some dispensational ones, err here by forcing details of the text, such as minor details of a parable, to take on a meaning that was not intended. In some cases it is a matter of reading one's preconceived doctrines (Level Three) into the Exegesis (Level Two). In others it results from using a preconceived application (Level Four) to reach an exegetical decision (Level Two). Both are wrong.

Interpreters from all schools of thought are quite susceptible to the dangers of this method. An awareness of biblical truth as a whole has often led interpreters to attribute a facet of that truth to the wrong text. It is possible to expound truth erroneously by relating it to a passage which does not teach it. "The lessons one draws from a passage may be true, that is, in general keeping with Scriptural facts and with reality, simply because one is sufficiently acquainted with the Bible to be able to draw conclusions which are congruous with it. However, this does not imply that one's conclusions represent a valid exegesis of the passage. For valid conclusions are those which legitimately grow out of a particular passage, and not merely those which generally correspond with Biblical truth" (Robert A. Traina, *Methodical Bible Study* [Robert A. Traina, 1952], pp. 17475).

Perhaps the allegorical method is most noted historically for its mishandling of historical narrative. The Alexandrian school during the first four centuries of the Christian era considered historical data to be of secondary importance compared to the spiritualized meaning conveyed by the account. The spiritual meaning was often derived through efforts to harmonize the Scripture with the philosophical teachings of ancient Greece.

The element of value which can be drawn from the allegorical method is a reminder that the literal framework of the Bible allows for figurative language to be incorporated into it. Yet the interpreter must use extreme caution in labeling something a figure. Otherwise, he runs the risk of not doing justice to the literal force of the text.

F. The Dogmatic (or Dialectical) Method

Preconceived doctrines, no matter what their source, have often twisted interpretations of individual passages. If the interpreter's beliefs precede his understanding of the Bible, he is in danger of falling into the dogmatic method. His beliefs may come from a variety of sources: instruction by someone else, his own "general survey" of the Bible, personal experiences, philosophical reasoning, pragmatic considerations, or others. Whatever his beliefs when he comes to a passage, they need to be put aside, or else he is vulnerable to this pitfall. He will inevitably mishandle a passage to force it to fit his own preconceived notions.

McClain deserves great respect as a theologian, but even he was not immune to this problem. He wrote, "A general survey of the Biblical material indicates that the concept of a `kingdom' envisages a total situation containing at least three essential elements: first, a *ruler* with adequate authority and power; second, a *realm* of subjects to be ruled; and third, the actual exercise of the function of *rulership*" (Alva J. McClain, *The Greatness of the Kingdom* [Grand Rapids: Zondervan, 1959], 17). This generalization may be accurate for many places in the Bible, but some passages such as Matthew 13 are exceptions to this general rule. To approach these "exception" passages with the preconceived generalization can but result in a violation of accurate Exegesis. The error puts Systematic Theology (Level Three) before Exegesis (Level Two).

It is commendable that this method looks to the Bible for authority to support doctrine. But the Bible's authority needs to be used properly if it is to count. One needs to begin with the Bible and use it as the basis for formulating his beliefs, and not let his beliefs precede his exegetical understanding.

G. The Fragmentary Method

The fragmentary method does violence to contextual considerations in its approach to interpretation. It treats the Bible as though it were merely a collection of statements unrelated to each other, i.e. as though each stood apart from its immediate and broad context. The practice most often arises from a desire for a "proof text" to support preconceived doctrine or a preconceived solution to a practical problem. As worthy as the doctrine may be or as adequate as the solution may seem to be, this use of Scripture is completely unjustified.

When one handles the Bible this way, he in effect accuses the Holy Spirit, who inspired the Bible, of being irrational. He treats the Bible as though there is no reason for putting the verses where they are. Very often this injustice is committed by a preacher or teacher who knows what topic he wants to present, but does not have the opportunity to search out the place (or places) in the Bible which teaches it. Under the pressure of time he simply goes to a statement which superficially seems to support what he has already decided to say. It is far better to leave a topic untreated than to relate it to the wrong text.

James 1:5 has frequently been misused this way, as a promise to students that God will help them pass examinations. The verse in its context teaches that God will supply wisdom to

Christians suffering adversity so that they will be able to accept their trials with joy. There is quite a difference between these two meanings.

A good remedy for the fragmentary error is to select whole paragraphs for discussion rather than single statements or parts of statements. This compels the interpreter to take into account the relationship between various parts of a context.

The area of merit derived from the fragmentary method is its recognition of the authority of Scripture. Advice is worthy only as it finds its support in the Bible. But the authority of the Bible does not include the license for an interpreter to construe its teachings in an irrational manner.

H. The Cross-Reference Method

The cross-reference method is similar to the fragmentary method with one added feature. Not only does it isolate statements from their contexts, but it seeks to relate those which present similar lines of teaching to each other. The result is that of interpreting one passage in light of what is taught in an entirely different section. To do this is to fail to examine each literary unit in its own peculiar setting and to arrive at a wrong interpretation. No two passages are exactly alike, but the cross-reference method assumes that they may be.

A wrong interpretation of 2 Peter 1:20 has been used to justify the cross-reference method. The verse reads in part, "No prophecy of Scripture is a matter of one's own interpretation" (NASB) or "No prophecy of scripture is of any private interpretation" (KJV). In reality, however, the word translated "interpretation" (ἐπιλύσεως) and the context of the statement show that the statement pertains to the origination of Scripture, not to how it should be interpreted, i.e. in concert with other parts of Scripture. Each prophecy did not come from a separate individual, but all prophecies came from God (2 Pet 1:21). This is the message of the verse and of the context. It has nothing to do with interpreting one Scripture in light of another.

Neither does 1 Cor 2:13, which has commonly been used in the same way, support the cross-reference method. "Comparing spiritual things with spiritual" (KJV) should be rendered, "Combining spiritual thoughts with spiritual words" (NASB). Inspired apostles and prophets transposed their God-given thoughts into words in transmitting their inspired messages to other Christians. This is the teaching of 1 Corinthians 2:13. The verse does not speak of how Scripture is to be interpreted, but of how it came into being.

It is, of course, perfectly legitimate and even necessary to study individual words and grammatical constructions in various passages where they occur. Without this resource the interpreter would be helpless. This is how he derives information for use in the grammatico-historical method. But this is far different from transferring the total teaching of one passage to another passage which seems to be similar.

Each passage must be handled as a separate entity. The practice of interpreting ambiguous passages in light of unambiguous ones is no exception to this rule. In practice there are no unambiguous passages when it comes to controversial issues, because various interpreters will always defend opposing viewpoints in these controversial passages. The only recourse is to resolve the ambiguities of each passage separately.

When the process of Exegesis has been completed, then and only then is it proper to combine interpretations from various passages into a meaningful system.

I. The Systematized Method

The systematized method presupposes that every scriptural teaching must fit into a preconceived system. This preconceived system is the snag, because it is man-made, not God-given. It is premature to apply a system to any passage until Exegesis is completed. Only then does God's system become apparent in all its facets. Fitting a passage into a system prior to that is tantamount to placing Systematic Theology (Level Three) before Exegesis (Level Two).

For example, the Sermon on the Mount has often been interpreted by some as being addressed to the church, because their system dictates that there must be such a body of ethical teaching for the church somewhere in Jesus' earthly ministry. The only compulsion that such be true, however, comes from a humanly constructed system that demands it. Nothing in the context or in the Sermon itself requires that it be addressed to the saved of this age. In fact, various historical features argue very strongly against such an interpretation. There are, of course, many important applications of the Sermon to the church, but these must be based on the one interpretation that does justice to its historical setting.

The value of this method is to remind the interpreter that there is system in the Scripture. He must be extremely careful not to settle for anything less than God's system, however.

J. Contemporary Breaches of Grammatico-Historical Interpretation

[See "How to Remedy Drifting" on next page]

How to Remedy the Drifting

One dare not leave a discussion of erroneous methods of exegesis without attention to a more recent approach among evangelicals. It resembles a situation faced by Paul while writing 2 Timothy, and can best be seen through the eyes of 2 Tim 2:15. Second Tim 2:15 provides the remedy that would halt the doctrinal slippage that was happening in Ephesus and is happening in present-day evangelicalism. That verse and its context bring out several key elements in halting the drift.

(1) **Timothy's goal**. Notice Paul does not tell Timothy to attack the problem directly. He tells him to use indirect means. In essence he says, "Don't limit yourself to confronting these men directly, though sometimes that may be necessary, as 2 Tim 4:2b indicates ("reprove, rebuke, exhort with all longsuffering"). Rather your goal, Timothy, is to gain the approval of God by making yourself an unashamed workman. Concentrate on the positive side of teaching the Word of truth. You are to be a God-pleaser, not a man-pleaser. You are not to allow yourself to be distracted by mere human considerations. You are to have an eye that is single toward His will and glory. You are looking for His seal of approval. Strive to maintain His standards so that you have nothing to be ashamed of before Him."

Δόκιμον, the word for "approved" in 2:15, includes two ideas, that of being tested and that of being approved. Some never have an opportunity of being tested that church leaders have. It is a great privilege to be tested, but how each one responds to the test is crucial?

A Christian leader should also have as his goal not to be ashamed because he has done a shoddy job. Nor should he be ashamed of his work before men. Note Paul's elaboration on this theme at 2 Tim 1:8, 12, 16. "Hold your head up, Timothy. Do the right kind of job and you will not have to apologize to anyone."

(2) **The means**. The instrumental participle ὀρθοτομοῦντα [English, "accurately handling"] in 2:15 tells how Timothy can satisfy the standard set earlier in the same verse: "cutting straight the word of truth" or "handling the word of truth accurately." What figure Paul had in mind with this participle is uncertain. Sometimes in secular Greek writings it referred to a mason squaring and cutting a stone to fit exactly into a predetermined opening. Other times it referred to a farmer's ploughing a straight furrow in his field or to a tentmaker cutting a piece of canvass to exactly the right size. Still other times it referred to a road-maker constructing a straight road.

Because of the word's use in the LXX of Prov 3:6 and 11:5 ("In all your ways acknowledge Him and he will make your paths straight"; "The righteousness of the blameless keeps their ways straight") and the use of similar terminology in Heb 12:13 ("make straight paths for your feet"), Paul probably had in mind the figure of road construction. The specifications for the construction have to be exactly right.

Some have objected to trying to understand just what figure Paul had in mind. They say that all we need to do is to be in the same ballpark with our interpretation. They claim that knowing the broad sense of the Word is sufficient, and pressing to figure out the specific meaning is an example of λογομαχεῖν ("striving with words," "hair splitting," 2 Tim 2:14) that Paul forbids in the verse just before 2:15. That is not what Paul meant by λογομαχεῖν, however. In 1 Tim 6:4 the word refers to quibbling over words, so here he probably refers to verbal disputes that distract from the close attention that should be given the word of truth. "Truth" highlights the contrast between God's unshakable special revelation and the worthless chatter of the novelty seekers in Ephesus. A correlation exists between the quality of a *detailed* analysis of Scripture and maintaining doctrinal orthodoxy.

In 2:15 the command instills in Timothy's mind the importance of precision. Learning the general idea of what Scripture teaches is not sufficient, because it gives the novelty teachers too much room to roam in justifying their innovations. It allows them to shade the truth a little bit this way or that way in order to integrate the Bible with psychology, science, philosophy, anthropology, sociology, mathematics, modern linguistics, or some other secular discipline that allegedly has come up with additional truth from God's general revelation. An expositor's handling of Scripture has to be right. It has to be accurate. It has to be right on target.

General Introduction

The topic of this article will take us through an assortment of general considerations related to biblical hermeneutics. The first thing to do is to review the role of hermeneutics in relation to other subjects in the theological curriculum. In view of limited space, the review comes most easily in Chart #1.

CHART #1 (see next page for Chart #1)

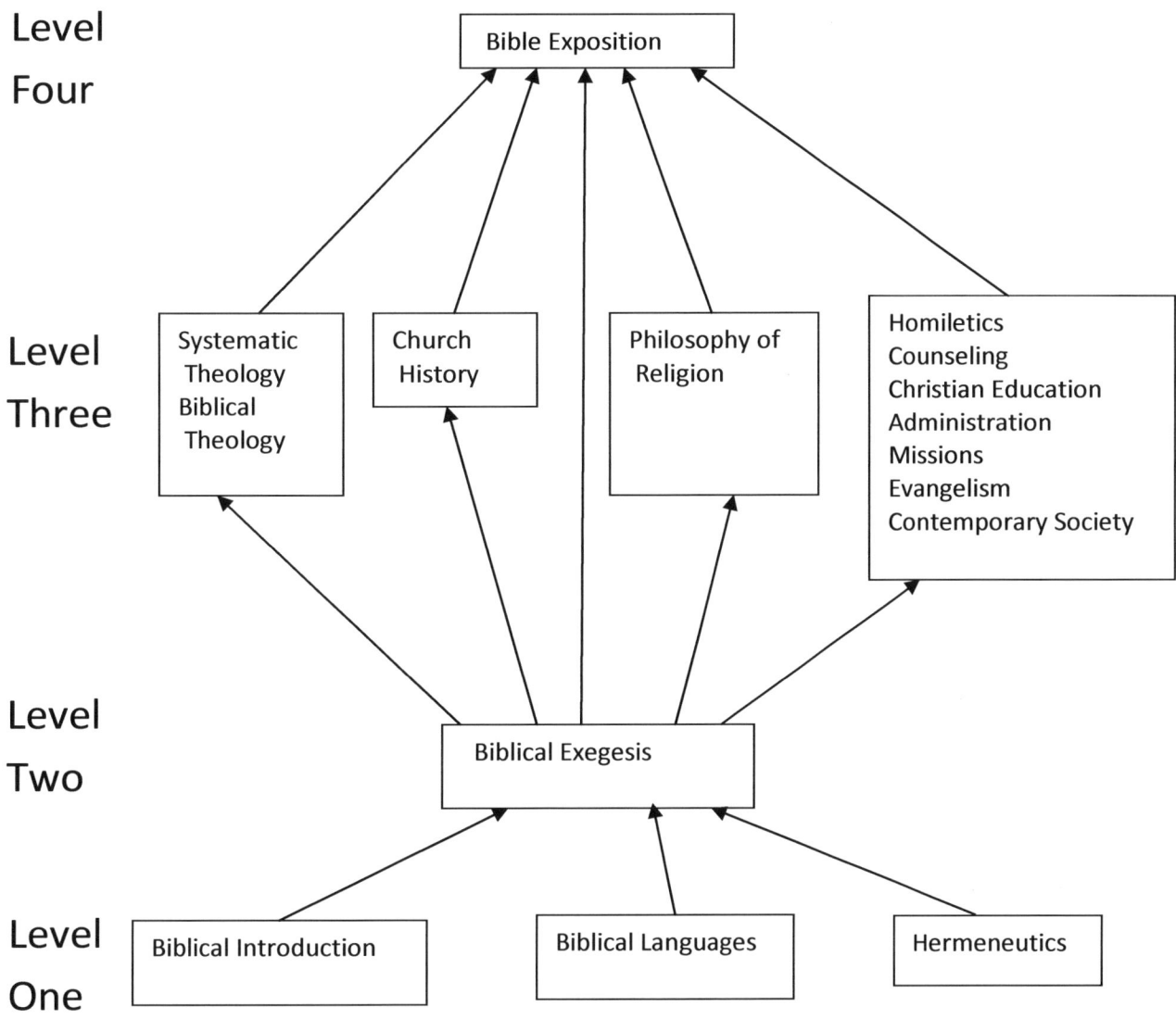

Level Four — Bible Exposition

Level Three — Systematic Theology / Biblical Theology · Church History · Philosophy of Religion · Homiletics, Counseling, Christian Education, Administration, Missions, Evangelism, Contemporary Society

Level Two — Biblical Exegesis

Level One — Biblical Introduction · Biblical Languages · Hermeneutics

Schema of Relationships Between Fields of Theological Study

Clarifying the Definition

      With the traditional grammatical-historical approach to exegesis, three areas of study constitute the foundational approach (i.e., Level One) to obtaining the meaning of a biblical text, if meaning is what you are seeking from a biblical text.

      At this point a parenthesis into the discussion is necessary because of recent confusion injected into biblical interpretation. Recent definitions of key terms have varied from traditional senses, making it necessary to recapture and emphasize the original senses. Four varying definitions of *hermeneutics* have in recent years been espoused,[1] but the correct definition is "a

---

[1] For a listing and a discussion of newly proposed definitions of various terms, see Robert L. Thomas, *Evangelical Hermeneuctics: The New Versus the Old* (Grand Rapids: Kregel, 2002), 20–27

set of principles." Of the four recently suggested meanings for *exegesis*, only "an implementation of valid interpretive principles" is correct. Recent proposals have listed as many as eight definitions of *meaning*, but only "the truth intention of the author" satisfies time-honored standards. The only one of four proposed definitions of *interpretation* that measures up to long-standing criteria is "an understanding of the truth intention of the author."

The proliferation of ramifications now attached to hermeneutical terminology is bewildering. No one intentionally created this state of confusion, but it is shameful that propounders of the new hermeneutical approaches did not utilize new terms for different meanings rather than assigning new meanings to old terms. It is almost as if there is an unconscious desire to retain a continuity with the past where little or no continuity exists. The practice of assigning new meanings to old words has resulted in an unusually high degree of uncertainty in communication among evangelicals. To what does one attribute such confusion?

Final answers to that question are evasive, but a proposal is that confusion in defining common hermeneutical terms has arisen at least in part from different hermeneutical principles that have come into play among evangelicals in recent years.

The Foundational Nature of Hermeneutics

Chart #1 shows the foundational role of hermeneutics, traditionally referred to as grammatical-historical principles. The grammar requires a knowledge of the principles of the biblical languages—Hebrew, Aramaic, and Greek. The history necessitates an awareness of the facts of history. Obviously, to utilize the principles of hermeneutics, a person must have a working knowledge of the original languages of the text of Scripture. He must know what books belong in the canon and must establish the exact text of the autographs of the books of the Bible. He gets help here from that portion of Biblical Introduction known as General Introduction with the area of Special Introduction furnishing him an understanding of the history surrounding the writing of each book.

Even here, however, confusion has arisen in the disciplines that stand beside hermeneutics at Level 1 as foundational to the practice of exegesis, which is at Level 2 in the Theological Curriculum. For one thing, traditional grammatical principles have come under assault by a relatively new discipline frequently referred to as Modern Linguistics. Modern Linguistics, though it still in a fluid stage of development, has challenged principles of grammar that have been a hinge and staple of grammar of long standing. Daniel Wallace's well-known *Greek Grammar Beyond the Basics* is full of the influence of Modern Linguistic principles that have strayed away from a centuries-old understanding of grammatical principles. A typical example of this is his "plenary genitive" in which he not only allows for but also advocates more than a single meaning for a specific grammatical construction.[2]

The English word "historical" has several meanings. It can be either history as a record of actual happenings simultaneous with the chronology of the narrative or history as interpreted by later chronological generations. Grammatical-historical principles have traditionally looked to the former of these definitions, but some evangelicals today are veering away from that meaning and opting for the dynamic concept of history. Progressive Dispensationalism is an example of

---

[2] E.g., D. B. Wallace, *Greek Grammar Beyond the Basics: An Exegetical Syntax of the New Testament* (Grand Rapids: Zondervan, 1996), 119–21.

the dynamic concept—i.e., an ongoing record of past events—versus a stable concept [past events connected with someone or some event].[3]

In light of such deviations from traditional definitions of various terms, when one speaks of following grammatical-historical principles of interpretation, he must be careful to define clearly what he means. Otherwise, his hermeneutical principles may be indistinguishable from those used by the new evangelical hermeneutics.

Recent Additions to the Foundation

Evangelical hermeneutics as now practiced in many and probably most evangelical environments has a complexion different from the traditional evangelical model. Level 1 in the Schema of Relationships Between Fields of Theological Study has a new member. The resulting new Schema looks like this.

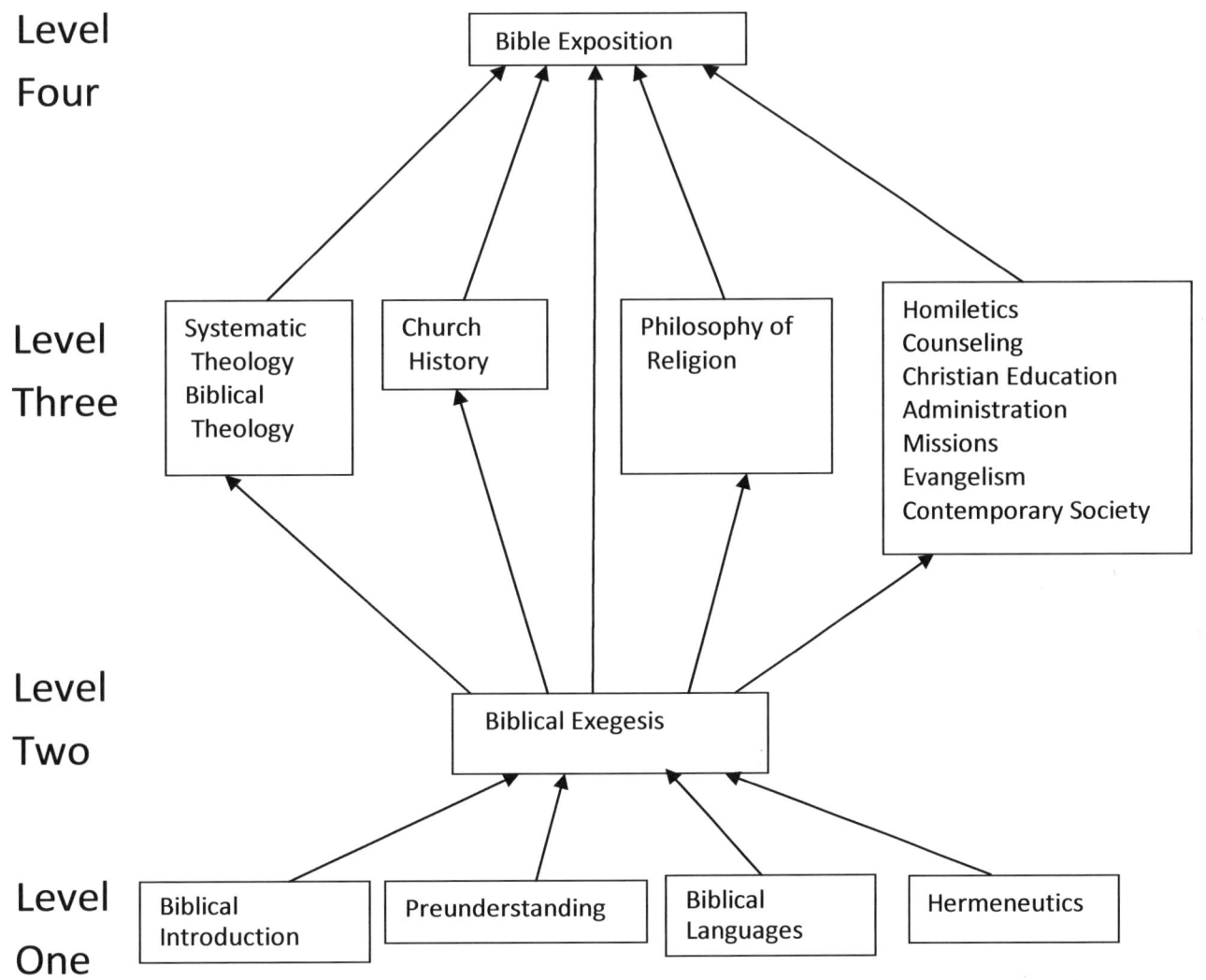

Schema of Relationships Between Fields of Theological Study

---

[3] E.g., Darrell L. Bock, "The Words of Jesus in the Gospels: Live, Jive, or Memorex?" in *Jesus under Fire*, eds. Michael J. Wilkins and J. P. Moreland (Grand Rapids: Zondervan, 1995), 81–84.

From the Schema one can see that the new resident at Level 1 is "Preunderstanding." Definitions of preunderstanding vary widely. The rise to prominence of an inclination toward an ill-defined preunderstanding is probably the most conspicuous difference from grammatical-historical practice in biblical interpretation. One has defined it as "hermeneutical self-awareness."[4] Many consider this addition to the arena of hermeneutical guidelines to be an absolute necessity and a healthy development.[5] The special attention devoted to the interpreter is ultimately the result of the Kantian philosophical emphasis on subjective reality as distinct from and more basic than objective reality.[6]

With many, preunderstanding is the principal determiner of one's eventual understanding of Scripture.[7] With others, it is possible to overcome preunderstanding partially and to approximate the text's objective meaning to some degree.[8] But with almost all, if not all, preunderstanding as a starting-point for the new evangelical hermeneutics is here to stay.[9]

What then is preunderstanding? For Silva, it is another name for prejudice and a commitment to the traditional view of inspiration,[10] but it also includes such things as a dispensational theology.[11] Another definition cited above is hermeneutical self-awareness[12] by which Osborne includes the impact of church history, contemporary meanings of word symbols, personal experiences, one's confessional tradition, and rational thinking.[13] McCartney and Clayton use "presuppositions" to speak of the same thing as "preunderstanding" and define them as one's views regarding life and ultimate realities and about the nature of the text being studied.[14]

KBH, following Ferguson, define preunderstanding as "a body of assumptions and attitudes which a person brings to the perception and interpretation of reality or any aspect of it."[15] They distinguish these from presuppositions, including in the latter such things as the inspiration of the Bible, its authoritativeness and truthfulness, its spiritual worth and

[4] G. R. Osborne, *The Hermeneutical Spiral: A Comprehensive Introduction to Biblical Interpretation* (Downers Grove, Ill.: InterVarsity, 1992) 7.

[5] Ibid., 267, 286–87; W. W. Klein, C. L. Blomberg, and R. L. Hubbard Jr. [hereafter KBH], *Introduction to Biblical Interpretation* (Dallas, Word, 1993) 7; M. Silva, in *An Introduction to Biblical Hermeneutics, The Search for Meaning*, co-authored by W. C. Kaiser, Jr., and M. Silva (Grand Rapids: Zondervan, 1994) 264. Blaising and Bock also recognize and welcome the change in evangelical hermeneutics with its incorporation of preunderstanding when they write, "And by the late 1980s, evangelicals became more aware of the problem of the interpreter's historical context and traditional preunderstanding of the text being interpreted. These developments . . . have opened up new vistas for discussion which were not considered by earlier interpreters, including classical and many revised dispensationalists" (Craig A. Blaising and Darrell L. Bock, *Progressive Dispensationalism* [Wheaton: Victor, 1993)] 35–36).

[6] For further discussion of when and how this recent change in evangelical hermeneutics came about, see Thomas, *Evangelical Hermeneutics*, 13–20,43–46.

[7] E.g., McCartney and Clayton, *Let the Reader Understand* 65; R. McQuilkin, *Understanding and Applying the Bible*, rev. ed. (Chicago: Moody, 1992) 19; M. J. Erickson, *Evangelical Interpretation: Perspectives on Hermeneutical Issues* (Grand Rapids: Baker, 1993) 88.

[8] For example, Klein et al., 115.

[9] E.g., Osborne, *Spiral* 286**Error! Main Document Only.**–87, 294; Erickson, *Evangelical Interpretation* 88.

[10] Silva, *Biblical Hermeneutics* 237, 245.

[11] Ibid., 264.

[12] Osborne, *Spiral* 7.

[13] Ibid., 14, 266, 267, 292.

[14] McCartney and Clayton, *Let the Reader* 13.

[15] Klein et al., *Biblical Interpretation* 99; cf. Duncan S. Ferguson, *Biblical Hermeneutics, An Introduction* (Atlanta: John Knox, 1986) 6.

effectiveness, its unity and diversity, its clarity, and a fixed canon of sixty-six books.[16] How this differs from preunderstanding is difficult to decipher, especially in light of their use of the same point—one's view of the miraculous—as an illustration of both preunderstanding and presuppositions.[17]

Johnson lists five hermeneutical premises which he apparently equates with preunderstanding: the literal, the grammatical, the historical, the textual design, and the theological.[18] McQuilkin's name for preunderstanding is presuppositions. He gives the following: as a supernatural book, the Bible is authoritative and trustworthy; as a natural book, it uses human communication.[19] Tate refers to preunderstanding as the interpreter's present horizon of understanding, i.e., the colored lenses through which the reader views the text.[20] He seems to distinguish preunderstanding, at least to some extent, from presuppositions which he classifies as reader presuppositions and theological presuppositions.[21]

Uncertainty among hermeneutical theoreticians regarding what constitutes preunderstanding is widespread, resulting in multiple understandings of "preunderstanding." They agree only regarding its influence on the outcome of the interpretive endeavor. In line with this acknowledged subjectivism, most advocate that one must view his own interpretive conclusions as tentative.[22] This relativism leads easily to divesting the Scripture of any value in stating propositional truth, though one writer would limit the uncertainty to ambiguous areas such as sovereignty and responsibility, the millennial issue, and church government.[23] Others pass off this uncertainty as tolerance of fellow believers for the sake of unity—i.e., "I don't agree with your conclusions . . . , but I concede your interpretation."[24] If allowed to progress to its logical end, however, this outlook leads eventually to a realization that what we have considered to be cardinal dogmas—such as the deity of Christ, His second coming, and His substitutionary atonement—are merely the myopic conclusions of Western, white, middle-class, male interpretations.[25] Such a hermeneutical approach spells the end of meaningful Christian doctrine, and plays right into the hands of postmodernism and deconstructionism.

Reasons Why the Current Foundation Is Shaky

The new and primary role given to preunderstanding in the exegetical process conflicts sharply with traditional grammatical-historical principles. It injects subjective elements into interpretation which, until the emergence of new hermeneutical principles in the 1970s and early 1980s, have been purposely and consciously shunned among evangelicals in quests for the meaning of Scripture.

Those who studied hermeneutics in many, if not most, evangelical colleges and seminaries during the 1950s and before learned the importance of seeking objectivity in

---

[16] Ibid., 88–93.

[17] Ibid., 94, 100. They distinguish preunderstanding from prejudice also by making the latter a subcategory of preunderstanding (ibid., 99 n. 34, 100).

[18] Johnson, E. E. Johnson, *Expository Hermeneutics: An Introduction* (Grand Rapids: Zondervan, 1990) 31–53.

[19] McQuilkin, *Understanding and Applying* 20–23.

[20] W. R. Tate, *Biblical Interpretation: An Integrated Approach* (Peabody, Mass.: Hendrickson, 1991) 166.

[21] Ibid., 166–70.

[22] E.g., Klein *et al.*, *Biblical Interpretation* 306; Kaiser, *Biblical Hermeneutics*, 88; McCartney and Clayton, *Let the Reader* 164; Osborne, *Spiral* 307.

[23] Osborne, *Spiral* 287.

[24] Klein *et al.*, *Biblical Interpretation* 150-51; cf. 139–44.

[25] Cf. Erickson, *Evangelical Interpretation* 125.

interpretation, i.e., letting the text speak for itself without imposing personal biases into what the meaning might be. Ramm has put it this way:

> The true philological spirit, or critical spirit, or scholarly spirit, in Biblical interpretation has as its goal to discover the original meaning and intention of the text. Its goal is *exegesis*—to lead the meaning out of the text and shuns *eisogesis*—bringing a meaning to the text. . . .
>
> It is very difficult for any person to approach the Holy Scriptures free from prejudices and assumptions which distort the text. The danger of having a set theological system is that in the interpretation of Scripture the system tends to govern the interpretation rather than the interpretation correcting the system. . . .
>
> Calvin said that the Holy Scripture is not a tennis ball that we may bounce around at will. Rather it is the Word of God whose teachings must be learned by the most impartial and objective study of the text.[26]

Before the hermeneutical revolution that began among evangelicals during the 1970s and 1980s, objectivity was the highest priority. Beginning study of a text with a conscious preunderstanding of what it would yield was unthought of, as Ramm so emphatically stated before he ever conceived that evangelicals would advocate letting subjective considerations become a part of interpretation. He allowed that such occurred with nonevangelicals such as Butlmann and Tillich, but insisted that it not happen among those of evangelical persuasions.[27]

Terry supported the same quest for objectivity, expressing it in different terms:

> The objectionable feature of these methods [i.e., the Apologetic and Dogmatic methods] is that they virtually set out with the ostensible purpose of maintaining a preconceived hypothesis. The hypothesis may be right, but the procedure is always liable to mislead. It presents the constant temptation to *find* desired meanings in words and ignore the scope and general purpose of the writer. There are cases where it is well to assume a hypothesis, and use it as a means of investigation; but in all such cases the hypothesis is only assumed tentatively, not affirmed dogmatically. In the exposition of the Bible, apology and dogma have a legitimate place. The true apology defends the sacred books against an unreasonable and captious criticism, and presents their claims to be regarded as the revelation of God. But this can be done only by pursuing rational methods, and by the use of a convincing logic. So also the Scriptures are profitable for dogma, but the dogma must be shown to be a legitimate teaching of the Scripture, not a traditional idea attached to the Scripture. . . .
>
> The systematic expounder of Scripture doctrine . . . must not import into the text of Scripture the ideas of later times, or build upon any words or passages a dogma which they do not legitimately teach. The apologetic and dogmatic methods of interpretation which proceed from the standpoint of a formulated creed, and appeal to all words and sentiments scattered here and there in the Scriptures, which may by any possibility lend support to a foregone conclusion, have been condemned already. . . . By such methods many false notions have been urged upon men as matters of faith. But no man has a right

---

[26] Bernard Ramm, *Protestant Biblical Interpretation: A Textbook of Hermeneutics* (Grand Rapids: Baker, 1970) 115–16.
[27] Ibid.

to foist into his expositions of Scripture his own dogmatic conceptions, or those of others, and then insist that these are an essential part of divine revelation. Only that which is clearly read therein, or legitimately proved thereby, can be properly held as scriptural doctrine.[28]

In his classic work on hermeneutics Terry insisted on letting the text speak for itself, without allowing ideas foreign to the text to intervene in its interpretation. Though he lived long before the notion of beginning the exegetical process with a preunderstanding of what it was going to say had made its appearance among conservatives, he clearly sought to obtain an objective awareness of what biblical writers intended when they penned the words of Scripture. The only assumption he made was unavoidable: he was dealing with an inspired book, not an uninspired one.[29]

That has always been the goal of grammatical-historical interpretation until the recent changeover in heremeneutical principles among some evangelicals. The method consciously seeks to rule out any personal biases or predispositions in order to let the rules of grammar and the facts of history of each text speak for themselves. That quest for objectivity has allowed the Bible to yield propositional truths that constitute a sure foundation for evangelical Christianity.

The present state of affairs among evangelicals is a far cry from the certainty God intended His people to have, however. He gave revelations to Paul and others "that we might know the things freely given to us by God" (1 Cor 2:12, emphasis added), not that we might tentatively theorize regarding what God may have given us.

Exegesis is not an exercise designed to correct my preunderstanding as the hermeneutical circle or hermeneutical spiral approaches contend. It is rather a scientific exercise designed to allow the text to speak for itself.

Often I hear the objection, "Impossible! A person cannot divest himself of a preunderstanding about what a text should mean. Every person is biased. He should recognize his own bias and let the text correct it. He should continue going back and forth between a corrected preunderstanding and the text a number of times, each time getting closer to what the text means." Note the frequency with which current evangelicals refer to the "Hermeneutical Circle" or the "Hermeneutical Spiral." Since the Reformation, Protestants have proposed that the interpreter should begin with a *tabla rasa*, a clean slate, and let the text speak for itself. Again, yet some still say, "Impossible."

The following analogy may help portray what an approach to hermeneutics should be. One's quest for objectivity in interpretation resembles his quest for Christian sanctification. Rather than expending all his energies explaining why he cannot attain absolute holiness, he should set his sights on the target of being holy as God is holy (1 Pet 1:16). The fact that he cannot attain unblemished holiness does not excuse him from continuing to pursue it without becoming preoccupied with reasons why he must fail. So it is in hermeneutics and exegesis. The goal is the objective meaning of Scripture. We cannot become distracted from pursuing it. It is within the capability of the Spirit-illumined believer to arrive at objective meaning—i.e., the meaning God intended to transmit through His human authors. This is possible, not because we are so expert in our interpretations, but because God is an expert communicator in His Word. A failure to have objectivity as a goal is just as serious as a failure to have Christian sanctification

---

[28] Milton S. Terry, *Biblical Hermeneutics: A Treatise on the Interpretation of the Old and New Testaments*, 2nd ed. (reprint; Grand Rapids, Zondervan, n.d.) 171-72, 583–84.
[29] Ibid., 137–50.

as a goal because of the lesson learned from Paul through 2 Tim 2:15. If Paul taught that lesson to Timothy in his study of Scripture, it certainly is a lesson for twenty-first-century Christians.

Traditional grammatical-historical guidelines have enough principles to enable exegetes to dispense with the "Circle" and the "Spiral" approaches to hermeneutics.

The Source of Preunderstandings

With the variety of understandings of "preunderstanding," settling a single source or even a specific number of sources for preunderstanding must be very selective, because each person's preunderstanding will differ from the next person's. Yet the probability is high that most preunderstandings draw from the disciplines at Levels 3 and 4 in the Theological Schema.

For example, a homiletician [i.e., Levels 3 and 4] might come up with a polished outline for the passage from which he wishes to preach before accomplishing his exegetical analysis. His exegetical analysis must then conform to the communicatively effective outline he has discovered. Suppose his exegetical study does not match his preconceived outline. That has a deleterious impact on his exegesis.

As suggested earlier in this discussion, Dispensationalism—another Level 3 discipline— can be a preunderstanding that needs to be corrected in the exegetical process. With some this may be true. Personally, I have leaned over backward to keep a theological system separate from an exegetical analysis of a passage. In doing so, I exert every effort to be first and foremost a grammatical-historical practioner. In implementing grammatical-historical principles, I find myself in the dispensational camp at Level 3. Yet I need to beware lest at any time the order should be reversed. If it should become reversed, I am just as guilty as the covenant theologian, the new covenant theologian, the kingdom theologian, or the progressive dispensational theologian in allowing preunderstanding a role in Level 1.[30]

A hot issue in contemporary society—a Level 3 category—is the effect of global warming on the environment. If I am convinced I need to deal with this in my Bible exposition, I will search high and low to find a passage that teaches the danger of global warming. Since I have made up my mind what I will find in a text, the principles of grammatical-historical exegesis will fall by the wayside as I look for a text dealing with that topic.

In the realm of historical theology—another Level 3 category—at a recent point in church history, the practice of historical criticism became prominent. If I am convinced that an inerrantist can use this device to enhance study of the Gospels, that will become my preunderstanding at Level 1. Yet that preunderstanding has proven to be badly mistaken.

Any pet subject, theological or otherwise, can become a preunderstanding at Level 1.

The above four suggestions amount to taking disciplines rightly belonging to Levels 3 and 4 and inserting them at Level 1 as preunderstandings, thus throwing the whole exegetical process out of balance. These are but a sampling of the endless number of assumptions that throw evangelical interpretations into a quagmire of subjectivism in tune with the contemporary deconstructionism of this postmodern era.

Principles of Grammatical-Historical Hermeneutics Frequently Undermined

With no pretense of being exhaustive, one could list a number of grammatical-historical principles that are violated by the new evangelical hermeneutics:

---

[30] Note my article in the Spring 2009 issue of *The Master's Seminary Journal*, entitled "Dispensationalism's Role in the Public Square."

(1) Cultural uniqueness of the biblical texts means that there is something special about the Hebrew, Aramaic, and Greek text of Scripture.[31]

(2) The uniqueness and superiority of special revelation demands that special revelation always deserves ultimate priority over anything that general revelation has to offer.[32]

(3) The principle of single meaning, the single meaning intended by the author and understood by the immediate readers, has dominant control over any legitimate practical application.[33]

(4) The distinction between interpretation and application must be maintained; that application must be completely distinct from interpretation but controlled by correct interpretation is mandatory.[34]

(5) Certainty resting on the biblical text is an exegete's responsibility. Scripture was given that we may know, not that we may question which meaning is correct.[35]

(6) Any personal addition to the grammatical-historical foundation of exegesis is a distortion.[36]

(7) Perspecuity of the biblical text—use of sound, not secret-coded, principles—will yield the correct meaning of the text.[37]

(8) Historical accuracy of the biblical text means that a correct hermeneutics yields precise facts of history.[38]

(9) Literal understanding is assumed unless the text justifies a nonliteral approach. Literal meaning is the first resort, not a last resort.[39]

(10) Inerrancy of the text is the first and only legitimate preunderstanding of a biblical text.

Recently Emerging Bogus Systems. *Evangelical Hermeneutics* describes five systems that have arisen in recent years, whose origins are traceable to the new evangelical hermeneutics. They are

> Progressive Dispensationalism[40]
> Evangelical Feminism[41]
> Evangelical Missiology[42]
> Theonomy[43]
> Open Theism.[44]

The list is growing at a rapid rate. With the growing inroads of preunderstanding at Level 1 in Theological Study, the rate is bound to increase. Since *Evangelical Hermeneutics* was released in

---

[31] Cf. Thomas, *Evangelical Hermeneutics*, 214–17.
[32] Ibid., 124–31.
[33] Ibid., 142–55.
[34] Ibid., 169-175
[35] Ibid., 201–3, 226–27.
[36] Ibid., 208–14.
[37] Ibid., 281–91.
[38] Ibid., 274–80.
[39] Ibid., 229–33.
[40] Ibid., 351–72.
[41] Ibid., 373–405.
[42] Ibid., 407–449.
[43] Ibid., 451–71.
[44] Ibid., 473–505.

2002, evangelicalism has already experienced the impact of such "-isms" as the New Perspective on Paul,[45] the Emerging Church, New Covenant Theology, a new allegedly Bible-based Noncessationist Movement.[46] Three new "-isms" that are currently arising among evangelicals are speech-act theory, intertextuality, and spiritual formation. All of this has happened since the incorporation of the new evangelical hermeneutics in the 1970s and early 1980s. When examined closely, each of these has its own preunderstanding that throws the exegetical process all out of whack.

The Needed Response

That theological slippage is targeting the evangelical church today as it did in the days of Paul's advice to Timothy in 2 Tim 2:15 is without question. Very obviously, the slippage results from the new evangelical hermeneutics that began taking its toll in the 1970s and 1980s. May God awaken His church to her need of restoring sound principles that let the biblical text speak for itself without imposing foreign meanings on it.

III. THE GRAMMATICO-HISTORICAL METHOD

A. The Definition

The Grammatico-historical method of exegesis is a study designed to discover the meaning of a text that is dictated by the principles of grammar and the facts of history. This is the method by which other books are interpreted. It seeks to find the meaning which the authors of Scripture intended to convey and the meaning comprehended by the recipients (Milton Terry, *Biblical Hermeneutics*, [Grand Rapids: Zondervan, n.d.] 173).

Of course, special allowances must be made for the inspiration of the Bible. It must be remembered that divine and human authors worked together to produce the inspired text. This raises the possibility that at times the Scripture may have a meaning that exceeds the comprehension of the human author ("a fuller sense," i.e. *sensus plenior*; cf. 1 Peter 1:1012). Provision must be made for such a situation.

Special provision must also be made for the prerogative of the Holy Spirit as the ultimate interpreter of the Scripture. Just as the Bible is a divine-human book with the divine element overshadowing the human, both perspectives are required for an adequate interpretation of it, with the stipulation that only the Holy Spirit can in the last analysis lead to a correct understanding.

A further stipulation that grows out of the first two is that of the inerrancy of the Bible. It is not the task of exegesis to prove inerrancy. It accepts inerrancy as the most probable alternative and builds upon this assumption.

Hence, a more specific definition of the Grammatico-historical method of Exegesis as applied to the Bible is "a study of inspired Scripture designed to discover under the guidance of the Holy Spirit the meaning of a text dictated by the principles of grammar and the facts of history."

---

[45] See Robert L. Thomas, "Hermeneutics of the New Perspective on Paul," *The Master's Seminary Journal* 16/2 (Fall 2005): 393–16.
[46] See Robert L. Thomas, "Hermeneutics of Noncessationism," *The Master's Seminary Journal* 14/2 (Fall 2003): 287–310.

B. The Practice

To practice the Grammatico-historical Method of Exegesis as defined specifically in relation to the Bible involves a thorough familiarity with and proficiency in the different aspects of the discipline. But it requires more than just this because of the nature of the Bible as an inspired book. There is also the spiritual dimension without which complete and accurate interpretations are impossible to attain. The Bible explicitly declares, "A natural man does not accept the things of the Spirit of God; for they are foolishness to him, and he cannot understand them, because they are spiritually appraised" (1 Cor 2:14). This declaration refers to the "depths (or deep things) of God" (1 Cor 2:10) that have been revealed through inspired men. This natural man is a non-Christian, one who is not indwelt by the Holy Spirit (cf. Rom 8:9). This is the reason the Bible's meaning is closed to him. Virkler is incorrect in holding that an unbeliever can intellectually comprehend the truths of Scripture just as well as a believer can by using the same criteria of interpretation (Henry A. Virkler, *Hemeneutics, Principles of Biblical Interpretation* [Grand Rapids: Baker, 1981], 29–31). Certain areas of meaning will be hidden to the natural man, presumably because he will lack the necessary spiritual guidance to use the exegetical data properly.

Only Christians are indwelt by the Spirit and therefore capable of experiencing His guidance in discovering the meaning of the Bible. But His indwelling does not automatically entail a correct understanding of Scripture. His filling of or control over the believer is necessary for this. Believers too can be blinded by sin. This blindness hinders a full appreciation of God's Word, because the Spirit is hindered from teaching as He otherwise would. Only a Christian's total commitment to the will of God can provide him this spiritual dimension of interpretation.

How to delineate how much or what part of Biblical Exegesis is attributable to mere human efforts and how much or what part comes from the Holy Spirit is difficult, if not impossible, to determine. Even an unenlightened unbeliever can glean some of the meaning if he follows correct procedure, but somewhere his efforts will go awry because he lacks spiritual insight. On the other hand, the enlightened believer will not, in most cases, be conscious of what has come from the Spirit as distinguished from what comes from the science of Exegesis. It will be the combined effect of the two that will bring him to the correct interpretation. Of course, he also needs the Spirit's guidance to apply the interpretation to life as it is now, but this is quite distinct from His help in illuminating the meaning of the passage in reference to its original setting.

An analogous situation existed with the apostles of Christ. Their witness for Christ in one sense was on a purely natural plane as they told about what they had seen with their own eyes and heard with their own ears. But it was not just that. The Holy Spirit also witnessed through them, and it was the combined effect of both that accomplished the purpose of their witnessing. John 15:2627 describes this dual witness: "When the Helper comes, whom I will send to you from the Father, that is the Spirit of truth, who proceeds from the Father, He will bear witness of Me, and you will bear witness also, because you have been with me from the beginning." It is highly doubtful that the apostles were ever able to distinguish clearly what came from the Spirit from what resulted from their personal experiences.

So it is in Exegesis. The guidance of the Spirit merges with a sane exercise of exegetical principles. He invariably utilizes accurate and normal rules of hermeneutics in guiding a believer to the correct interpretation. Only He can give a proper sensitivity in applying the rules. So the interpreter is ultimately dependent on Him for the right balance in the grammatico-historical Method of Exegesis.

The Method consists of two main parts, the preparation for interpretation and the interpretation proper.

1. *Preparation for Interpretation.* The "Preparation for Interpretation" step could also be called the "observation" step. It should not be confused with the "Level One" disciplines, Biblical Introduction especially. Before coming to this "preparation" step, one ideally has already settled issues related to canonicity, biblical backgrounds, and textual criticism. In practice it must be recognized that the ideal is not always possible, and therefore, there may be times when a variant reading, for example, may have to be decided upon in conjunction with the exegetical process. Even when this is the case, however, the decision regarding the correct reading should be separated as much as possible from decisions related to the interpretation of the text.

Five stages in the Preparation for Interpretation may be suggested:

a. *Historical Background.* Observation includes a specialized attention to background data related to the book designated for exegetical study. A more generalized study of biblical backgrounds is presupposed prior to this (Level One). Now the interpreter gives more particular attention to matters related to this writer, these readers, their city, the church in this city, and other data of special relevance to the portion being studied.

Four types of sources may be suggested for this aspect of observation. One is the group of works devoted to New Testament Introduction. These will often have extensive discussion related to the individual books. Another consists of Bible dictionary or encyclopedia articles. A third source is the introductory material found in introductions to many substantial commentaries. Oftentimes the authors of these works have made more valuable contributions in their introductions than they have in the commentaries proper. A fourth source is works devoted exclusively to topics of New Testament history.

It is almost impossible to overestimate the importance of historical background, both general and special, in the Grammatico-historical Method. It should be kept in mind at this stage, however, that interpretation itself has not yet begun. One should therefore, guard himself zealously against conclusions in regard to controversial areas. He should assimilate only such information as is non-prejudicial on debatable points at this stage of study.

b. *The Greek Text.* With the historical background well established, the exegete should proceed to familiarize himself with the Greek text. There are definite advantages to observing a whole book at a time, but sometimes limitations of time make this impractical. When these limitations exist, the exegete can work with a smaller section and still gain rich benefits from observing the Greek text.

The initial translation should be done using only standard language tools. The small amount of extra time consumed by not using "short cut" lexicons or interlinear texts is abundantly rewarded by the additional insight gained from the standard works. After the initial translation is done, there should be repeated readings of the Greek text. Very quickly the exegete will come to feel at home in the Greek text, much the same as he does in the English. He will find that his reading in the Greek will go as fast as that in the English. He should then spend every spare moment reading the text. He should read it many times, the more, the better. His purpose is to become thoroughly conversant with text. This kind of familiarity will guard him from accepting some of the careless comments that he may pick up in his use other sources. Even the best of commentators have lapses now and then, and the exegete needs to be equipped to catch them.

In his repeated readings of the Greek text one will notice characteristics that arouse attention. These may be by way of uniqueness, difficulty, or some other special interest category. It is impossible to classify all the possible things to note, since they are of such wide variety and they will vary from person to person. But a sample list of some types of observations is helpful for illustrative purposes. The examples are taken from 1 Thessalonians.

(1) *The same word used repeatedly.* An example of this in 1 Thessalonians would be the word παρουσία which occurs here with a greater frequency rate than in any other book of the New Testament. When speaking of words that are used repeatedly, words like δέ or καί which are used over and over again without any unusual force are not included; instead ones that are not as frequent in other literature should be singled out.

(2) *Different forms of the same verb.* Even though it may not be the same form of a verb every time, different stems from the same verb will stimulate interest. The verb οἶδα in 1 Thessalonians is used over and over again, but it is found in different forms, sometimes in the perfect, sometimes in the pluperfect, sometimes in the infinitive, etc. Thus one is immediately alerted to the fact that Paul makes frequent reference to knowledge. Further investigation reveals that it is the knowledge of his readers. He alludes to their knowledge repeatedly for some reason yet to be discovered in the exegetical process.

(3) *An unusual word occurring only once.* Here again, what is unusual? Well, the more one reads in Greek the more he will become alert to what is unusual. In this particular epistle the word that appears in 2:8, ὁμειρόμενοι, which is found only once in the New Testament and is extremely rare in the Greek Bible as well as in other literature. It is so scarce that scholars have difficulty in tracing the meaning of the word. This, of course, will point out an area that needs further investigation as the exegesis proceeds.

(4) *An unusual word occurring several times.* Here again a broad background in reading Greek will increase one's alertness. A word to illustrate is the adverb ἀδιαλείπτως. This word is found three times in 1 Thessalonians and only one other time in the New Testament. It has certain characteristics every time it is found, and turns out to be quite fruitful as an area for investigation.

(5) *An unusual grammatical (syntactical) construction.* Once again, one's increased familiarity with grammar will give him an increased basis for picking out what is unusual. Also, he may find that he has difficulty in making a smooth English rendition of a verse or phrase. Further investigation of this type of situation may reveal something that is an irregularity. An example of this is in 1 Thess 4:1. No one can make a smooth English translation here because of the two occurrences of ἵνα: "Finally therefore, brethren, I ask you and beseech you in the Lord *that* just as you received from us how it is necessary for you to walk and to please God, just as also you walk, *that* you abound more." From the standpoint of grammar, the second ἵνα is unnecessary because the περισσεύητε at the end of the verse is governed by the first ἵνα. But

because of two rather lengthy comparative clauses which Paul inserts in the the middle, he uses the particle a second time. This is the type of thing that is not normal. It is not an error, but simply a grammatical peculiarity. The step of observation can be quite beneficial in locating these peculiarities.

(6) *Repeated grammatical (syntactical) constructions.* A number of comparative clauses, while relatively infrequent in other parts of the New Testament, are found in 1 Thessalonians. Notice the frequency with which καθώς and ώς are found in a comparative sense. "Just as you know" comes time and again in this epistle. Paul found it a very forceful device in proving his argument, to remind his readers of something in their past knowledge. This is the most frequent use of the comparative clauses, but also he uses comparisons in other connections.

(7) *Syntactical problems.* An instance of this is found in 2:13 where there is the relative pronoun ὅς. The relative can have as its antecedent either λόγος or θεοῦ. It can be "which also works in you who believe" or "who also works in you who believe." The two nouns are both masculine, and the relative agrees with both in gender and number. Immediately one wonders, "Which one is the antecedent?" This question should be stored away until a future occasion in the process when there is better opportunity to come back and study it with the aid of additional data.

Thus, reading the Greek text repeatedly until it becomes very familiar is a second part in preparing for interpretation.

c. *Reviewing English translations.* Having become thoroughly familiar with the Greek text, the exegete should move to familiarize himself with a number of English translations. A bare minimum would be the King James Version, the American Standard Version, and the New American Standard Bible. But the more English translations a person can read, the more his understanding of the text will be enhanced from the standpoint of observation. The above-listed examples are literal (formal equivalence) translations. Some dynamic equivalence translations which could be consulted are Phillips Modern English, the Living Bible, Today's English Version, and the New International Version. There are at least three advantages in consulting the versions:

(a) They are a good source for suggestions of modern idioms. Translators have spent much time pondering how one would convey this expression in English, i.e. which is the English idiom that most closely corresponds to this Greek idiom. An example of help of this type is the rendering of Beck in 1 Thess 3:1; he effectively translates μηκέτι στέγοντες by "when we couldn't stand it any longer," which is a much more modern idiom than "when we could no longer forbear," the reading of the King James Version. (Cf. William F. Beck, *The New Testament in the Language of Today* [St. Louis: Concordia, 1963], 360.)

(b) In some cases versions may reveal a problem, e.g. when there are discrepant renderings of the same word. In 1 Thess 2:17 where ἀπορφανισθέντες occurs, practically every version expresses the thought differently. Since the rendering of verse 17 varies in different versions, there is help to alert the interpreter as to possibilities of meaning.

(c) Another advantage in consulting versions lies in learning the viewpoint of translators on points of syntax. For example, in 1 Thess 2:2 the two participles are rendered differently in the RSV and in the New English Bible. The RSV says, "Though we suffered before and were insulted," and the NEB says, "After we had suffered before and were insulted." The RSV understands a concessive clause, and the New English Bible takes it as a temporal clause. A matter over which there is a difference of opinion is thereby pinpointed. Much can be learned from translations, because translators in most cases did not quickly fly through and make the first rendering that came to mind. Instead they evaluated the various possibilities before finalizing their translations.

d. *Greek commentaries*. Having looked at various English versions, one may pursue a further step in preparing for interpretation. This is still the process of observation, not interpretation proper. Here the exegete looks at the works of other men with a view to increasing his own knowledge of the text, not with a view to forming conclusions. This latter would be premature.

Some have objected to consulting the interpretive works of men in the process of exegesis, both preparing for interpretation and in interpretation proper. They feel that this limits or excludes the possibility of the Holy Spirit's teaching ministry to the individual. This approach insists that the correct interpretation is communicated only when the Spirit illuminates the interpreter directly. It does not accept the possibility of the Spirit's using an indirect means of teaching the meaning of a passage.

Undoubtedly the Holy Spirit does illuminate believers by a direct ministry to them. But to say that He does not use means to do so also is antiscriptural. First Corinthians 12:28, 29 and Eph 4:11, 12 are extremely specific in showing that teaching is a prominent gift of the Spirit to the body of Christ and that that teachers have a major role in promoting the growth of this body. These teachers teach through an oral ministry, but they also teach through a written ministry. A rich storehouse of Spirit-given teaching based on the Bible is available in the writings of these teachers whom Christ has given to His church, and it should not be ignored. It should be used by Christians just as they use what they receive from the pulpit or in the classroom. It should not be viewed as data that excludes what the Spirit teaches directly, but should used alongside it as a supplement to it. Otherwise, a large category of truth that He desires to transmit is missed.

Hence, it is legitimate and even necessary for the conscientious interpreter to consult what men have written in the way of interpretations of the books the Bible. Insofar as the preliminary step of observation is concerned, a good guideline to follow is first to consult A. T. Robertson's *Word Pictures in the New Testament* (Broadman) and two or three other substantial commentaries dealing with the Greek text. Robertson's work goes verse by verse through each book of the New Testament and treats the text in a rather strict grammatical way. While Robertson does not allude to everything significant in the passage, he does a good job of calling attention to the more prominent features of exegetical significance. His work affords an excellent means for initial exposure to the text and can provide an excellent foundation in one's preparation for interpretation.

Then two or three other substantial commentaries should be consulted. The notes on the text should be read carefully in a progressive fashion, making comparison of the text with the comments and vice versa as one progresses through a passage or book. It should be kept in mind that familiarization with content is the objective at this stage of study.

e. *English commentaries.* The final step of observation is to look at a few commentaries dealing with the English text. The English commentaries will go much faster than the Greek. They will not be as helpful as those on the Greek text, but they will contribute a bird's-eye view of the book which is not often available in the more technical works.

This concludes the step of observation in preparation for exegesis. At this point one has not read to form conclusions, but to gain knowledge, familiarity with the text, e.g. what the problems of the text are (without solving the problems). This step simply acquaints the interpreter with the atmosphere in which he is moving, and to that extent draws him closer to the mind of the author and readers and ultimately that of the Holy Spirit who inspired the text.

2. *The Interpretation Proper.* The Interpretation Proper consists of five parts: Lexical Exegesis, Syntactical Exegesis, Synthesis and Outline, Resolving of Difficulties, and Re-evaluation. Some have suggested a step of Rhetorical Exegesis following Syntactical Exegesis in which various types of figurative language are analyzed, but the procedure recommended here handles all figures of speech and figurative language in conjunction with either lexical or syntactical exegesis.

a. *Lexical Exegesis.* The individual words of Scripture have held a unique fascination for all connected with Christianity for many years, especially those who adhere to the verbal inspiration viewpoint. Investigation of these words is the task of Lexical Exegesis. This step consists of a study of the "terms" of the text. By "terms" one does not mean the same as "words," because "words" take on different meanings in different contexts. A "term," however, has only one meaning, and that is the one defined by the background of its development and the demands of the specific context in which it is used. For example, λόγος is a word having a number of possible meanings, but λόγος in Heb 4:12 is a term having one clear-cut meaning. To illustrate further, λόγος in Heb 4:13 is the same word as in Heb 4:12, but as a term, it has an entirely different meaning. Thus a term may be defined as "a given word in a particular passage."

Some terms are more crucial than others. Therefore, a distinction should be made between two types of terms in the text, the routine terms and the nonroutine terms. The routine terms are those upon which no special emphasis is placed; they simply complete the meaning of the sentence, being somewhat subordinated to the terms upon which the author wished to fix special attention. On the other hand, the nonroutine terms are those which are invested with unusual significance and outstanding importance. What is routine and what is nonroutine may be discerned in many different ways. Two examples may be given to illustrate the types of conditions that set a term apart as being nonroutine:

(1) Ἥμαρτον in Romans 5:12 is nonroutine because of its usage in two earlier passages in Romans (2:12; 3:23) and because of the far-reaching theological implications in one's interpretation of the statement πάντες ἥμαρτον.

(2) Ὑπερεπερίσσευσεν in Romans 5:20 is nonroutine because of the prepositional prefix. The verb περισσεύω alone carries the meaning "to be over and above," and the preposition alone carries the meaning "to be over and above," and the preposition ὑπέρ intensifies this meaning because it too means "over" in composition.

The task of Lexical Exegesis, then, is to discover the nonroutine terms and to define the meaning of these terms as dictated by the context in which they are used and by the scope of meanings permitted by the background of the word.

It is practically impossible to overemphasize the importance of the immediate context in which a term is used. This is the principal factor in the study of a term. One's conclusion in regard to the meaning of the term must harmonize with the progression of thought in the passage. Nevertheless, a meaning which is far from what the word has in other literature must be subject to serious scrutiny before being accepted. An instance where there is an apparent clash between the context and the meaning of a word in other contexts is found in the term κατάκριμα in Rom 8:1. In this passage the context demands that it refer to the release of the Christian from bondage to his sin nature, but earlier usage in Romans seems to refer it to the release of the sinner from the penalty for his sins (Rom 5:16, 18).

In studying the usage of a word in other passages, the most value is almost always derived from another occurrence of the same word in the same immediate context. A general principle is, "the nearer the context, the more likelihood there is that the words are used in the same sense." An ever-widening circle of contexts may be suggested; the smallest circle is the same sentence, then the same paragraph, the same book, the same author, the New Testament, the Greek Old Testament, nonbiblical Greek. To illustrate once again, in Ephesians 2:20 τῶν ἀποστόλων καὶ προφήτων is often taken to refer to New Testament apostles and Old Testament prophets. But when the use of προφήτης in Ephesians 3:11 is considered, it is clear that Paul has reference to New Testament prophets instead of Old Testament prophets. Use of the word in the Greek Old Testament, for example, does not have nearly the influence of its uses in the same book.

(1) *Sources for Lexical Exegesis*. The following sources will be found helpful in studying Lexical Exegesis:

(a) *Lexicons*. Lexicons are useful in giving the etymology of a word, in classifying its usages and in giving information in regard to synonyms. Various lexicons give various types information, and therefore it is advisable not to limit one's study to just one. Much information is available from a lexicon when the student becomes familiar with the various symbols and abbreviations found in it. An example of the rich resources may be cited in connection with the word ἐνεργέω; Abbott-Smith notes parenthetically at the beginning of the paragraph, "for full lexical treatment, v. AR, *Eph.*, 243 ff." Upon examination of this resource (J. Armitage Robinson, *St. Paul's Epistle to the Ephesians*, 243 ff.), one derives a good bit of valuable information in regard to the word which can be used in the process of Lexical Exegesis.

A point to be kept carefully in mind in the use of lexicons, however, is the subjective element that is present in every lexicon. In compiling lexical categories of a particular word, the lexicographer must first interpret the passage to see which of the word's possible meanings has been used in the passage. In regard to the noun βασιλεία, for example, there is no debate that it refers to the territory or people over whom the king rules in Matt 4:8; there could hardly be any other interpretation. But the same word used in Luke 1:33 or Acts 1:6 has been subject to two interpretations, and the lexicographer must settle upon one of these before including these two references in the category of meanings headed by "sovereignty, royal power, dominion" (Abbott-Smith, 77). The lexicographer may not have made the right choice. The interpreter, therefore, should not take lexical classifications as absolutely binding.

(b) *Concordances*. In one sense concordances are even more valuable than lexicons. Studying a word using this type of resource is more purely inductive, even though it is more time consuming. With a concordance it is possible to find all the places where a word is used and to go to the primary sources to learn firsthand the shades of meaning a word has. Such a study as this guards against the subjective interpretations that may be encountered in a lexicon. Also it provides an opportunity to glean additional information not included in a lexicon. For instance, when studying the word κοιμάω, one discovers from the lexicon that the word is used metaphorically to speak of death, but the lexicon does not mention the fact that κοιμάω is used only for a believer's death in the New Testament. In anticipation of resurrection the death of a believer is looked upon as only temporary, comparable to falling asleep with the anticipation of being awakened. Hence, the verb meaning "sleep" is quite appropriate.

(c) *Bible dictionaries and encyclopedias*. Bible dictionaries and encyclopedias afford excellent opportunity for gathering historical data about specific words of Scripture. They are particularly helpful in such matters as locations, weights and measures and the like. Included under this heading also are the valuable theological dictionaries and treatments of synonyms. Many such works have incorporated helpful background studies of words.

(d) *Critical exegetical works*. The value of thorough commentaries cannot be overestimated. In addition to the conclusions reached, these works will tell where information was found and suggest places for the student to look in order to obtain more detailed treatments.

(e) *Periodical literature*. Theological and exegetical periodicals often contain studies that have been done on individual words or groups of words. These are a strong contributing resource in lexical study.

(f) *Topical works*. Sometimes works of a topical nature will be built around lexical treatments of crucial words. Leon Morris's work *Apostolic Preaching of the Cross* is of this type. The book deals with a number of words related to the atonement of Christ, such as propitiation (ἱλασμός), redemption (λύτρωσις), and wrath (ὀργή).

(g) *Unpublished works*. Some theses and dissertations found in the libraries of various theological institutions both in this country and in others consist of thorough lexical investigations of the words of Scripture. Consulting these in the process of lexical study brings very beneficial input for Lexical Exegesis.

(2) *Categories of Lexical Exegesis*. The scope of Lexical Exegesis is best grasped by listing some of the types of information that one may expect to encounter in this area of study. This list of possible categories is not exhaustive. It is intended to be illustrative only. In the discussion of each category specific examples have been included to facilitate a more thorough understanding of the category.

Many of the examples chosen are those which involve interpretive difficulties. This is not typical in Lexical Exegesis. By far most of the data accumulated in this type of study is noncontroversial. But in an introductory study such as this the controversial types of examples help to emphasize the importance of the categories and bring to the forefront more readily how indispensable each area of study is.

(a) *A Study of Etymology*. Etymology is defined as "the history of a linguistic form shown (1) by tracing its development since its earliest recorded occurrence in the language where it is found, (2) by tracing its transmission from one language to another, (3) by analyzing it into its component parts, (4) by identifying its cognates in other languages, or (5) by tracing it and its cognates to a common ancestral form in an ancestral language" (*Webster's Seventh New Collegiate Dictionary*, 1961, p. 286).

The broad definition may be narrowed down and illustrated best by pursuing a simple discussion of a Greek word, to show how the various parts of the etymological study are carried out in a particular instance. The word selected for this purpose is δόξα, "glory."

Historically, δόξα finds its origin in the verb δοκέω, "to think," "seem," "appear." In Plato's writings this verb is used as an antithesis to εἶναι, "to be." "What appears to be" stands in contrast to "what is." Mere appearance is the opposite of the real state of affairs.

In nonbiblical Greek from Homer's time onward the noun δόξα carried the connotation of "what one thinks," that is, his "opinion." At times it is bad opinion and at times good opinion. In the latter cases the noun began to gain the favorable sense of "reputation" or "renoun."

The verb δοκέω maintained its neutral flavor consistently in both secular and biblical writings; it was not used in either a predominantly bad or a predominantly good sense. The same was not true with δόξα. It remained noncommittal only in nonbiblical writings. Outside biblical writings there is only a very slight hint of the uniformly favorable sense that the word carries in the Greek Bible. There is only a barely noticeable tendency in the writings of Josephus and Philo to approach the meanings of "splendor" and "glory."

In the New Testament usage of δόξα the old and extrabiblical meaning "opinion" has disappeared completely. There is a remnant of the favorable senses of "reputation" or "honor" (Luke 14:10; 1 Cor 11:15; 1 Thess 2:6), but there is a profound change when the sense of "radiance" or "glory" are conveyed in the New Testament (Matt 4:6; 6:29; Rev 21:24, 26). This added dimension is unparallelled in profane writings prior to New Testament times.

The use of the word δόξα in the New Testament which is still predominant and striking is in relation to God. In this case it seems to convey a concept beyond human comprehension. It is as though one's "opinion" about God has become completely colored, enveloped and overwhelmed by the majesty and splendor of His person. It is beyond man's ability to understand. This connotation of the word is unknown outside biblical Greek.

When one turns to investigate the interaction of this noun with other languages, the results are equally enlightening. Of course, the English noun "doxology" traces its origin to the high connotation of δόξα in relation to God in the New Testament; it means "an expression of praise to God." But the impact of a cognate Hebrew noun is of much greater help in determining the force of the Greek noun since the subsequent impact of δόξα on the English language is of negligible value in the exegetical process. In fact, a great puzzle is solved by recourse to the Hebrew counterpart, the puzzle of why the Greek noun underwent such a radical change in meaning in the New Testament.

A major part of the reason lies in the Hebrew term which δόξα translates in the Greek Old Testament: כָּבוֹד (*kabod*). Stemming from the verb כָּבֵד (*kabed*), "to be heavy," the noun carries the idea of "abundance," "honor" or "glory" in the Old Testament. Thus the Greek translator of the Old Testament initiated a linguistic change of far-reaching significance, giving to the Greek term δόξα a distinctiveness in sense which could hardly be surpassed. He took a word which reflected only subjective opinion and made it express something absolutely objective, i.e., the reality of God.

Within the New Testament δόξα has various categories of meaning: (1) visible brightness or splendor; (2) brightness radiating from the presence of God; (3) majesty or goodness of God manifested to men; (4) the perfections of God as communicated to man through Christ.

It is through the development of δόξα that another cognate verb derives its meaning. This verb is δοξάζω. Though related in history and form with δοκέω, in the Greek Old and New Testaments it does not reflect a kinship in meaning with it. To be sure, outside biblical writings the two verbs coincide closely in meaning "to have an opinion," but in the LXX and New Testament the only meaning of δοξάζω that is found is that related to the distinctive sense of δόξα. Under the influence of the ending -άζω the verb conveys the idea of "causing glory," "honor," "extol," "glorify," "clothe with splendor," or "magnify."

In comparing the above with the definition of "etymology" quoted at the outset of this discussion several observations may be made:

1) The majority of the discussion lies in the area of part one ([1]) of the definition with somewhat less material in the areas of parts two and four ([2] and [4]). In the case of this particular word only a very small amount is devoted to part three ([3]).

2) It is extremely rare that any help can be gleaned from part five ([5]) of the definition because of the obscurity in which the origins of the Greek language are wrapped.

3) A strong note of caution should be sounded in relation to the use of etymological research. Care should always be utilized in taking into account the *total* picture of the word's history. All too often, something such as inattention to context or homiletical expediency has resulted in the use of only part of the background, the part which happened to fit the exigencies of the occasion. Such a partial treatment unduly limits the broad scope of the word's possibilities, and therefore does not allow for a consideration of all the possible meanings in each context.

(b) *Synonyms.* One of the broadest fields of study in Lexical Exegesis is in the area of synonyms. A synonym is defined as "one of two or more words or expressions of the same language that have the same essential meaning in some or all senses" (*Webster's Seventh New Collegiate Dictionary*, 1961, 894). The goal of studying synonyms is to discover the aspects of meaning where two or more words coincide and where they differ. No two words have the same etymology, and hence, differences must always be present, even if they are only very slight and are discovered only with great difficulty. But sometimes the differences are not in the author's mind when he uses the word; rather he draws upon areas of meaning common to the words. Clarification of the areas of coincidence and difference is thus the challenge of studying synonyms.

Synonyms in the New Testament occur in great abundance, and may be illustrated by the following examples:

The Greek words for "love" are ἀγαπᾶν, φιλεῖν, and ἐρᾶν. Perhaps there have been no synonyms discussed more frequently than these. Yet there remains great confusion and even outright error in the minds of many about them. The error stems partially from oversimplified discussions of them and partially from a misunderstanding of the true nature of a synonym. An instance of such a mistreatment is the oft-stated distinction between ἀγαπᾶν and φιλεῖν, that the former refers to divine love and the latter to human love. This distinction is only partially true, and from the broad standpoint, could be called a misrepresentation of the correct meanings.

Φιλεῖν does not refer exclusively to human love, for example; at times God exercises this love (John 5:20) just as He does the other type (John 3:35).

Yet one must not go to the other extreme and say that there is no distinction between the words. There *is* a difference in emphasis maintained. The delicate task consists in stating this difference accurately. By basing the distinctions on the majority (not necessarily the entirety) of uses of each word, the following definitions result:

a) Ἐρᾶν, a word not found in New Testament writings, is a passionate love which desires the other for selfish reasons. It is a sort of sensual intoxication which came to be associated with religious worship. This concept caused enormous sexual activity in connection with the temples of the heathen goddesses. While Plato and Aristotle raised the word above the sensual connotations by making it figurative, it still retained the idea of seeking in others the fulfillment of one's own hunger. By virtue of its predominant usage the word became associated with an ethic much lower and more degraded than the Christian standard.

b) Φιλεῖν, on another hand, is used in both secular and New Testament writings. In the former it is the most noble word for love. Its overshadowing of ἀγαπᾶν in extrabiblical writings is more frequent. This love is more a spontaneous natural affection without the sensual elements of ἐρᾶν. It is an emotional response to an object which appeals to the lover. It is an instinctive act in which the intellect and the will play little or no part. This is the love of friends for each other because they find mutual compatibility. The Bible never commands this type of love nor does it forbid it.

c) The final word, ἀγαπᾶν, is used only sparingly in prebiblical writings, but comes to be the predominant word in the New Testament. This seems to result in part from the unfavorable senses of other words in secular writings. Through its biblical usage the word acquires the meaning of intelligent and purposeful love. It does not exclude emotions, but emotions do not dominate. The intellect and the will are controlling factors, and the total personality is involved. This is love which gives and acts on the other's behalf. It is not self-oriented as are the other two words. The cause of this love is found solely in the one loving and has nothing to do with the desirability or compatibility of love's object. Since this love is volitional and not instinctive, it can be commanded as a duty.

From the above remarks a clear distinction in emphasis can be seen. Nevertheless, allowance should always be made for cases where the words may convey a meaning which is covered by all the words. In such cases the writer is not emphasizing the difference, but the similarity between the words. This could explain the use of both ἀγαπᾶν and φιλεῖν for the Father's love of the Son (John 3:35; 5:20), His love for the disciples (John 14:21; 16:27), Jesus' love for John (John 13:23; 20:2) and other instances where the words could carry the same general meaning of love. Note that in such cases where the word meanings overlap, the words are widely separated from one another and there is no attempt to contrast by placing them in juxtaposition. Hence, no great problem is posed if ἀγαπᾶν, for example, rather than ἐρᾶν is used to express sensual love, as it is in the Greek Old Testament; no comparison of terms was intended in such cases.

Another situation is encountered, however, when two or more words are placed in close proximity to each other. It is highly questionable that any New Testament writer varied his vocabulary for purely stylistic reasons. It is safe to assume that the appearance of synonyms close to one another almost always finds its explanation in the author's desire to play upon the meanings which distinguish the words from each other. Such is surely the case in the classical passage John 21:15-17 where ἀγαπᾶν and φιλεῖν are contrasted in Christ's dealings with Peter. Even though Christ and Peter possibly spoke in Aramaic, the fact remains that they did find a means, perhaps by resorting to Greek for clarification, of distinguishing the two words used. The differences in these two words are not in the nature of opposites, but rather that each has its own emphasis and neither one is necessarily a derogatory term.

In summary, the following schema is offered to illustrate the relationships of synonyms:

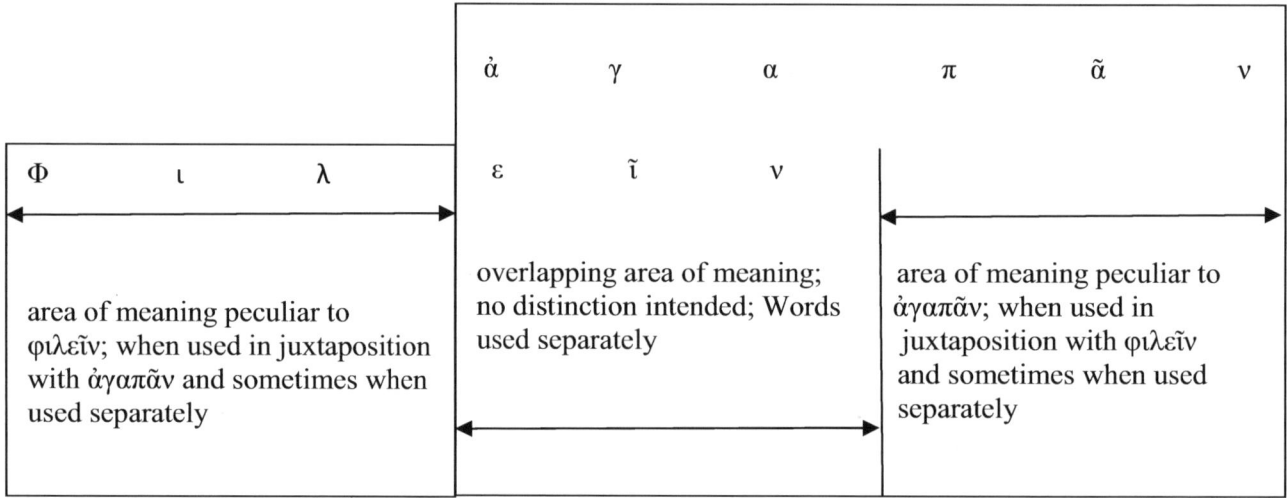

(c) *Biblical usage of words.* It stands to reason that the greatest help in fixing word meanings in the New Testament will come from other uses of the same word elsewhere in biblical Greek. Such a conclusion is verified by actual experience in Lexical Exegesis. Though some help is derived from outside the Bible, the fact remains that the nearer context of thought within Scripture provides the most insight to aid interpretation.

1) In most cases a given writer will consistently use the same word in the same sense in the same book. To illustrate, the writer of Hebrews uses ἐπιλαμβάνομαι in two verses of his epistle (2:16; 8:9). In the earlier verse the King James Version shows gross neglect of this principle when it gives the verb the sense "appropriate for oneself," a sense which also does injustice to the context of chapter two. Had the translators consulted the other occurrence (8:9), they would have inserted the proper sense which is that of "help." The Son did not come to help angels, but to help Abraham's seed, says the author of 2:16.

Another case in point is μετάνοιαν in Heb 6:6. A wrong definition of "repentance" can be quite detrimental to a correct understanding of this difficult passage. But it is completely unnecessary to misunderstand the author, when he gives elsewhere a clear statement to define μετάνοια as a turning away "from dead works" (6:1). The "dead works" are, in turn, clarified in

Heb 9:14; they are works of the Aaronic ritual which have been superceded by the work of Christ. Hence, "repentance" in Hebrews 6:6 is a turning away from the Old Testament ritual, and not necessarily the accompaniment of a decision to trust Jesus Christ for salvation as it may be elsewhere in the New Testament.

2) The same writer writing in different books will usually use the same word in the same sense, but not quite so consistently as in the same book. For example, διαθήκη is used consistently by Paul in his epistles to mean "covenant," with the possible exception of Gal 3:15 where a few have defended the meaning "testament" or "will." The word always relates to dealings between God and man except in the disputed Galatians passage, and is preferred over συνθήκη because of a desire to escape the connotation that the parties making the covenant stand on equal terms. Most commentators feel that the meaning of "covenant" is also demanded by the context in Galatians 3:15.

3) Agreement between different writers of the New Testament in vocabulary use is another general rule, even though the exceptions here are more frequent than in "2)" above. This also can be illustrated by the consistent use of διαθήκη in the New Testament. Five different authors regularly use the word in the same way. In spite of this the Revised Standard Version unfortunately overlooks this characteristic in Heb 9:15–20. In this passage the noun διαθήκη occurs five times, and its sense is to be understood once in addition (9:18). In four cases the translation given is "covenant," but in two instances the translators chose "will" (9:16 –17). This difference obscures the continuity of the passage which is obvious in Greek. Διαθήκη means "covenant" in every other case in Hebrews, and throughout the New Testament, for that matter (again, with the possible exception of Gal 3:15). Considerations from the immediate context of Heb 9:16–17 caused the translators to make the change in these two verses, but it is doubtful that the changes are of sufficient weight to offset the evidence for the other meaning. "Covenant" provides a satisfactory meaning in verses 16 and 17, just as it does throughout the rest of the paragraph. One word of caution about applying this rule of interpretation should be added. At times there may be contextual reasons which are sufficient to override considerations from word usage. Two examples will suffice to illustrate this:

In Rom 10:16–17 there is an interesting sequence revolving about the noun ἀκοή. In verse 16 it must have the meaning "the thing heard," but if the same meaning is followed in verse 17, there is conflict with the meaning of ῥῆμα which refers to "the word uttered" about Christ. Thus, the best solution is to see a distinction in meaning and to take the noun in verse 16 as "the thing heard" and in verse 17 as "the act of hearing." See a similar situation with ἀκοή in Gal 3:2.

Another illustration is καλέω in Rom 9:24–26 where the first occurrence appears to refer to an effectual call to salvation and the last two to the act of "calling by name."

(d) *Words used in antithesis.* An antithesis is "a rhetorical contrast of ideas by means of parallel arrangements of words, clauses, or sentences" (*Webster's Seventh New Collegiate Dictionary* [1961], 40). The present discussion will be limited to cases where only words are involved in antithetical expressions. Quite often, obscure passages are made plain simply by attention to words which are used in opposition to one another in a given context. Two pairs of antonyms will illustrate the value of this facet of Lexical Exegesis.

1) Σάρξ and πνεῦμα. The nature of the opposites depited by two words will not always be the same in every case, as illustrated by σάρξ and πνεῦμα. The context must determine this.

In John 3:6 the two words occur twice each. The former occurrence of σάρξ refers to humanity in its present constitution while the former occurrence of πνεῦμα contrasts the Holy Spirit with such humanity. The latter occurrence of σάρξ depicts the nature of the natural man and the latter πνεῦμα the nature of the regenerate man. The former nature is of an inferior essence and is unfit to see the kingdom of God, but the latter merits entrance into that kingdom.

Romans 1:3–4 also utilizes this pair of words. In 1:3 "flesh" depicts the human nature of Christ and in 1:4 "spirit" is a representation of His divine nature. The antithesis between these two words is a chief reason for ruling out any reference to the Holy Spirit in that verse.

Many have found in 1 Pet 3:18 a relationship between the Holy Spirit and the resurrection of Christ, because they have failed to observe the force of the antithesis there. The presence of this combination in the said passage demands that the πνεῦμα be a reference to the immaterial part of Christ's person, not the Holy Spirit. This is the only way it can furnish a suitable opposite to the σάρξ which refers to His material body.

It should be noted that in each of the above passages there is a common ground which forms the basis for the contrast. Whether it be the source of birth, the nature of man, the nature of Christ, the composition of His person or some other, the context must supply a common entity that furnishes the substance around which the antithesis builds. Then in each case σάρξ represents the lower side of the contrast, and πνεῦμα points to the higher side. Examples of this pair of words in combination abound in the New Testament.

2) Another combination which is of great interest is that of νήπιος and τέλειος. A study of these two is particularly helpful in connection with "that which is perfect" in 1 Cor 13:10. A survey of antitheses involving these words is quite revealing:

Heb 5:13–14 - A babe is contrasted to one of full age (individual Christians); ability to receive teaching about Christ[s priesthood typified by Melchizedek.

Eph 4:13–14 - A mature man is contrasted to children (growth of the collective body of Christ).

1 Cor 2:6; 3:1 - Those who are mature are contrasted to babes in Christ (individual Christians; ability to receive truth by the Spirit).

1 Cor 14:20 - Children are contrasted with full-grown men (individual Christians; willingness to recognize the shortcomings of tongues in a Christian gathering).

In each case the juxtaposition gives τέλειος the meaning of "mature" rather than "perfect," i.e., relative maturity instead of absolute perfection. Hence, when the two antonyms come together in 1 Cor 13:10–11, the writer must be speaking of relative maturity, and more specifically in the context of 1 Corinthians 12–14, the increasing maturity of the body of Christ through the period of its existence on earth (cf. Eph 4:13–14). Certain gifts were appropriate to the infancy and childhood stages of the church, but as maturity developed, these were discarded as being inappropriate and unnecessary for the adult stage.

In each of the above illustrations the common ground is the normalcy of growth from immaturity to maturity according to the pattern of human development, but in some cases it relates to individuals while in others, to a group growth. The contrast lies in the relatively undeveloped stage which is the lower side of the comparison and the stage of development which is relatively high and therefore more desirable. The lower side may or may not be derogatory in itself, but it of necessity in some way falls short of the higher.

(c) *Figures of speech.* Certain figurative expressions belong under the heading of Lexical Exegesis. For example, there is *onomatopoeia*, "the meaning of a thing or action by a vocal imitation of the sound associated with it" (e.g., "buzz," "hiss"; *Webster's Seventh New Collegiate Dictionary* [1961], 590). New Testament examples of this may be found in John 6:41, ἐγόγγυζον ("murmur"), or James 2:19, φρίσσουσιν ("bristle," "shiver").

Another figure of speech included in Lexical Exegesis is *metonomy*, "the use of the name of one thing for that of another of which it is an attribute or with which it is associated" (ibid., 534) To illustrate, σταυρός ("cross") is frequently used by metonomy in the New Testament to depict Christ's death on the cross (1 Cor 1:17; Gal 5:11; 6:12, 14; Eph 2:16; Phil 3:18).

(f) *Familiarization with lexical difficulties.* In carrying out the procedure for Lexical Exegesis, instances will arise in which opinions differ in regard to the meanings of terms. In such cases the various alternatives should be listed, and the term should be noted as being subject to differences of opinion. Such terms are thus set aside for study at a later stage in the process of exegesis, when the interpreter is in better position to weigh the various threads of evidence.

(g) Other illustrations or categories of Lexical Exegesis are *hapax legomena* (words used only one time) and cognate words (words built from the same root).

(3) *Distinguishing "nonroutine" terms from "routine" ones.* A method for recognizing which terms are "nonroutine" and which are not may be suggested. As pointed out earlier during the observation step, some terms will be discovered which are obviously non-routine. In addition, use of the various sources for Lexical Exegesis will focus the interpreter's attention on some words as being more crucial to a statement's meaning. The terms that commented upon by all or nearly all of those who have written on a passage, are obviously non-routine. But a term that is commented upon by one writer only may be nonroutine also. In this latter case the interpreter has to use his own judgment about inclusion in or exclusion from the non-routine category. Usually, however, it proves to be the safer course to include the term rather than risk leaving out something that may later prove to be beneficial in interpretation. In reaching such a decision a wide margin for error is provided for, so that even if the interpreter makes a wrong choice, a later part of the exegetical process will reveal it and enable him to correct his wrong decision.

b. *Syntactical Exegesis.* After Lexical Exegesis as been accomplished, the next step is "Syntactical Exegesis." Without this step interpretation would be pervaded by a high degree of confusion. Any word standing alone is capable of a number of meanings, but only one meaning is allowable when the word is in a grammatical combination with others. Webster defines *syntax* as "the way in which words are put together to form phrases, clauses or sentences." As this definition suggests, the step of Syntactical Exegesis deals with the relationships between words, just as Lexical Exegesis deals with definitions narrowed down to a single word. Stated in other terms, Syntactical Exegesis deals with the structure of the text, a study involving all the relations and interrelations which bind terms together into a literary unit. It includes the methods of connection between words and words, phrases and phrases, and clauses and clauses within the sentence. Structural study, however, cannot be limited to the sentence unit. It must extend to include logical sequence from one sentence to the next, from one paragraph to the next, from one section to the next, and so on. Accordingly, an interpretation of the genitive θεοῦ in Rom 1:17 is a matter of Syntactical Exegesis, but so is the asyndeton of Rom 9:1, which helps to define the relationship between Romans 1–8 and Romans 9–11. "Syntax thus treats of the binding of words together in all relations" (A. T. Robertson, large *Grammar*, 385).

The wide variety of relationships may be divided into two types of connections: the grammatical and the literary. The grammatical connections are the most frequent and the most easily identified. Included in this area are such things as the significance of the presence or absence of the article, interpretation of the cases of the noun or the tenses of the verb, the meaning of conjunctions and connective particles, the word order of the sentence and many other features pertaining to syntax from a strictly grammatical point of view.

A point similar to one made in connection with Lexical Exegesis deserves special mention. The vast majority of grammatical relationships fall under the heading of "routine." These need not be given special attention. But those connections which for one reason or another are of special importance to a context should be made the objects of concentrated study. To illustrate, one could scarcely make a big point of the aorist tense of ὤφθη in 1 Corinthians 15:6, but the conjunctions ἔπειτα . . . ἔπειτα . . . εἶτα are the key that opens up the nature of the structural relation between parts of the sentence. It is that of temporal sequence.

The other type of connection, the literary, is not so easily discerned, because it involves a logical connection, a connection in thought only. There is no special grammatical clue that reflects the logical progression. Grammatical connections are logical too, but sometimes there are thought relationships that cannot be tied to a specific grammatical phenomenon. An instance of this is in the repetition of the same word or cognate words which bind the sentences together (cf. πειρασμόν and πειραζόμενος, James 1:12–13). Another example of the literary connection is the question and answer method of logical development (cf. Rom 3:1–2). In this area a background in the study of logic is very helpful.

(1) *Sources for Syntactical Exegesis.* Though sources for Syntactical Exegesis are not as numerous as those for Lexical, they are still rather plentiful and are certainly ample.

(a) Grammar books. An extensive knowledge of grammatical principles is of inestimable value, but to supplement what may come to mind from previous study, many grammars have Scripture indices to point out which verses are discussed under their different headings. An illustration of how a grammar book can be used is seen in the δικαιοῦσθε of Gal 5:4 which Dana and Mantey classifies as a "tendential present." The tendential present tense is used of action which purposed or attempted but does not actually take place. This factor helps clear up a matter which might otherwise be a problem in a context which deals with justification by faith. Paul does not say that anyone is being justified by works, only that some are trying to be justified by works.

(b) *Commentaries.* Substantial works dealing with the original text will prove valuable in studying the structure of the text. From these more critical works one will derive information on both the grammatical and the literary connections. From the works based on the English text it will be principally the literary connections that are derived. For example, from a technical work one derives the follow comment: "ὥστε marks the conclusion from the preceding statements, and especially from ἐφρουρούμεθα" (Eadie [writing on Gal 3:24], 282). An example from a noncritical work is from Alexander; after commenting on fhe clause "and He is the propitiation for our sins" in 1 John 2:2, Alexander writes. "Then, as if suddenly fired by a great thought, St. John's view broadens over the whole world beyond the limits of the comparatively little group of believers whom his words at that time could reach" (*The Expositor's Bible*, 103). The latter illustration gives a connection in thought between the two parts of the verse, while the former comment is more grammatical in nature.

(c) *Periodical literature*. Periodicals of a theological or exegetical type often have treatments of grammatical themes. These can be of great benefit if related to a construction of a type encountered in the passage under study. Indices of periodical literature are the most convenient means for locating useful articles. These will usually be indexed under both a subject and a Scripture reference.

(d) *Unpublished works*. Some theses and dissertations in libraries of various institutions in this country and in others are devoted to topics of a grammatical nature. Lists of these are usually available. The titles of these studies will usually reveal their possible relevance to a grammatical phenomenon that may be the subject of special study. Even if no direct help is obtained from an unpublished work, its bibliography quite often will have suggestions of works to be consulted in further study of Syntactical Exegesis.

(2) *Categories of Syntactical Exegesis*. The following categories of Syntatical Exegesis may be suggested:

(a) *Familiarization with syntactical difficulties*. There will be differences of opinion in some matters of Syntactical Exegesis. Every non routine structural phenomenon will not be explained in the same way by everyone. Minor differences should not be a cause for further concern; if the case in favor on one particular explanation seems rather clear-cut, the matter should not be considered problematical, even though one or two sources may express divergent ideas. But when the evidence is more evenly divided, various alternatives should be noted and a detailed examination of each view provided for at a later stage in the process of interpretation.

(b) *Grammatical relationships*. Grammar is a field of study all its own. To help comprehend the importance of grammatical studies in Exegesis, several miscellaneous types of grammatical contributions will be discussed and illustrated in detail. Then an overview of the grammatical discipline known as "syntax" will follow. In this latter discussion illustrations will be more abundant, but discussion of each will be abbreviated.

1) *The contribution of grammatical studies to Exegesis*. As the name of the method indicates, grammar is the heart of the Grammatico-Historical Method of Exegesis. Its part in Exegesis is so vital and its kinds of contributions to exegetical study so numerous that it is impossible to list all the ways that grammar is used in Exegesis. The following are offered as samples of how grammar leads to correct interpretations of Scripture.

a) *Verb tense*. The tense of the Greek verb is such that it is quite valuable as an aid to interpretation. It is impossible to list all the areas of benefit, so only three passages will be offered as examples.

In Rom 6:1213 a contrast between the present and aorist tenses presents valuable lessons in regard to Christian doctrine and daily Christian living. Two present imperatives, βασιλευέτω and παριστάνετε, are opposed to an aorist imperative, παραστήσατε. Several observations grow out of this antithesis:

One is the conclusion that the readers, although already justified, had not allowed Christ to be Lord of their lives. This observation grows out of the nature of the present imperative preceded by μή. Grammarians are unanimous in agreeing that such a combination encourages the cessation of an action already in progress, unless there is a definite contextual factor to indicate otherwise. Since there is no such exception here, it is to be understood that these Roman Christians were engaged in letting sin reign in their mortal bodies and in yielding their members as instruments of unrighteousness to sin, until the reception of this letter. Hence, Paul exhorts, "Stop letting sin reign . . . and stop yielding. . . ."

A second observation is that the aorist imperative παραστήσατε must represent an instantaneous act because of its contrast with the two present imperatives. This is not true of every aorist tense (cf. John 2:20 where οἰκοδομήθη speaks of action covering a forty-six year period), but is necessitated in a case where such an antithesis is involved. It is the teaching of this verse, therefore, that the regenerate person who has not done so already should at one particular time in his life yield himself to God, recognizing the claim of Christ as Lord of his life.

A last observation about the Romans passage is that the aorist infinitive παραστῆσαι in Rom 12:1 should be interpreted in light of the tense significance in Rom 6:13. Again the apostle beseeches his readers to offer a once-for-all presentation of their bodies to God.

An interesting insight into the lives of the readers of the Ephesian letter is gained by observing the same rule about the present imperative preceded by μή. They were actively engaged in sin ("stop letting the sun go down on your wrath," 4:26); they were allowing the devil a prominent place ("stop giving place to the devil," 4:27); they were thieves (4:28); they were using corrupt language (4:29); they were grieving the Holy Spirit (4:30); fornication, uncleanness and covetousness were spoken of among them (5:3); they were partakers with those who used vain words (5:7); they were partaking of the unfruitful works of darkness (5:11); they were foolish (5:17); and they were drunkards (5:18). These Christians apparently rivaled the Corinthians in their loose living, a characteristic that is discerned only by close attention to the verb tenses. Paul commands them to depart from these evil practices.

One final illustration of the value of verb tense may be drawn from Col 2:1112. The time of the aorist passive participle συνταφέντες (2:12) is determined in relation to the finite verb of the sentence, περιετμήθητε (2:11). Most would agree that the circumcision not made with hands occurred at the moment of initial faith in Christ. It follows, then, that the time of burial together with Him in baptism must be either prior to or simultaneous with the moment of saving faith, because the adverbial aorist participle in the New Testament cannot depict action subsequent to the main verb (Dana and Mantey are in error on this point; cf. Robertson's large *Grammar*). Since a baptism prior to saving faith is an absurdity in this context, it is concluded that the baptism referred to here is simultaneous with the act of God imparting eternal life to a person. This grammatical phenomenon is to a large degree decisive in deciding between the meaning of spiritual baptism and that of water baptism in this passage. Two alternatives exist: the writer means water baptism and hence the doctrine of baptismal regeneration, or else he has reference to the spiritual act by which a person is placed into the body of Christ. It is obvious that the former alternative which speaks of an external ordinance is ruled out in a context where the writer is emphasizing spiritual transactions (cf. ἀχειροποιήτῳ, 2:11). His words must be referred to the placing of his readers into the spiritual body, the church (cf. Col 1:18), which is accomplished by a purely spiritual act.

b) *Conjunctions*. A conjunction is "an uninflected linguistic form that joins together sentences, clauses, phrases, or words" (*Webster's Seventh Collegiate Dictionary* [1961], 176). It is impossible to follow an author's logic without close attention to the conjunctions he uses. There is a sense in which conjunctions constitute the skeleton on which the meaning of the New Testament hangs. The meaning assigned to each statement to some degree grows out of the connective word used to introduce it.

This is an area where there is substantial difference between Hebrew and Greek. Hebrew is extremely limited as to variety of conjunctions. The *vav* does duty for all sorts of thought patterns. But with Greek the opposite is true; there is a specific means for expressing practically every shade of transition when a writer moves from one thought to the next. This linguistic characteristic of the Greek serves notice of the importance of this area of study.

For example, much misunderstanding of "Eye hath not seen, nor ear heard . . ." (1 Cor 2:9) could have been avoided by attention to the conjunction ἀλλά which introduces the verse. Since ἀλλά is normally a strong adversative conjunction, the sense of the verse must be such as to be in contrast to something that precedes. That verse 9 could speak of heaven is thus summarily ruled out, for there is no suitable opposite to heaven in verses 7–8. But there is an opposite to possession of the wisdom of God: the ignorance of that wisdom on the part of "the princes of this world" (v. 8). It can be seen, hence, that ἀλλά determines the sense in which the familiar quotation is to be understood.

English translations are often misleading in their handling of connectives. The King James Version commits a serious error in Rom 3:20 where διότι is translated "therefore." This rendering tells the reader that verse 20 is a logical inference, a sort of concluding statement in summary of the previous paragraph. This is not true at all. Διότι is never inferential; it is always causal. The correct relationship sees verse 20 as assigning the cause of which verse 19 is the effect. The inability of the works of law to justify (v. 20) results in the stopping of every mouth and the guilt of the whole world before God (v. 19).

Another serious translation error in the King James Version is the omission of the ἤ ("or") of Rom 7:1. The absence of "or" from the English text of the KJV completely obscures Paul's presentation of an alternative which is coupled with the one stated in 6:14b. His readers must either admit to the truth that they are no longer under law (6:14–23), or else they are ignorant about the true nature of law (7:1–6).

A further discrepancy in the KJV is found in Rom 8:8. The δέ is rendered "so then," making verse 8 an inference derived from verse 7. But closer examination reveals that δέ is not an inferential conjunction. It may be adversative, continuative, explanatory or emphatic, but never inferential. So Rom 8:8 adds a further thought to verse 7, but does not draw a conclusion from it. The mind of the flesh is enmity against God (v. 7), and those who are in the flesh cannot please God (v. 8).

Nor are modern translators free from this tendency. F. F. Bruce in his expanded paraphrase of Gal 1:10 discovered the difficulty in understanding the γάρ in Gal 1:10, and so left it untranslated (*The Letters of Paul*, 21). To be sure, this makes for smoother English, but it fails to bring out the causal or explanatory nature of the connection between verses nine and ten.

One of the most difficult connections in the New Testament relates to the last verse of Matthew 6. Having stressed in 6:19–33 the need to be free from anxiety over daily needs, the Lord Jesus draws a logical conclusion (οὖν) in verse 34: "Do not be anxious about tomorrow, for the morrow will be anxious for itself; sufficient for the day is its trouble." On one hand, He forbids all anxiety, but in deriving His conclusion He permits anxiety about any given day. The solution may be found by noting that in His conclusion Christ draws special attention to tomorrow's anxieties, whereas earlier He has dealt with anxieties in general. Without implying the propriety of anxieties about today, He adduces an additional reason for avoiding anxieties about tomorrow. Even if it be granted that today's anxieties are permissible, it is useless to add to today's burdens by anticipating those that belong to another day. Whether proper or improper, they should not be borrowed from one day to the next.

A favorite proof-text of nondispensationalists for showing that the church is spiritual Israel is Gal 6:16. In fact, this is the only such verse which can be adduced to make such an identification, and the correctness of the conclusion hinges upon one's understanding of καί (the last of the three occurrences in the verse). The issue is whether "the Israel of God" is epexegetic of "those who walk according to this rule," in which case καί is translated "even," or whether it supplies an additional category not specifically referred to previously, in which case καί means "and" or "even" in an ascensive rather than an explicative sense. In spite of the fact that the New Testament nowhere else refers to the church as Israel, advocates for the epexegetic use lean strongly on the unlikelihood in this context that Paul would pronounce blessing on anyone who does not walk according to "this rule." To offset this factor, however, is the failure of Paul in any other place to use καί with so marked an explicative force as this would demand. The strength of this stylistic trait along with other considerations makes a reference to two distinct groups the stronger possibility: those who walk according to this rule and those believers in the church who are of the physical lineage of Abraham.

So regular are the occurrences of conjunctions in most of the New Testament that special explanation is required when a connective is not found. Such an instance is in Rom 9:1 where the Apostle opens a new section without a connective particle. Such a phenomenon is called an "asyndeton." It is usually indicative of strong emotion on the part of the author. This indicator of emotion is quite interesting at this point, since there are several other indications in the early verses of chapter nine that the apostle is deeply moved over the spiritual plight of his kinsmen according to the flesh. All of these factors combine to show Paul's very strong concern for the people of Israel.

c) *Middle Voice*. The middle voice is very helpful in understanding the emphasis of New Testament writers. The added emphasis to the subject which is supplied by the middle comes in different ways, in each case the type of emphasis being made clear by the context.

Romans 3 contains at least three interesting uses of the middle voice. In verse 9 προεχόμεθα has been variously understood. A passive "Are we surpassed?" is ruled out because it would require a Gentile speaker, an impossibility in this context. The middle presents two possibilities: "Do we put ourselves forward as better?" or "Are we in our own opinion better?" The former meaning, a direct middle, is ruled out because no such use of προέχω has been discovered elsewhere. The latter, an indirect middle, gives an additional emphasis to the subject which would not be present with the active voice. Hence, in this case the middle brings to the forefront the subjective feeling of those designated by "we": "Do *we* think ourselves better?"

In Rom 3:23 the force of ὑστεροῦνται, the middle voice, is well illustrated by two uses of the same verb in the gospels. In Matt 19:20 the rich young ruler asked, "What do I still lack?" This is an active voice of the same verb, and reflects no particular self-attention on the speaker's part. But regarding the prodigal son in Luke 15:14 it is said, "He began to be in need." This time the verb is middle voice, in which case it indicates not only the need, but also the son's sense of his lack: "He began to be in need and to feel it." Since Rom 3:23 uses the verb in the middle voice, a subjective awareness of falling short is to be understood.

Another illustration is προέθετο in Rom 3:25, where the middle voice indicates that it is for His own purpose that God has set forth Christ as a "propitiatory" or "mercy seat." His self-involvement is highlighted by the middle.

Hebrews 9:12 uses εὑράμενος to speak of Christ's accomplishment of eternal redemption. The middle participle in this instance focuses attention on His personal role in this transaction. The Aaronic priests offered sacrifices which were separate from themselves, but Christ offered Himself.

The KJV translators created great problems in a number of places by rendering middle verbs in the passive. One such passage is 2 Pet 2:22: "the sow which was washed to her wallowing in the mire." To render λουσαμένη passively gives the impression that the apostate had at one time been cleansed by an agent outside himself, i.e. the blood of Christ. Closer scrutiny reveals, on the other hand, that this is a direct middle "the sow who had washed herself." This presents the picture of reformation rather than regeneration; the apostate merely underwent what appeared to be regeneration, and his relationship to Christ was at no time genuine.

Then there is the rendering "ye are washed" for the middle form ἀπελούσασθε in 1 Cor 6:11. Standing in parallel with two passives, ἡγιάσθητε and ἐδικαιώθητε, the middle voice is even more noticeable. This appears to be a permissive middle: "you permitted yourselves to be washed." A similar usage is found in 1 Cor 10:2 where the middle ἐβαπτίσθησαν is the correct reading. The children of Israel "allowed themselves to be baptized into (i.e., identified with) Moses."

One final case to illustrate the need for close attention to the middle voice is Acts 22:16. "Be baptized and wash away your sins" in the KJV is misleading. Βάπτισαι and ἀπόλουσαι are aorist middle imperatives, and in neither case is the work to be done directly by the person addressed. Rather, they are causative middles: "Get yourself baptized and get your sins washed away." In each case the action is accomplished by an agent outside the person addressed, the baptism by a human agent and the washing away by a divine agent. The aorist middle participle ἐπικαλεσάμενος with its phrase expresses the means by which one gets his sins washed away: "by calling (on your own behalf) on His name."

d) *The Genitive Case.* An understanding of the options open to a writer in New Testament times is vital. Of the several choices presenting themselves to him, one would doubtless be better than the others to express the exact shade of meaning in his mind. To appreciate the shades of meaning fully, therefore, the interpreter of Scripture must know the habits of communication prevailing in the first century Greek world. Only by knowing them can one reach an intelligent decision about an author's intent.

There is no more obvious place to prove the importance of such awareness that in the use of the genitive case. This case, referred to as the case of definition or description, is used in at least nine distinct ways in literature of the Koine Greek period. Each occurrence of a genitive, then, presents a challenge to the student who would interpret the Word of God carefully. Which of the nine relationships was in the writer's mind when he penned this passage? This question must be answered before one's understanding of a passage is complete.

Seemingly limitless are examples of this type of decision. Two are frequently discussed passages in Ephesians. Ephesians 2:20 uses the genitives (or ablatives) τῶν ἀποστόλων καὶ προφητῶν following the noun τῷ θεμελίῳ. The nature of "the foundation" hinges on the syntactical relationship of "the apostles and prophets" to it. One suggestion is a genitive of apposition: "the foundation which is the apostles and prophets." The principal objection to this viewpoint is its mixing of figures of speech: the apostles and prophets cannot be at the same time a part of the house (2:19) and the foundation on which the house is built (2:20). The other main possibility is sometimes referred to as a genitive of originating cause, but in terms of the eight case system it would be an ablative of source: "the foundation issuing from the apostles and prophets," in the sense that they laid the foundation. This view looks at the preaching of the apostles and prophets as the foundation of the church. Of this preaching Jesus Christ is the prominent part, i.e. the chief cornerstone.

Ephesians 4:9 is a second instance of a genitive that has been debated extensively. How does τῆς γῆς relate to τὰ κατώτερα [μέρη]? Only by answering this question can a reader decide what phase of Christ's activity Paul is depicting here. A genitive (or more correctly, an ablative) of comparison has been one suggestion, "the parts lower than the earth" being a reference to the grave. The word order of the verse is against this conclusion, however. Others would understand a genitive of apposition, "the lower parts which are the earth." This would be a reference to to the incarnation of Christ. But in a context where Christ's bestowal of gifts is in view, one would expect a reference to an event located nearer His ascension. Another sense is rendered by a genitive of possession, "the lower parts belonging to the earth." This was His descent into Hades, and is a suitable opposite to "far above all the heavens" (4:10). This meaning is hard to justify in the context, however. Probably the genitive of apposition carries the least objection of these three possibilities.

In Gal 3:2 Paul asks his readers whether they received the Holy Spirit "by works of the law" or "by the hearing of faith." This furnishes an interesting parallelism between the two genitives νόμου and πίστεως. The former is obviously a subjective genitive: "works which the law requires or produces," which gives principal emphasis to works. This would lead one to expect a subjective genitive in the latter case also, but this yields a very difficult sense: "the report (or hearing) which faith (or the things believed) produces," which emphasizes the report. Since Paul's emphasis in the context is not on the report (i.e., the message preached) but on faith, the subjective genitive is highly improbable. It appears that Paul resorts to an objective genitive in the second part of the antithesis: "the hearing which produces faith." This gives prominence to faith and thus strengthens the contrast between works and faith which pervades the rest of the context.

Commentators occasionally become rather vague in their handling of the genitive. Burton (I.C.C.) and Ridderbos (N.I.C.) refer to τὴν ἐπαγγελίαν τοῦ πνεύματος in Gal 3:14 as a "metonymic phrase" meaning "the promised Spirit." The parallel passages cited by Burton to justify such a construction are unconvincing. No such Hebraic construction of the genitive case is common in the New Testament. Eadie, on the other hand, calls this an objective genitive, i.e., the promise which looks forward to the Spirit's coming. This, however, might imply that the Galatians had only received the promise at this juncture, and not the Spirit Himself. In comparison with these suggestions it seems quite obvious that Abbott-Smith has hit on the correct solution when he calls this an epexegetic genitive (a genitive of apposition; cf. p. 163): "that Him who was promised, the Spirit, we might receive through faith." In fact, Eadie mentions this as sort of an afterthought, calling it a genitive of nearer specification or definition. Cf. also Acts 2:33; Heb 9:15.

It would be difficult to find a genitive with more significance than the one found in the title of the Apocalypse. Revelation 1:1 begins Ἀποκάλυψις Ἰησοῦ Χριστοῦ. Opinion has been evenly divided between the subjective genitive, picturing Christ as the revealer, and the objective genitive, picturing HIm as the one revealed. Favoring the subjective genitive is the context of the book throughout which Christ acts in the capacity of the revealer (e.g., the opening of the seals). He does not become the revealed one until chapter 19. On the other side, ἀποκάλυψις is almost always followed by an objective genitive in the New Testament (the nature of the genitive following this noun in Gal 2:12 is debated also). Some have sought a solution to this matter by accepting both the subjective and the objective senses, but such follows an untenable hermeneutical procedure. A decision must be made, and in this case the weight of evidence is in favor of the subjective genitive.

Grammarians are not infallible in their application of grammatical principles. In Rom 1:5 A. T. Robertson considers ὑπακοὴν πίστεως to be a subjective genitive, "the obedience which faith produces," but comparison with the context of Romans lends more credence to a genitive of apposition, for Rom 10:16 equates obedience and faith. In Rom 6:6 he finds a descriptive genitive in τὸ σῶμα τῆς ἁμαρτίας, "the sinful body." But the body is not inherently sinful. Charles Hodge, on the other hand, takes it as an appositional genitive, looking at sin as a heavy mass. This, however, is contrary to a parallel usage in 6:1213 where σῶμα is the human body. The possessive genitive (Sanday and Headlam) gives the best sense in this passage: "the body of which sin has taken possession."

Ἀγάπη is practically always followed by a subjective genitive in the New Testament. Two clear examples of objective genitives are found (2 Thess 2:10; Luke 11:42). Other examples of objective uses are possible, but "the love of Christ" (2 Cor 5:14) is Christ's love for us, and "the love of God" (Rom 5:5), God's love for us, according to the general rule that prevails.

There are many other areas of grammatical study, of course. Some of them are summarized in the following section.

2) *Summary of selected syntactical relationships.* "Syntax" has been defined and discussed above. A complete treatment of the subject is beyond the scope of this work, but a discussion of selected themes of syntax is beneficial in a consideration of the Grammatico-historical Method of Exegesis. The basis for selecting themes to be treated is the degree of usefulness of these themes in Exegesis, i.e., the items discussed in the following pages are more than likely the ones that will be most often encountered in interpretive study. For further discussion of these and other parts of syntax, the work by H. E. Dana and Julius R. Mantey, *A Manual Grammar of New Testament Greek* (New York: Macmillan, 1957) should be consulted. The page numbers following the initials "D. & M." in the following discussion are references to this work.

1.1 *Definition and nature of syntax* (D. & M., 59–62). A sentence is a "conventional unit of connected speech or writing, usually containing a subject and predicate, beginning with a capital letter and ending with an end mark (period, question mark, exclamation point . . .)" (*Webster's New World Dictionary of the American Language*, 1327). It is also "a word or group of words stating, asking, commanding, requesting, or exclaiming something" (*Webster's*, 1327).

Among other things, *syntax* is a study of the manner in which words in a sentence relate to each other. People may express themselves in a wide variety of ways, but within a given period of time these ways will become fairly stereotyped for a given language. Otherwise, interpersonal communication would be impossible. For example, those who used Koine Greek during the general period of the New Testament fell into the habit of speaking and writing according to certain patterns that were common in their time. It is the task of *syntax* to discover these habits, to analyze them and to put them into well defined categories. Or, in other words, *"syntax is the process of analyzing and classifying the modes of expression presented by a language"* (D. & M., 59).

Syntax is an indispensable "science" in the study of any language which has long ago ceased to be generally used. It is impossible to project oneself back into an ancient cultural and linguistic situation so as to become intuitively sensitive to various nuances of meaning conveyed by different word and grammatical combinations. These shades of meaning were obvious to people when they were using the language every day, but the twentieth century student of Scripture must find another means for tracing out correct interpretations. This alternate means is none other than *syntax* which enables him to examine analytically the various options of expression which were available to the first century Koine Greek writer. By considering the various possibilities for a particular inflectional form in the light of its context and other factors, one can with a high degree of probability establish the meaning which was in the writer's mind when he wrote. Without the analysis and classification of the various forms of expression which *syntax* provides, this would not be possible.

Special attention needs to be drawn to the fact that *syntax* does not consist of a previously contrived set of rules that New Testament writers were obliged to follow. This is not the nature of *syntax*. The final authority for syntactical principles was the people who used the language. There were no absolutes of grammar to which New Testament Greek could be compared. No source to which one can refer is available to discover syntactical categories. These categories must arise from an inductive examination of what has been written in that language. Fortunately much Greek literature is available, both biblical and non-biblical, and many have undertaken the challenge of syntactical analysis and classifications. It is now necessary only to become familiar with the possibilities so that any passage under investigation can be interpreted most in accord with the linguistic patterns of the day.

The purpose of language, both written and spoken, is communication from one party to another. It is the means of bridging the gap between the thought processes of one person and the thought processes of another. The name given to the device for bridging that gap is "sentence." The objective of the Bible interpreter is to examine the "sentences" of Scripture carefully so as to ascertain the thoughts of the writer (or speaker) and the thoughts suggested to the minds of the readers (or listeners). When this is accomplished, the interpreter has also learned in most cases the meaning of the Spirit who inspired the writer. The exceptions to this rule include some statements of Scripture where the manner of inspiration precluded the writer's understanding the full meaning of his own words. Instances of this exceptional situation will be obvious because of the nature of the literature or some unusual contextual feature. The general rule for interpreting, however, is to determine the thoughts of the writer and those produced in the reader. This is done, first of all, by scrutinizing each "sentence."

In the definition of a sentence given above, it is seen to consist of two parts, a subject and a predicate. Turner puts it this way:

The minimal form of the sentence is Subject and Predicate. The Subject is usually expressed by a noun and the Predicate by a verb; and this verb may need a direct or indirect Object. But often the Predicate too may be a noun or its substitute (Nigel Turner, *Syntax*, Vol. III of *A Grammar of New Testament Greek* by James Hope Moulton).

As Turner points out, the part of speech usually associated with the subject is the noun and that normally used in the predicate is the verb. In the second clause of John 1:1, ὁ λόγος ἦν πρὸς τὸν θεόν, has a subject, ὁ λόγος and a predicate, ἦν πρὸς τὸν θεόν. Λόγος is a noun, and ἦν which controls the predicate is a verb. A noun is a means for representing a fact of consciousness or a "picture" in the mind of the writer. A verb makes some assertion concerning the noun, either some action in which it is involved or a state in which it is found.

The syntax of a sentence can conveniently be divided into two broad classifications of study: those which relate most readily to the noun and those usually related to the verb. It is true, as Turner says in the above quotation, that nouns are sometimes found involved in the predicate of a sentence. It is also true that verbs are sometimes found in the subject of a sentence. Nevertheless, the usual pattern is to express a subject by a noun and a predicate by a verb. It is natural, therefore, to divide syntactical discussions into two categories, those related to the noun and those related to the verb.

1.2 *Classifications of syntactical study* (D. &. M., pp. 63–64).   60

2.1 *The Noun.* John 1:1–9 is used for illustrative purposes in this section. Noun-related areas of *syntax* include the following:

3.1 CASE. This pertains to the noun's function in relation to the rest of the sentence. What role does it play? Is it the subject of the sentence? Is it a direct object? Is it an indirect object? Does it play some other part filling out the sentence's meaning?

3.2 PREPOSITIONS. The preposition is a part of speech that makes a noun's function in a sentence more explicit than does the case of the noun. For example, in John 1:4 the thought of ἐν αὐτῷ, a preposition followed by a pronoun, could also have been expressed by αὐτῷ, a pronoun in the locative case without a preposition. The former method of expressing the thought "in him" is more explicit, however, because αὐτῷ alone may have other meanings such as "to him" or "of him."

{John 1:4} - ἐν αὐτῷ ζωὴ ἦν, καὶ ἡ ζωὴ ἦν τὸ φῶς τῶν ἀνθρώπων·

3.3 ADJECTIVES. When one wishes to describe some quality of a noun, he may use an adjective. In John 1:9a, Ἦν τὸ φῶς τὸ ἀληθινόν, the last word ἀληθινόν is an adjective which gives an added feature of φῶς. It is the "true" light.

{John 1:9} - Ἦν τὸ φῶς τὸ <u>ἀληθινόν</u>, ὃ φωτίζει πάντα ἄνθρωπον, ἐρχόμενον εἰς τὸν κόσμον.

3.4 PRONOUNS. If a fact of consciousness had to be referred to by the same word every time, communication would become very monotonous. Hence, language has developed parts of speech called "pronouns." For instance, John 1:2–4 without pronouns would have read, "The word was in the beginning with God. All things were made through the word, and without the word not even one thing which has come into being has been made. In the word was life, and the life was the light of men." The recurrence of "the word" several times in these three verses becomes offensive to the mind of the reader, especially after its use three times in v. 1. Through the use of οὗτος (1:2), αὐτοῦ (1:3), αὐτοῦ (1:3), and αὐτῷ (1:4), this offense is removed.

{John 1:2} - <u>οὗτος</u> ἦν ἐν ἀρχῇ πρὸς τὸν θεόν.

{John 1:3} - πάντα δι' <u>αὐτοῦ</u> ἐγένετο, καὶ χωρὶς <u>αὐτοῦ</u> ἐγένετο οὐδὲ ἕν. ὃ γέγονεν

{John 1:4} - ἐν <u>αὐτῷ</u> ζωὴ ἦν, καὶ ἡ ζωὴ ἦν τὸ φῶς τῶν ἀνθρώπων·

3.5 THE ARTICLE. The Greek article adds yet another dimension to the noun. Its presence with an object of thought marks that object as specific. Its absence changes the focus of attention from the object's identity to a qualitative view of it. Thus it is of interpretive significance that in John 1:1 τὸν θεόν differs from θεὸς in that one identifies and the other stresses quality. A similar comparison may be made between ζωὴ and ἡ ζωὴ in John 1:4.

{John 1:1} - Ἐν ἀρχῇ ἦν ὁ λόγος, καὶ ὁ λόγος ἦν πρὸς <u>τὸν θεόν</u>, καὶ <u>θεὸς</u> ἦν ὁ λόγος.

{John 1:4} - ἐν αὐτῷ <u>ζωὴ</u> ἦν, καὶ <u>ἡ ζωὴ</u> ἦν τὸ φῶς τῶν ἀνθρώπων·

2.2 *The Verb*. John 1:19 is used for illustrative purposes in this section. As stated above, the verb is the heart of the predicate of a sentence. The thought of action or state of the subject is expressed by the verb.

3.1 The verb possesses wide capabilities in designating action or state.

4.1 PERSON. It may speak of that action with the subject himself involved (first person). The action may involve the person addressed (second person) or an object of consciousness separate from either of the above (third person). The verb inflection allows for all three of these. All the finite verbs in John 1:1–9 are third person.

4.2 NUMBER. Inflectional forms of verbs may also reflect whether the subject is one or more than one in number. In John 1:1–9 all the verb forms are singular except for πιστεύσωσιν in 1:7. The first ἐγένετο in 1:3 is singular even though its subject is plural (πάντα), but this is a special case and does not represent the usual situation.

4.3 VOICE. The verb may involve the subject in its action in various ways. The subject may perform, receive or in some other way be involved in the action. This characteristic of the verb is referred to as "voice." Φαίνε ιin John 1:5 is active voice. Ἐγένετο in John 1:6 is middle voice. There is no passive form of a finite verb in John 1:1–9.

{John 1:5} - καὶ τὸ φῶς ἐν τῇ σκοτίᾳ <u>φαίνει</u>, καὶ ἡ σκοτία αὐτὸ οὐ κατέλαβεν.

{John 1:6} - <u>Ἐγένετο</u> ἄνθρωπος, ἀπεσταλμένος παρὰ θεοῦ, ὄνομα αὐτῷ Ἰωάννης

4.4 MOOD. The concept of reality by a writer when he makes a statement is also reflected in the verb's inflectional form. The indicative mood, for example ἦλθεν in John 1:7, conceives of an action as actual. The subjunctive, for example πιστεύσωσιν in John 1:7, conceives of an action as potential. There is no imperative or optative mood in John 1:19.

{John 1:7} - οὗτος <u>ἦλθεν</u> εἰς μαρτυρίαν ἵνα μαρτυρήσῃ περὶ τοῦ φωτός, ἵνα πάντες <u>πιστεύσωσιν</u> δι' αὐτοῦ.

4.5 TENSE. A further feature of the Greek verb is its capability of expressing how an action is conceived of by a writer. He may think of it and express it as being in progress, as being completed, or as a combination of the two, or else he may chose to leave it undefined. This aspect of the verbal form is called "tense." Samples of different kinds of action from John 1:1–9 may be cited:

1:1 ἦν   action in progress in the past

{John 1:1} - Ἐν ἀρχῇ <u>ἦν</u> ὁ λόγος, καὶ ὁ λόγος <u>ἦν</u> πρὸς τὸν θεόν, καὶ θεὸς <u>ἦν</u> ὁ λόγος.

1:3 ἐγένετο   undefined action in the past

{John 1:3} - πάντα δι' αὐτοῦ <u>ἐγένετο</u>, καὶ χωρὶς αὐτοῦ <u>ἐγένετο</u> οὐδὲ ἕν. ὃ γέγονεν

1:6 ἀπεσταλμένος   completed action

{John 1:6} - Ἐγένετο ἄνθρωπος, <u>ἀπεσταλμένος</u> παρὰ θεοῦ, ὄνομα αὐτῷ Ἰωάννης

1:7 μαρτυρήσῃ   undefined action

{John 1:7} οὗτος ἦλθεν εἰς μαρτυρίαν ἵνα <u>μαρτυρήσῃ</u> περὶ τοῦ φωτός, ἵνα πάντες πιστεύσωσιν δι' αὐτοῦ.

1:9 φωτίζει   an action in progress in the present.

{John 1:9} - Ἦν τὸ φῶς τὸ ἀληθινόν, ὃ <u>φωτίζει</u> πάντα ἄνθρωπον, ἐρχόμενον εἰς τὸν κόσμον.

4.6 INFINITIVES AND PARTICIPLES. The Greek verb may also assume forms in which it partakes of certain characteristics of nouns and adjectives. These are called infinitives and participles. In these forms verbs still retain their characteristics of voice and tense. In the participial form they have the added capability expressing gender and case. In John 1:6 ἀπεσταλμένος is a participle. No infinitive appears in John 1:1–9.

{John 1:6} - Ἐγένετο ἄνθρωπος, <u>ἀπεσταλμένος</u> παρὰ θεοῦ, ὄνομα αὐτῷ Ἰωάννης

3.2 ADVERBS. Adverbs normally modify verbs, adjectives or other adverbs. In relation to verbs they somehow qualify or clarify the action expressed by the verb. In John 1:5 οὐ negates κατέλαβεν, and therefore is an adverb, though some grammarians choose to call it a negative particle. In John 1:3 οὐδέ is an example of an adverb used to qualify an adjective (ἕν).

{John 1:3} - πάντα δι' αὐτοῦ ἐγένετο, καὶ χωρὶς αὐτοῦ ἐγένετο <u>οὐδὲ</u> ἕν. ὃ γέγονεν.

3.3 CONJUNCTIONS. A sentence may contain more than one subject and predicate. When this happens, conjunctions are used to connect the different units of a sentence. In John 1:1 καί is used twice to connect three subject-predicate combinations which compose the sentence. In John 1:7 ἵνα is used twice to connect the three subject-predicate combinations in that sentence. Another conjunction, ἀλλά, divides the sentence of John 1:8 to show contrast between the two parts.

{John 1:1} Ἐν ἀρχῇ ἦν ὁ λόγος, καὶ ὁ λόγος ἦν πρὸς τὸν θεόν, καὶ θεὸς ἦν ὁ λόγος.

_____
_____

{John 1:7} - οὗτος ἦλθεν εἰς μαρτυρίαν ἵνα μαρτυρήσῃ περὶ τοῦ φωτός, _ἵνα_ πάντες πιστεύσωσιν δι’ αὐτοῦ.

_____
_____

{John 1:8} - οὐκ ἦν ἐκεῖνος τὸ φῶς, ἀλλ’ ἵνα μαρτυρήσῃ περὶ τοῦ φωτός.

_____
_____

3.4 PARTICLES. Particles are variously defined by different grammarians. For most purposes, it is sufficient to consider them to include a miscellaneous group of words to convey the thought of emphasis or uncertainty.

1.3 CASE USAGES

2.1 THE NOMINATIVE CASE (D. & M., 68–71)

3.1 PREDICATE NOMINATIVE - a substantive (or adjective) in the predicate stands in apposition with (i.e. is a further definition of or description of) the subject of the sentence.

John 1:14 -   σάρξ is a definition of ὁ λόγος. The "flesh" is the same as "the word."

{John 1:14} - Καὶ ὁ λόγος σὰρξ ἐγένετο καὶ ἐσκήνωσεν ἐν ἡμῖν, καὶ ἐθεασάμεθα τὴν δόξαν αὐτοῦ, δόξαν ὡς μονογενοῦς παρὰ πατρός, πλήρης χάριτος καὶ ἀληθείας.

_____
_____

John 1:19 -   "the testimony" is equivalent to "this"

{John 1:19} - Καὶ <u>αὕτη</u> ἐστὶν <u>ἡ μαρτυρία</u> τοῦ Ἰωάννου, ὅτε ἀπέστειλαν [πρὸς αὐτὸν] οἱ Ἰουδαῖοι ἐξ Ἱεροσολύμων ἱερεῖς καὶ Λευίτας ἵνα ἐρωτήσωσιν αὐτόν, Σὺ τίς εἶ;

_____

_____

_____

John 1:19 -   "Who" is the same as "you"

{John 1:19} - Καὶ αὕτη ἐστὶν ἡ μαρτυρία τοῦ Ἰωάννου, ὅτε ἀπέστειλαν [πρὸς αὐτὸν] οἱ Ἰουδαῖοι ἐξ Ἱεροσολύμων ἱερεῖς καὶ Λευίτας ἵνα ἐρωτήσωσιν αὐτόν, <u>Σὺ</u> <u>τίς</u> εἶ;;

_____

_____

_____

John 1:20 -   The equivalency of "the Christ" with "I" is denied by οὐκ.

{John 1:20} - καὶ ὡμολόγησεν καὶ οὐκ ἠρνήσατο, καὶ ὡμολόγησεν ὅτι <u>Ἐγὼ</u> οὐκ εἰμὶ <u>ὁ</u> <u>Χριστός</u>.

_____

_____

John 1:21 -   The question asks whether "Elijah" is the same as "you."

{John 1:21} - καὶ ἠρώτησαν αὐτόν, Τί οὖν; <u>Σὺ</u> <u>Ἡλίας</u> εἶ; καὶ λέγει, Οὐκ εἰμί. Ὁ προφήτης εἶ σύ; καὶ ἀπεκρίθη, Οὔ.

_____

_____

John 1:21 -   The question asks whether "the prophet" is an accurate identification of "you."

{John 1:21} - καὶ ἠρώτησαν αὐτόν, Τί οὖν; Σὺ Ἡλίας εἶ; καὶ λέγει, Οὐκ εἰμί. <u>Ὁ</u> <u>προφήτης</u> εἶ <u>σύ</u>; καὶ ἀπεκρίθη, Οὔ.

_____

_____

3.2 NOMINATIVE OF APPELLATION - limited to proper names.

John 1:6 -   ὄνομα αὐτῷ Ἰωάννης is set off to itself with no grammatical tie-in to the rest of the sentence. The proper name is thus placed in the nominative case.

{John 1:6} - γένετο ἄνθρωπος, ἀπεσταλμένος παρὰ θεοῦ, <u>ὄνομα αὐτῷ Ἰωάννης</u>·

John 3:1 -   Νικόδημος ὄνομα αὐτῷ is also a sort of parenthesis. Hence, Νικόδημος is nominative.

{John 3:1} - Ἦν δὲ ἄνθρωπος ἐκ τῶν Φαρισαίων, <u>Νικόδημος ὄνομα αὐτῷ</u>, ἄρχων τῶν Ἰουδαίων·

John 13:13 - One would have expected Ὁ διδάσκαλος and Ὁ κύριος to be accusative, to agree with με, but it is a nominative of appellation.

{John 13:13} - ὑμεῖς φωνεῖτέ <u>με Ὁ διδάσκαλος καὶ Ὁ κύριος</u>, καὶ καλῶς λέγετε, εἰμὶ γάρ.

Rev 1:4 -   ὁ ὢν καὶ ὁ ἦν καὶ ὁ ἐρχόμενος. Ordinarily the substantive following ἀπό has a genitive inflectional ending, but in this instance it is the nominative because it is construed as an indeclinable proper noun.

{Rev 1:4} - Ἰωάννης ταῖς ἑπτὰ ἐκκλησίαις ταῖς ἐν τῇ Ἀσίᾳ· χάρις ὑμῖν καὶ εἰρήνη <u>ἀπὸ ὁ ὢν καὶ ὁ ἦν καὶ ὁ ἐρχόμενος</u> καὶ ἀπὸ τῶν ἑπτὰ πνευμάτων ἃ ἐνώπιον τοῦ θρόνου αὐτοῦ,

3.3 INDEPENDENT NOMINATIVE - the nominative has no grammatical relation to the rest of the sentence, i.e. no action or state is represented by a verb in connection with it.

John 7:38 -   ὁ πιστεύων is a nominative participle used as a substantive, but it is connected with no finite verb in its sentence. The αὐτοῦ later in sentence picks up the sense of ὁ πιστεύων in the clause following.

{John 7:38} - <u>ὁ πιστεύων</u> εἰς ἐμέ, καθὼς εἶπεν ἡ γραφή, ποταμοὶ ἐκ τῆς κοιλίας <u>αὐτοῦ</u> ῥεύσουσιν ὕδατος ζῶντος.

John 1:6; 3:1 -   In both verses ὄνομα is used without relationship to a verbal idea in the sentence. Hence, it is an independent nominative in each case.

{John 1:6} - Ἐγένετο ἄνθρωπος, ἀπεσταλμένος παρὰ θεοῦ, <u>ὄνομα</u> αὐτῷ Ἰωάννης·

{John 3:1} - Ἦν δὲ ἄνθρωπος ἐκ τῶν Φαρισαίων, Νικόδημος <u>ὄνομα</u> αὐτῷ, ἄρχων τῶν Ἰουδαίων·

John 1:29 -   ὁ ἀμνὸς is not used as the subject of a verbal idea and therefore is an independent nominative.

{John 1:29} - Τῇ ἐπαύριον βλέπει τὸν Ἰησοῦν ἐρχόμενον πρὸς αὐτὸν καὶ λέγει, Ἴδε <u>ὁ ἀμνὸς</u> τοῦ θεοῦ ὁ αἴρων τὴν ἁμαρτίαν τοῦ κόσμου.

Rev 3:12 -   ὁ νικῶν stands by itself, being picked up by the αὐτόν in the next clause.

{Rev 3:12} - <u>ὁ νικῶν</u> ποιήσω αὐτὸν στῦλον ἐν τῷ ναῷ τοῦ θεοῦ μου καὶ ἔξω οὐ μὴ ἐξέλθῃ ἔτι καὶ γράψω ἐπ' <u>αὐτόν</u> τὸ ὄνομα τοῦ θεοῦ μου καὶ τὸ ὄνομα τῆς πόλεως τοῦ θεοῦ μου, τῆς καινῆς Ἰερουσαλὴμ ἡ καταβαίνουσα ἐκ τοῦ οὐρανοῦ ἀπὸ τοῦ θεοῦ μου, καὶ τὸ ὄνομά μου τὸ καινόν.

Rev 3:21 -   In this case the independent ὁ νικῶν is picked up by the αὐτῷ of the next clause. The next clause could have been written τῷ νικῶντι if the independent nominative had not been used.

{Rev 3:21} - <u>ὁ νικῶν</u> δώσω <u>αὐτῷ</u> καθίσαι μετ' ἐμοῦ ἐν τῷ θρόνῳ μου, ὡς κἀγὼ ἐνίκησα καὶ ἐκάθισα μετὰ τοῦ πατρός μου ἐν τῷ θρόνῳ αὐτοῦ.

3.4 NOMINATIVE OF EXCLAMATION - special emotion usually involved here.

Rom 6:17 -   χάρις is a nominative without verbal relations. It is a special expression of gratitude.

{Rom 6:17} - <u>χάρις</u> δὲ τῷ θεῷ ὅτι ἦτε δοῦλοι τῆς ἁμαρτίας ὑπηκούσατε δὲ ἐκ καρδίας εἰς ὃν παρεδόθητε τύπον διδαχῆς,

Rom 7:24 -   ταλαίπωρος . . . ἄνθρωπος· conveys special misery. The exclamation may
               also express remorse.

{Rom 7:24} - <u>ταλαίπωρος</u> ἐγὼ <u>ἄνθρωπος</u>· τίς με ῥύσεται ἐκ τοῦ σώματος τοῦ θανάτου
τούτου;

Rom 7:25 -   χάρις. Here is a special thanksgiving because of victory.

{Rom 7:25} - <u>χάρις</u> δὲ τῷ θεῷ διὰ Ἰησοῦ Χριστοῦ τοῦ κυρίου ἡμῶν. ἄρα οὖν αὐτὸς ἐγὼ
τῷ μὲν νοῒ δουλεύω νόμῳ θεοῦ τῇ δὲ σαρκὶ νόμῳ ἁμαρτίας.

Rom 11:33 -   βάθος expresses wonder over the qualities and capabilities of God. Here is
               utter amazement.

{Rom 11:33} - Ὦ <u>βάθος</u> πλούτου καὶ σοφίας καὶ γνώσεως θεοῦ· ὡς ἀνεξεραύνητα τὰ
κρίματα αὐτοῦ καὶ ἀνεξιχνίαστοι αἱ ὁδοὶ αὐτοῦ.

---

1 Cor 15:57 - Here is another χάρις without a finite verb and hence without a complete
               sentence. This is a victory over death through resurrection.

{1 Cor 15:57} - τῷ δὲ θεῷ <u>χάρις</u> τῷ διδόντι ἡμῖν τὸ νῖκος διὰ τοῦ κυρίου ἡμῶν Ἰησοῦ
Χριστοῦ.

2.2 THE VOCATIVE CASE (D. & M., 71–72)

When the writer (or speaker) uses the name (or other designation) of the person he is
addressing so as to attract his attention or add some kind of emphasis, the vocative is the case
used.

John 17:1 -   In His prayer Christ uses Πάτερ as a designation of the one He is
               addressing. The relationship of Father and Son is a close one, and His use
               of "Father" calls special attention to its intimacy. The inflectional form for
               the vocative in this instance differs from the nominative (Πατήρ).

{John 17:1} - Ταῦτα ἐλάλησεν Ἰησοῦς καὶ ἐπάρας τοὺς ὀφθαλμοὺς αὐτοῦ εἰς τὸν οὐρανὸν εἶπεν, <u>Πάτερ</u>, ἐλήλυθεν ἡ ὥρα· δόξασόν σου τὸν υἱόν, ἵνα ὁ υἱὸς δοξάσῃ σέ,

John 17:21 -   Here the inflectional form of πατήρ is nominative in some ancient manuscripts, but the case is vocative. The whole prayer is punctuated with these direct addresses of the Father.

{John 17:21} - ἵνα πάντες ἓν ὦσιν, καθὼς σύ, <u>πατήρ</u>, ἐν ἐμοὶ κἀγὼ ἐν σοί, ἵνα καὶ αὐτοὶ ἐν ἡμῖν ὦσιν, ἵνα ὁ κόσμος πιστεύῃ ὅτι σύ με ἀπέστειλας.

2.3 THE GENITIVE CASE (D. & M., 72–81) - (Genitive Inflectional Form).

The genitive answers the question, "What kind is it?" In doing so, it falls into different categories of meaning:

3.1 GENITIVE OF DESCRIPTION - this is the broadest use of the genitive, and therefore the least definitive of all. It is the category for a use of the genitive that will fit nowhere else.

Eph. 2:23 -   τῆς ἀπειθείας is descriptive of τοῖς υἱοῖς. They are "disobedient" sons. Essentially the same meaning could have been obtained by using an adjective to describe the sons.

-   we were "wrathful" children. The genitive ὀργῆς tells the nature of τέκνα.

{Eph 2:2} - ἐν αἷς ποτε περιεπατήσατε κατὰ τὸν αἰῶνα τοῦ κόσμου τούτου, κατὰ τὸν ἄρχοντα τῆς ἐξουσίας τοῦ ἀέρος, τοῦ πνεύματος τοῦ νῦν ἐνεργοῦντος ἐν <u>τοῖς υἱοῖς τῆς ἀπειθείας</u>·

{Eph 2:3} - ἐν οἷς καὶ ἡμεῖς πάντες ἀνεστράφημέν ποτε ἐν ταῖς ἐπιθυμίαις τῆς σαρκὸς ἡμῶν ποιοῦντες τὰ θελήματα τῆς σαρκὸς καὶ τῶν διανοιῶν, καὶ ἤμεθα <u>τέκνα</u> φύσει <u>ὀργῆς</u> ὡς καὶ οἱ λοιποί·

3.2 GENITIVE OF POSSESSION

John 1:14 -   αὐτοῦ tells whose glory was beheld. It was the possession "of Him," i.e. the word.

{John 1:14} - Καὶ ὁ λόγος σὰρξ ἐγένετο καὶ ἐσκήνωσεν ἐν ἡμῖν, καὶ ἐθεασάμεθα τὴν δόξαν αὐτοῦ, δόξαν ὡς μονογενοῦς παρὰ πατρός, πλήρης χάριτος καὶ ἀληθείας.

_____

_____

_____

John 7:38 -   αὐτοῦ identifies the person from whose belly living waters will flow. The belly belongs to him "who believes in Me."

{John 7:38} - ὁ πιστεύων εἰς ἐμέ, καθὼς εἶπεν ἡ γραφή, ποταμοὶ ἐκ τῆς κοιλίας αὐτοῦ ῥεύσουσιν ὕδατος ζῶντος.

_____

_____

_____

Rev 1:4 -   αὐτοῦ clarifies that the throne is the property of "the one who is and the one who was and the one who is coming."

{Rev 1:4} - Ἰωάννης ταῖς ἑπτὰ ἐκκλησίαις ταῖς ἐν τῇ Ἀσίᾳ· χάρις ὑμῖν καὶ εἰρήνη ἀπὸ ὁ ὢν καὶ ὁ ἦν καὶ ὁ ἐρχόμενος καὶ ἀπὸ τῶν ἑπτὰ πνευμάτων ἃ ἐνώπιον τοῦ θρόνου αὐτοῦ

_____

_____

_____

Rev 3:12 -   τοῦ θεοῦ shows that my "God" is the owner of the temple (or sanctuary).

{Rev 3:12} - ὁ νικῶν ποιήσω αὐτὸν στῦλον ἐν τῷ ναῷ τοῦ θεοῦ μου καὶ ἔξω οὐ μὴ ἐξέλθῃ ἔτι καὶ γράψω ἐπ' αὐτὸν τὸ ὄνομα _τοῦ θεοῦ_ μου καὶ τὸ ὄνομα τῆς πόλεως τοῦ θεοῦ μου, τῆς καινῆς Ἰερουσαλὴμ ἡ καταβαίνουσα ἐκ τοῦ οὐρανοῦ ἀπὸ τοῦ θεοῦ μου, καὶ τὸ ὄνομά μου τὸ καινόν.

_____

_____

_____

3.3 GENITIVE OF RELATIONSHIP - used only for kinds of blood relationships (including marriage)

John 21:2 -   οἱ τοῦ Ζεβεδαίου. "Those of Zebedee" understands that it was "the sons" of Zebedee who were referred to. The context of the four gospels makes this clear enough, so that the blood relationship in the mind of John when he wrote need not be in doubt.

{John 21:2} - ἦσαν ὁμοῦ Σίμων Πέτρος καὶ Θωμᾶς ὁ λεγόμενος Δίδυμος καὶ Ναθαναὴλ ὁ ἀπὸ Κανὰ τῆς Γαλιλαίας καὶ <u>οἱ τοῦ Ζεβεδαίου</u> καὶ ἄλλοι ἐκ τῶν μαθητῶν αὐτοῦ δύο.

_____

_____

_____

John 21:15 -   Σίμων Ἰωάννου. That Peter was the son of a man named John has already been specified earlier by the writer John (John 1:42).

{John 21:15} - Ὅτε οὖν ἠρίστησαν λέγει τῷ Σίμωνι Πέτρῳ ὁ Ἰησοῦς, <u>Σίμων Ἰωάννου</u>, ἀγαπᾷς με πλέον τούτων; λέγει αὐτῷ, Ναὶ κύριε, σὺ οἶδας ὅτι φιλῶ σε. λέγει αὐτῷ, Βόσκε τὰ ἀρνία μου.

_____

_____

_____

3.4 ADVERBIAL GENITIVE - The adverbial genitive has three shades of meaning which it expresses:

4.1 Of Time

John 3:2 -   νυκτὸς does not indicate the point in time of Nicodemus' coming (locative), nor does it tell how long he stayed (accusative). It rather tells the kind of time he chose for coming to Christ. He chose to come during the nighttime rather than the daytime.

{John 3:2} - οὗτος ἦλθεν πρὸς αὐτὸν <u>νυκτὸς</u> καὶ εἶπεν αὐτῷ, Ῥαββί, οἴδαμεν ὅτι ἀπὸ θεοῦ ἐλήλυθας διδάσκαλος· οὐδεὶς γὰρ δύναται ταῦτα τὰ σημεῖα ποιεῖν ἃ σὺ ποιεῖς, ἐὰν μὴ ᾖ ὁ θεὸς μετ' αὐτοῦ.

_____

_____

_____

1 Thess 2:9 -   νυκτὸς καὶ ἡμέρας tells the nature of the time periods during which Paul and his associates labored. They worked to support themselves in periods of both darkness and daylight. It was an around-the-clock effort.

{1 Thess 2:9} - μνημονεύετε γάρ, ἀδελφοί, τὸν κόπον ἡμῶν καὶ τὸν μόχθον· <u>νυκτὸς καὶ ἡμέρας</u> ἐργαζόμενοι πρὸς τὸ μὴ ἐπιβαρῆσαί τινα ὑμῶν ἐκηρύξαμεν εἰς ὑμᾶς τὸ εὐαγγέλιον τοῦ θεοῦ.

_____

_____

_____

4.2 Of Place (rare in the N. T.)

Luke 16:24 -	ὕδατος tells the place where the rich man requests Lazarus to dip his finger.

{Luke 16:24} - καὶ αὐτὸς φωνήσας εἶπεν, Πάτερ Ἀβραάμ, ἐλέησόν με καὶ πέμψον Λάζαρον ἵνα βάψῃ τὸ ἄκρον τοῦ δακτύλου αὐτοῦ <u>ὕδατος</u> καὶ καταψύξῃ τὴν γλῶσσάν μου, ὅτι ὀδυνῶμαι ἐν τῇ φλογὶ ταύτῃ.

———
———
———

Luke 19:4 -	ἐκείνης points out the place (by the sycamore tree) by which Jesus was about to pass.

{Luke 19:4} - καὶ προδραμὼν εἰς τὸ ἔμπροσθεν ἀνέβη ἐπὶ συκομορέαν ἵνα ἴδῃ αὐτὸν ὅτι <u>ἐκείνης</u> ἤμελλεν διέρχεσθαι.

———
———

4.3 Of Reference - that with reference to which the force of an adjective applies.

John 1:14 -	χάριτος καὶ ἀληθείας define the areas of fullness. Πλήρης is an adjective, for which these two genitives specify the realms where the fullness applies.

{John 1:14} - Καὶ ὁ λόγος σὰρξ ἐγένετο καὶ ἐσκήνωσεν ἐν ἡμῖν, καὶ ἐθεασάμεθα τὴν δόξαν αὐτοῦ, δόξαν ὡς μονογενοῦς παρὰ πατρός, πλήρης <u>χάριτος καὶ ἀληθείας</u>.

———
———
———

1 Cor 11:27 -	The liability for eating the bread and drinking the cup unworthily is in two regards: the body and the blood of the Lord. The adjective which is further defined in this case is ἔνοχος.

{1 Cor 11:27} - Ὥστε ὃς ἂν ἐσθίῃ τὸν ἄρτον ἢ πίνῃ τὸ ποτήριον τοῦ κυρίου ἀναξίως, <u>ἔνοχος</u> ἔσται τοῦ σώματος καὶ τοῦ αἵματος τοῦ κυρίου.

———
———

3.5 GENITIVE WITH NOUNS OF ACTION -- the verbal idea of the noun of action need not be strong. If there is even a slight verbal idea latent in the noun, this is a likely identification. The genitive with nouns of action is of two types:

4.1 Subjective Genitive - the noun in the genitive which accompanies the noun of action is the one accomplishing the action involved in the verbal idea.

John 4:10 -   τὴν δωρεὰν has the verbal idea of "giving" and τοῦ θεοῦ is a genitive which tells who does the giving. Hence, this is a subjective genitive. This is not far from the idea of an ablative of source. The verbal idea of the noun is sufficient to indicate a genitive (subjective) with a noun of action.

{John 4:10} - ἀπεκρίθη Ἰησοῦς καὶ εἶπεν αὐτῇ, Εἰ ᾔδεις <u>τὴν δωρεὰν</u> <u>τοῦ θεοῦ</u> καὶ τίς ἐστιν ὁ λέγων σοι, Δός μοι πεῖν, σὺ ἂν ᾔτησας αὐτὸν καὶ ἔδωκεν ἄν σοι ὕδωρ ζῶν.

---

1 Tim 4:1 -   διδασκαλίαις δαιμονίων. The demons are the ones who carry out the teaching suggested in the noun of action. Therefore, this is a subjective genitive.

{1 Tim 4:1} - Τὸ δὲ πνεῦμα ῥητῶς λέγει ὅτι ἐν ὑστέροις καιροῖς ἀποστήσονταί τινες τῆς πίστεως προσέχοντες πνεύμασιν πλάνοις καὶ <u>διδασκαλίαις δαιμονίων,</u>

4.2 Objective Genitive - the noun in the genitive which accompanies the noun of action is the object of the action of the verbal idea.

John 2:17 -   The sense is that the zeal is directed toward God's house. Ὁ ζῆλος contains the notion of action and τοῦ οἴκου is the genitive that is the object of that zeal. Hence, an objective genitive is the correct identification.

{John 2:17} - Ἐμνήσθησαν οἱ μαθηταὶ αὐτοῦ ὅτι γεγραμμένον ἐστίν, <u>Ὁ ζῆλος</u> <u>τοῦ οἴκου</u> σου καταφάγεταί με.

John 3:1 -   Since Nicodemus ruled (with others) over (ἄρχων) the Jews in his leadership capacity, τῶν Ἰουδαίων· is an objective genitive.

{John 3:1} - Ἦν δὲ ἄνθρωπος ἐκ τῶν Φαρισαίων, Νικόδημος ὄνομα αὐτῷ, <u>ἄρχων</u> <u>τῶν Ἰουδαίων·</u>

John 7:13 -   The verbal idea of fearing is involved in τὸν φόβον. The ones feared were "the Jews" (τῶν Ἰουδαίων), i.e. they were the objects of the fear.

{John 7:13} - οὐδεὶς μέντοι παρρησίᾳ ἐλάλει περὶ αὐτοῦ διὰ <u>τὸν φόβον</u> <u>τῶν Ἰουδαίων</u>.

3.6 GENITIVE of APPOSITION - the noun in the genitive is in some sense identical with the noun it modifies. It further defines it in some way.

John 2:21 -   τοῦ σώματος designates the same thing as τοῦ ναοῦ. Hence, it is a genitive of apposition. It is in apposition to (i.e. placed beside so as to explain) τοῦ ναοῦ. In this case "the temple (or sanctuary)" is figurative and is followed by "His body" which explains what He meant by "the temple."

{John 2:21} - ἐκεῖνος δὲ ἔλεγεν περὶ <u>τοῦ ναοῦ</u> <u>τοῦ σώματος</u> αὐτοῦ.

John 11:13 -   τῆς κοιμήσεως is ambiguous. It could refer to death or physical sleep. The genitive τοῦ ὕπνου as an appositional explanation decides the issue between the two. The disciples thought He referred to physical sleep.

{John 11:13} - εἰρήκει δὲ ὁ Ἰησοῦς περὶ τοῦ θανάτου αὐτοῦ, ἐκεῖνοι δὲ ἔδοξαν ὅτι περὶ <u>τῆς κοιμήσεως</u> <u>τοῦ ὕπνου</u> λέγει.

3.7 PARTITIVE GENITIVE - the noun in the genitive designates a whole group or body. The substantive that it modifies refers to a part of that group or body. Though close to the ablative and its root idea, in the partitive genitive separation is not the emphasis as it is with the ablative.

Mark 14:43 -   εἷς is part of a larger body which is designated by τῶν δώδεκα. The latter expression is referred to as a partitive genitive.

{Mark 14:43} - Καὶ εὐθὺς ἔτι αὐτοῦ λαλοῦντος παραγίνεται Ἰούδας <u>εἷς τῶν δώδεκα</u> καὶ μετ᾽ αὐτοῦ ὄχλος μετὰ μαχαιρῶν καὶ ξύλων παρὰ τῶν ἀρχιερέων καὶ τῶν γραμματέων καὶ τῶν πρεσβυτέρων.

Rev 8:7 -   Both τῆς γῆς and τῶν δένδρων designate totality. A part of that in each case is τὸ τρίτον. The genitives are therefore partitive.

{Rev 8:7} - Καὶ ὁ πρῶτος ἐσάλπισεν· καὶ ἐγένετο χάλαζα καὶ πῦρ μεμιγμένα ἐν αἵματι καὶ ἐβλήθη εἰς τὴν γῆν, καὶ <u>τὸ τρίτον τῆς γῆς</u> κατεκάη καὶ <u>τὸ τρίτον τῶν δένδρων</u> κατεκάη καὶ πᾶς χόρτος χλωρὸς κατεκάη.

_____

_____

_____

3.8 GENITIVE ABSOLUTE - the noun or pronoun and the participle in the genitive case are without grammatical relationship to the rest of the sentence.

John 2:3 -   "And the wine having failed (or when the wine failed), the mother of Jesus says to Him. . . ." The noun οἴνου and the participle ὑστερήσαντος are genitives and have no grammatical connection with the rest of the sentence.

{John 2:3} - καὶ <u>ὑστερήσαντος οἴνου</u> λέγει ἡ μήτηρ τοῦ Ἰησοῦ πρὸς αὐτόν, Οἶνον οὐκ ἔχουσιν.

_____

_____

John 4:9 -   γυναικὸς Σαμαρίτιδος οὔσης. "Samaritan (gen. of description) woman" is made up of two genitives with γυναικός furnishing a part of the genitive absolute. The participle in the genitive is οὔσης. "Since I am a Samaritan woman." Γυναικός is actually a predicate agreeing with an understood ἐμοῦ.

{John 4:9} - λέγει οὖν αὐτῷ ἡ γυνὴ ἡ Σαμαρῖτις, Πῶς σὺ Ἰουδαῖος ὢν παρ' ἐμοῦ πεῖν αἰτεῖς <u>γυναικὸς Σαμαρίτιδος οὔσης</u>; οὐ γὰρ συγχρῶνται Ἰουδαῖοι Σαμαρίταις.

_____

_____

_____

3.9 GENITIVE WITH VERBS - the nature of the verbal idea requires a genitive to complete its meaning. There are four types of verbal ideas that require genitive objects: sensation, emotion, sharing, and ruling.

Mark 10:42 -   This verse contains three verbs that denote *ruling*: ἄρχειν, κατακυριεύουσιν, and κατεξουσιάζουσιν. Each is followed by a genitive case: τῶν ἐθνῶν, αὐτῶν, and αὐτῶν.

{Mark 10:42} - καὶ προσκαλεσάμενος αὐτοὺς ὁ Ἰησοῦς λέγει αὐτοῖς, Οἴδατε ὅτι οἱ δοκοῦντες <u>ἄρχειν τῶν ἐθνῶν</u> <u>κατακυριεύουσιν αὐτῶν</u> καὶ οἱ μεγάλοι αὐτῶν <u>κατεξουσιάζουσιν αὐτῶν</u>.

_____

_____

_____

John 10:8 -   ἀκούω is a verb of hearing, a root idea of *sensation* which requires the genitive case in its object. Hence, the text reads αὐτῶν rather than αὐτούς (accusative).

{John 10:8} - πάντες ὅσοι ἦλθον [πρὸ ἐμοῦ] κλέπται εἰσὶν καὶ λησταί, ἀλλ᾽ οὐκ <u>ἤκουσαν</u> <u>αὐτῶν</u> τὰ πρόβατα.

2.4 THE ABLATIVE CASE - (Genitive Inflectional Form) (D. & M., pp. 81–83). The ablative is the "whence" case. Having the root idea of separation, it focuses upon "that from which."

3.1 ABLATIVE OF SEPARATION (rare in the N.T.)

1 Cor 9:21 -   ἄνομος θεοῦ. The idea of the phrase is "without law away from God." The notion of independence or separation from God is prominent.

{1 Cor 9:21} - τοῖς ἀνόμοις ὡς ἄνομος, μὴ ὢν <u>ἄνομος θεοῦ</u> ἀλλ᾽ ἔννομος Χριστοῦ, ἵνα κερδάνω τοὺς ἀνόμους·

Eph. 2:12 -   The Gentile readers of the epistle were not included in the provisions of God's covenants with Israel. They were "strangers separated from the covenants of promise."

{Eph 2:12} - ὅτι ἦτε τῷ καιρῷ ἐκείνῳ χωρὶς Χριστοῦ, ἀπηλλοτριωμένοι τῆς πολιτείας τοῦ Ἰσραὴλ καὶ <u>ξένοι τῶν διαθηκῶν τῆς ἐπαγγελίας</u>, ἐλπίδα μὴ ἔχοντες καὶ ἄθεοι ἐν τῷ κόσμῳ.

3.2 ABLATIVE OF SOURCE

Rom 1:17 -   δικαιοσύνη . . . θεοῦ. God is the source of this righteousness. The genitive should not be construed as subjective, i.e., "a righteousness which God produces." Though the idea is very close to a subjective genitive, the notion of God's acting is not prominent in δικαιοσύνη or in the context. The source from which the righteousness comes (i.e., an ablative of source), blends better with the flow of thought.

{Rom 1:17} <u>δικαιοσύνη</u> γὰρ <u>θεοῦ</u> ἐν αὐτῷ ἀποκαλύπτεται ἐκ πίστεως εἰς πίστιν, καθὼς γέγραπται, Ὁ δὲ δίκαιος ἐκ πίστεως ζήσεται.

Heb 13:7 -   The readers are to observe carefully "that which issues from (τὴν ἔκβασιν τῆς ἀναστροφῆς) their leaders' (ὧν . . . τῶν ἡγουμένων ὑμῶν) behavior." Exemplary behavior is a source from which comes an outflow or consequences which other believers are to watch carefully.

{Heb 13:7} Μνημονεύετε <u>τῶν ἡγουμένων ὑμῶν</u>, οἵτινες ἐλάλησαν ὑμῖν τὸν λόγον τοῦ θεοῦ, <u>ὧν</u> ἀναθεωροῦντες <u>τὴν ἔκβασιν τῆς ἀναστροφῆς</u> μιμεῖσθε τὴν πίστιν.

3.3 ABLATIVE OF MEANS (includes agency also)

John 6:45 -   διδακτοὶ θεοῦ, "taught by God." God is also the source of the teaching, but the verbal adjective διδακτοί dictates that His agency in teaching be the force of the ablative here.

{John 6:45} ἔστιν γεγραμμένον ἐν τοῖς προφήταις, Καὶ ἔσονται πάντες <u>διδακτοὶ θεοῦ</u>· πᾶς ὁ ἀκούσας παρὰ τοῦ πατρὸς καὶ μαθὼν ἔρχεται πρὸς ἐμέ.

Rom 1:7 -   The Roman recipients are "beloved by God." Again, as is often the case, the genitive inflectional ending (θεοῦ) following a verbal adjective (ἀγαπητοῖς) is an ablative of agency (or means).

{Rom 1:7} πᾶσιν τοῖς οὖσιν ἐν Ῥώμῃ <u>ἀγαπητοῖς θεοῦ</u>, κλητοῖς ἁγίοις, χάρις ὑμῖν καὶ εἰρήνη ἀπὸ θεοῦ πατρὸς ἡμῶν καὶ κυρίου Ἰησοῦ Χριστοῦ.

3.4 ABLATIVE OF COMPARISON

John 1:15 -   πρῶτός μου compares the time of the Word's existence with that of John the Baptist. John says the Word existed earlier.

{John 1:15} Ἰωάννης μαρτυρεῖ περὶ αὐτοῦ καὶ κέκραγεν λέγων, Οὗτος ἦν ὃν εἶπον, Ὁ ὀπίσω μου ἐρχόμενος ἔμπροσθέν μου γέγονεν, ὅτι <u>πρῶτός μου</u> ἦν.

John 4:12 -   μείζων . . . τοῦ πατρὸς . . . Ἰακώβ. The woman questions whether Jesus is greater than Jacob. The ablative is used in comparisons quite frequently in the NT.

{John 4:12} μὴ σὺ μείζων εἶ τοῦ πατρὸς ἡμῶν Ἰακώβ, ὃς ἔδωκεν ἡμῖν τὸ φρέαρ καὶ αὐτὸς ἐξ αὐτοῦ ἔπιεν καὶ οἱ υἱοὶ αὐτοῦ καὶ τὰ θρέμματα αὐτοῦ;

3.5 ABLATIVE WITH VERBS - the verbal idea requires an ablative for its object.

Gal 5:4 -   τῆς χάριτος. Trying to be justified by law automatically entails being separated from the grace method of justification. The two cannot mix. The ἐκ prefix of ἐκπίπτω adds the idea of separation to πίπτω. This is a verb of departure.

{Gal 5:4} κατηργήθητε ἀπὸ Χριστοῦ, οἵτινες ἐν νόμῳ δικαιοῦσθε, τῆς χάριτος ἐξεπέσατε.

James 1:5 -   Verbs of lacking such as λείπεται need an ablative object. To lack wisdom (σοφίας) is to be separated from it.

{Jas 1:5} Εἰ δέ τις ὑμῶν λείπεται σοφίας, αἰτείτω παρὰ τοῦ διδόντος θεοῦ πᾶσιν ἁπλῶς καὶ μὴ ὀνειδίζοντος καὶ δοθήσεται αὐτῷ.

---

1 Pet 4:1 -   Separation is involved in the verbal idea of ceasing (πέπαυται). Hence, ἁμαρτίας, an ablative, and not ἁμαρτίαν, an accusative, is used.

{1 Pet 4:1} Χριστοῦ οὖν παθόντος σαρκὶ καὶ ὑμεῖς τὴν αὐτὴν ἔννοιαν ὁπλίσασθε, ὅτι ὁ παθὼν σαρκὶ πέπαυται ἁμαρτίας

2.5 THE DATIVE CASE (Dative Inflectional Ending) (D. & M., 83–86)

3.1 DATIVE OF INDIRECT OBJECT - with an indirect object in English a "to" or "for" may be stated, or understood but not stated.

John 4:9 -   "She says to Him." The pronoun αὐτῷ specifies the person to whom the action of λέγει is directed.

{John 4:9} λέγει οὖν <u>αὐτῷ</u> ἡ γυνὴ ἡ Σαμαρῖτις, Πῶς σὺ Ἰουδαῖος ὢν παρ᾽ ἐμοῦ πεῖν αἰτεῖς γυναικὸς Σαμαρίτιδος οὔσης; οὐ γὰρ συγχρῶνται Ἰουδαῖοι Σαμαρίταις.

_____
_____
_____

John 4:10 -   σοι, μοι, and σοι are indirect objects. "Give me to drink" is the same as
               "give to me to drink." These are two ways of expressing an indirect object
               in English.

{John 4:10} ἀπεκρίθη Ἰησοῦς καὶ εἶπεν αὐτῇ, Εἰ ᾔδεις τὴν δωρεὰν τοῦ θεοῦ καὶ τίς ἐστιν ὁ λέγων <u>σοι</u>, Δός <u>μοι</u> πεῖν, σὺ ἂν ᾔτησας αὐτὸν καὶ ἔδωκεν ἄν <u>σοι</u> ὕδωρ ζῶν.

_____
_____
_____

John 4:42 -   τῇ . . . γυναικί is the person "to whom" the words were directed.

{John 4:42} <u>τῇ</u> τε <u>γυναικὶ</u> ἔλεγον ὅτι Οὐκέτι διὰ τὴν σὴν λαλιὰν πιστεύομεν, αὐτοὶ γὰρ ἀκηκόαμεν καὶ οἴδαμεν ὅτι οὗτός ἐστιν ἀληθῶς ὁ σωτὴρ τοῦ κόσμου.

_____
_____
_____

3.2 DATIVE OF ADVANTAGE OR DISADVANTAGE

John 3:26 -   ᾧ is a pronoun designating the person "for whose sake" John had testified
               (μεμαρτύρηκας). The context demands a stronger emphasis on personal
               benefit than is provided by the indirect object, which says an action is
               done "for" someone.

{John 3:26} καὶ ἦλθον πρὸς τὸν Ἰωάννην καὶ εἶπαν αὐτῷ, Ραββί, ὃς ἦν μετὰ σοῦ πέραν τοῦ Ἰορδάνου, <u>ᾧ</u> σὺ μεμαρτύρηκας, ἴδε οὗτος βαπτίζει καὶ πάντες ἔρχονται πρὸς αὐτόν.

_____
_____

Rev 21:2 -   The bride is adorned (κεκοσμημένην) for the advantage of her husband
               (τῷ ἀνδρί). Personal interest is highlighted in such a relationship and
               activity.

{Rev 21:2} καὶ τὴν πόλιν τὴν ἁγίαν Ἰερουσαλὴμ καινὴν εἶδον καταβαίνουσαν ἐκ τοῦ οὐρανοῦ ἀπὸ τοῦ θεοῦ ἡτοιμασμένην ὡς νύμφην <u>κεκοσμημένην</u> <u>τῷ ἀνδρὶ</u> αὐτῆς.

_____
_____

3.3 DATIVE OF POSSESSION

John 1:6; 3:1 -   αὐτῷ in both verses goes with ὄνομα, "John's or
Nikodemus's name." It specifies the one to whom the name
belongs.

{John 1:6} Ἐγένετο ἄνθρωπος, ἀπεσταλμένος παρὰ θεοῦ, ὄνομα <u>αὐτῷ</u> Ἰωάννης·

_____

_____

{John 3:1} Ἦν δὲ ἄνθρωπος ἐκ τῶν Φαρισαίων, Νικόδημος ὄνομα <u>αὐτῷ</u>, ἄρχων τῶν
Ἰουδαίων·

_____

_____

John 18:39 -   The custom of releasing one at Passover was the possession of those
addressed. Thus the second person pronoun ὑμῖν qualifies συνήθεια. (The
second and third occurrences of ὑμῖν in the verse tells for whose sake
someone was released.)

{John 18:39} ἔστιν δὲ συνήθεια <u>ὑμῖν</u> ἵνα ἕνα ἀπολύσω <u>ὑμῖν</u> ἐν τῷ πάσχα· βούλεσθε οὖν
ἀπολύσω <u>ὑμῖν</u> τὸν βασιλέα τῶν Ἰουδαίων;

_____

_____

3.4 DATIVE OF REFERENCE

Rom 6:2 -   τῇ ἁμαρτίᾳ stipulates that with reference to which the death (ἀπεθάνομεν)
took place.

{Rom 6:2} μὴ γένοιτο. οἵτινες <u>ἀπεθάνομεν</u> <u>τῇ ἁμαρτίᾳ</u>, πῶς ἔτι ζήσομεν ἐν αὐτῇ;

_____

_____

Rom 6:11 -   Since such a death (νεκρούς) with reference to sin (τῇ ἁμαρτίᾳ) occurred,
the believer is to count on such a death in his own mental outlook. Also
since Christ lives with reference to God (6:10), the believer is to take into
account his own life (ζῶντας) with reference to God (τῷ θεῷ).

{Rom 6:11} οὕτως καὶ ὑμεῖς λογίζεσθε ἑαυτοὺς [εἶναι] <u>νεκροὺς</u> μὲν <u>τῇ ἁμαρτίᾳ</u> <u>ζῶντας</u>
<u>δὲ τῷ θεῷ</u> ἐν Χριστῷ Ἰησοῦ.

_____

_____

3.5 DATIVE with VERBS - the verbal idea has personal interest as a prominent part. This includes verbs of trusting, obeying, worshiping, serving, pleasing and commanding.

John 3:36 -   τῷ υἱῷ is the direct object of ἀπειθῶν, a verb of disobeying. In this case it is a verb expressing the absence of personal interest.

{John 3:36} ὁ πιστεύων εἰς τὸν υἱὸν ἔχει ζωὴν αἰώνιον· ὁ δὲ <u>ἀπειθῶν</u> <u>τῷ υἱῷ</u> οὐκ ὄψεται ζωήν, ἀλλ' ἡ ὀργὴ τοῦ θεοῦ μένει ἐπ' αὐτόν.

John 4:21 -   μοι is the object of a verb of trust, and τῷ πατρί is the object of a verb of worship.

{John 4:21} λέγει αὐτῇ ὁ Ἰησοῦς, Πίστευέ <u>μοι</u>, γύναι, ὅτι ἔρχεται ὥρα ὅτε οὔτε ἐν τῷ ὄρει τούτῳ οὔτε ἐν Ἱεροσολύμοις προσκυνήσετε <u>τῷ πατρί</u>.

Rom 7:25 -   νόμῳ (both occurrences) is the object of δουλεύω. This expresses the personal interest of service, in this verse a divided interest.

{Rom 7:25} χάρις δὲ τῷ θεῷ διὰ Ἰησοῦ Χριστοῦ τοῦ κυρίου ἡμῶν. ἄρα οὖν αὐτὸς ἐγὼ τῷ μὲν νοῒ <u>δουλεύω</u> <u>νόμῳ</u> θεοῦ τῇ δὲ σαρκὶ <u>νόμῳ</u> ἁμαρτίας.

Rom 8:8 -   Pleasing (ἀρέσαι) is a very obvious example of personal interest. Hence, the dative θεῷ as an object to complete the verb's meaning.

{Rom 8:8} οἱ δὲ ἐν σαρκὶ ὄντες <u>θεῷ</u> <u>ἀρέσαι</u> οὐ δύνανται.

2.6 THE LOCATIVE CASE (Dative Inflectional Ending) (D. & M., pp. 8688)

The locative is the "where" case. It points to the location, whether it be in space, in time, or in concept.

3.1 LOCATIVE OF PLACE - here the location is geographical. (very rare in the NT)

John 21:8 -   τῷ πλοιαρίῳ specifies the location of "the other disciples" as they came (ἦλθον). This could possibly be construed as an instrumental of means, telling the means by which they came, but the balance of probability is on the side of the locative of place.

{John 21:8} οἱ δὲ ἄλλοι μαθηταὶ <u>τῷ πλοιαρίῳ ἦλθον</u>, οὐ γὰρ ἦσαν μακρὰν ἀπὸ τῆς γῆς ἀλλὰ ὡς ἀπὸ πηχῶν διακοσίων, σύροντες τὸ δίκτυον τῶν ἰχθύων.

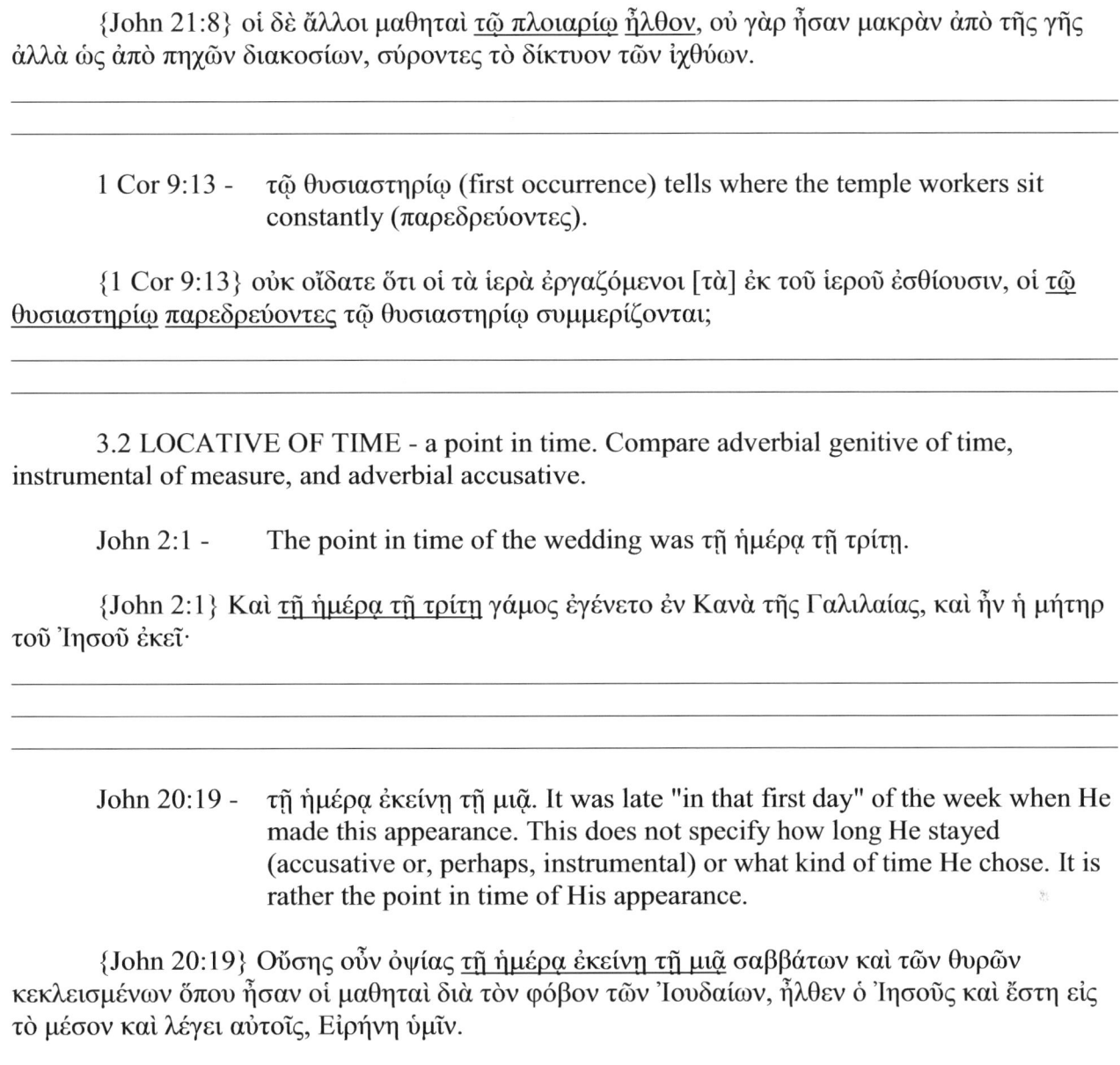

1 Cor 9:13 -   τῷ θυσιαστηρίῳ (first occurrence) tells where the temple workers sit constantly (παρεδρεύοντες).

{1 Cor 9:13} οὐκ οἴδατε ὅτι οἱ τὰ ἱερὰ ἐργαζόμενοι [τὰ] ἐκ τοῦ ἱεροῦ ἐσθίουσιν, οἱ <u>τῷ θυσιαστηρίῳ</u> <u>παρεδρεύοντες</u> τῷ θυσιαστηρίῳ συμμερίζονται;

3.2 LOCATIVE OF TIME - a point in time. Compare adverbial genitive of time, instrumental of measure, and adverbial accusative.

John 2:1 -   The point in time of the wedding was τῇ ἡμέρᾳ τῇ τρίτῃ.

{John 2:1} Καὶ <u>τῇ ἡμέρᾳ τῇ τρίτῃ</u> γάμος ἐγένετο ἐν Κανὰ τῆς Γαλιλαίας, καὶ ἦν ἡ μήτηρ τοῦ Ἰησοῦ ἐκεῖ·

John 20:19 -   τῇ ἡμέρᾳ ἐκείνῃ τῇ μιᾷ. It was late "in that first day" of the week when He made this appearance. This does not specify how long He stayed (accusative or, perhaps, instrumental) or what kind of time He chose. It is rather the point in time of His appearance.

{John 20:19} Οὔσης οὖν ὀψίας <u>τῇ ἡμέρᾳ ἐκείνῃ τῇ μιᾷ</u> σαββάτων καὶ τῶν θυρῶν κεκλεισμένων ὅπου ἦσαν οἱ μαθηταὶ διὰ τὸν φόβον τῶν Ἰουδαίων, ἦλθεν ὁ Ἰησοῦς καὶ ἔστη εἰς τὸ μέσον καὶ λέγει αὐτοῖς, Εἰρήνη ὑμῖν.

3.3 LOCATIVE OF SPHERE - location in the realm of ideas.

1 Cor 14:20 -   ταῖς φρεσὶν (first occurrence) tells the sphere in which they were to stop being children (μὴ παιδία γίνεσθε). The readers were encouraged to be infants (νηπιάζετε) in the realm of malice (τῇ κακίᾳ). In the realm of their minds (ταῖς . . . φρεσὶν) they were told to be mature (τέλειοι γίνεσθε) τέλειοι γίνεσθε.

{1 Cor 14:20} Ἀδελφοί, μὴ παιδία γίνεσθε ταῖς φρεσὶν ἀλλὰ τῇ κακίᾳ νηπιάζετε, ταῖς δὲ φρεσὶν τέλειοι γίνεσθε.

Rom 12:10–13 - Each of the following tells the appropriate sphere of the behavior related to it: τῇ φιλαδελφίᾳ (12:10), τῇ τιμῇ (12:10), τῇ σπουδῇ (12:11), τῷ πνεύματι (12:11), τῇ ἐλπίδι (12:12), τῇ θλίψει (12:12), τῇ προσευχῇ (12:12), ταῖς χρείαις (12:13).

{Rom 12:10} τῇ φιλαδελφίᾳ εἰς ἀλλήλους φιλόστοργοι, τῇ τιμῇ ἀλλήλους προηγούμενοι,

{Rom 12:11} τῇ σπουδῇ μὴ ὀκνηροί, τῷ πνεύματι ζέοντες, τῷ κυρίῳ δουλεύοντες,

{Rom 12:12} τῇ ἐλπίδι χαίροντες, τῇ θλίψει ὑπομένοντες, τῇ προσευχῇ προσκαρτεροῦντες,

{Rom 12:13} ταῖς χρείαις τῶν ἁγίων κοινωνοῦντες, τὴν φιλοξενίαν διώκοντες.

2.7 THE INSTRUMENTAL CASE (Dative Inflectional Ending) (D. & M., 88–91)

This case frequently involves the idea of association as well as that of means.

3.1 INSTRUMENTAL OF MEANS

1 Pet 1:18–19 - φθαρτοῖς, ἀργυρίῳ, and χρυσίῳ express means by which redemption was not obtained. τιμίῳ αἵματι tells the means by which it was obtained.

{1 Pet 1:18} εἰδότες ὅτι οὐ φθαρτοῖς, ἀργυρίῳ ἢ χρυσίῳ, ἐλυτρώθητε ἐκ τῆς ματαίας ὑμῶν ἀναστροφῆς πατροπαραδότου

{1 Pet 1:19} ἀλλὰ τιμίῳ αἵματι ὡς ἀμνοῦ ἀμώμου καὶ ἀσπίλου Χριστοῦ,

3.2 INSTRUMENTAL OF CAUSE

Rom 4:20 - τῇ ἀπιστίᾳ, "because of unbelief," dismisses unbelief as a cause for doubt. It did not cause Abraham to doubt. Possibly τῇ πίστει gives the cause of his becoming strong, but it may more easily depict the sphere in which he was strengthened.

{Rom 4:20} εἰς δὲ τὴν ἐπαγγελίαν τοῦ θεοῦ οὐ διεκρίθη <u>τῇ ἀπιστίᾳ</u> ἀλλ᾽ ἐνεδυναμώθη <u>τῇ πίστει</u>, δοὺς δόξαν τῷ θεῷ

Gal 6:12 - The Galatian Judaizers feared being persecuted "because of the cross" (τῷ σταυρῷ) of Christ.

{Gal 6:12} - ὅσοι θέλουσιν εὐπροσωπῆσαι ἐν σαρκί, οὗτοι ἀναγκάζουσιν ὑμᾶς περιτέμνεσθαι, μόνον ἵνα <u>τῷ σταυρῷ</u> τοῦ Χριστοῦ μὴ διώκωνται.

3.3 INSTRUMENTAL OF MANNER

John 3:29 - χαρᾷ tells the manner of the friend's rejoicing (χαίρει). "Rejoicing with joy" is a very intense activity.

{John 3:29} ὁ ἔχων τὴν νύμφην νυμφίος ἐστίν· ὁ δὲ φίλος τοῦ νυμφίου ὁ ἑστηκὼς καὶ ἀκούων αὐτοῦ <u>χαρᾷ χαίρει</u> διὰ τὴν φωνὴν τοῦ νυμφίου. αὕτη οὖν ἡ χαρὰ ἡ ἐμὴ πεπλήρωται.

---

1 Cor 8:7 - τῇ συνηθείᾳ. Certain ones eat "according to the custom" of the idol until now. They continue to do so in the same manner until now.

{1 Cor 8:7} - Ἀλλ᾽ οὐκ ἐν πᾶσιν ἡ γνῶσις· τινὲς δὲ <u>τῇ συνηθείᾳ</u> ἕως ἄρτι τοῦ εἰδώλου ὡς εἰδωλόθυτον ἐσθίουσιν, καὶ ἡ συνείδησις αὐτῶν ἀσθενὴς οὖσα μολύνεται.

3.4 INSTRUMENTAL OF MEASURE

Luke 8:27 - χρόνῳ ἱκανῷ. Two points, a beginning point and an end point, which was the time of this encounter, are separated by means of "a long time." This is the force of the instrumental of measure

{Luke 8:27} ἐξελθόντι δὲ αὐτῷ ἐπὶ τὴν γῆν ὑπήντησεν ἀνήρ τις ἐκ τῆς πόλεως ἔχων δαιμόνια καὶ <u>χρόνῳ ἱκανῷ</u> οὐκ ἐνεδύσατο ἱμάτιον καὶ ἐν οἰκίᾳ οὐκ ἔμενεν ἀλλ᾽ ἐν τοῖς μνήμασιν.

John 2:20 - Τεσσεράκοντα καὶ ἓξ ἔτεσιν tells the measure of time separating the beginning of construction and the point of progress reached at the time Jesus cleansed the temple.

{John 2:20} εἶπαν οὖν οἱ Ἰουδαῖοι, <u>Τεσσεράκοντα καὶ ἓξ ἔτεσιν</u> οἰκοδομήθη ὁ ναὸς οὗτος, καὶ σὺ ἐν τρισὶν ἡμέραις ἐγερεῖς αὐτόν;

3.5 INSTRUMENTAL OF ASSOCIATION - the one thus designated furnished the means of association.

John 1:37 - τῷ Ἰησοῦ. Since it follows a verb that always requires the associative idea in its object, ἀκολουθέω, it is an instrumental of association.

{John 1:37} καὶ ἤκουσαν οἱ δύο μαθηταὶ αὐτοῦ λαλοῦντος καὶ <u>ἠκολούθησαν τῷ Ἰησοῦ</u>.

John 4:9 - συγχρῶνται, as the verb meaning clearly shows, has an associative instrumental (Σαμαρίταις) as its object.

{John 4:9} λέγει οὖν αὐτῷ ἡ γυνὴ ἡ Σαμαρῖτις, Πῶς σὺ Ἰουδαῖος ὢν παρ᾽ ἐμοῦ πεῖν αἰτεῖς γυναικὸς Σαμαρίτιδος οὔσης; οὐ γὰρ <u>συγχρῶνται</u> Ἰουδαῖοι <u>Σαμαρίταις</u>.

3.6 INSTRUMENTAL OF AGENCY

Luke 23:15 - αὐτῷ names the agent by whom nothing worthy of death had been done.

{Luke 23:15} ἀλλ᾽ οὐδὲ Ἡρῴδης, ἀνέπεμψεν γὰρ αὐτὸν πρὸς ἡμᾶς, καὶ ἰδοὺ οὐδὲν ἄξιον θανάτου ἐστὶν πεπραγμένον <u>αὐτῷ</u>·

1 Tim 3:16 - ἀγγέλοις names the agents by whom Christ was seen.

{1 Tim 3:16} καὶ ὁμολογουμένως μέγα ἐστὶν τὸ τῆς εὐσεβείας μυστήριον· Ὃς ἐφανερώθη ἐν σαρκί, ἐδικαιώθη ἐν πνεύματι, ὤφθη <u>ἀγγέλοις</u>,

---

2.8 THE ACCUSATIVE CASE (D. & M., 91–95) - the case of limitation.

3.1 ACCUSATIVE OF DIRECT OBJECT

1 Thess 1:6 -   τὸν λόγον limits the action of δεξάμενοι to "the word." Hence, τὸν λόγον is the direct object of the participle.

{1 Thess 1:6} καὶ ὑμεῖς μιμηταὶ ἡμῶν ἐγενήθητε καὶ τοῦ κυρίου, <u>δεξάμενοι</u> <u>τὸν λόγον</u> ἐν θλίψει πολλῇ μετὰ χαρᾶς πνεύματος ἁγίου,

---

1 Thess 1:9 -   ὁποίαν εἴσοδον in the relative clause introduced by ὁποίαν serves as the direct object of ἔσχομεν. It limits the action of "we had."

{1 Thess 1:9} - αὐτοὶ γὰρ περὶ ἡμῶν ἀπαγγέλλουσιν <u>ὁποίαν εἴσοδον</u> <u>ἔσχομεν</u> πρὸς ὑμᾶς, καὶ πῶς ἐπεστρέψατε πρὸς τὸν θεὸν ἀπὸ τῶν εἰδώλων δουλεύειν θεῷ ζῶντι καὶ ἀληθινῷ

3.2 ADVERBIAL ACCUSATIVE - the verbal action is limited in an adverbial way rather than by an object. There are three forms of adverbial limitation.

4.1 Measure - may be time or space.

Luke 24:1(23:56b) - τὸ . . . σάββατον places a limit on the time they rested (ἡσύχασαν, accusative of time). The accusative tells the length of their rest. In this same verse note two other cases with time designations: τῇ . . . μιᾷ, "on the first (day)," (locative of time) which tells the point at which they came, and ὄρθρου βαθέως, "by early dawn," (genitive of time) which tells the kind of conditions prevailing at their coming.

{Luke 23:56b} Καὶ <u>τὸ</u> μὲν <u>σάββατον</u> ἡσύχασαν κατὰ τὴν ἐντολήν.

{Luke 24:1} τῇ δὲ μιᾷ τῶν σαββάτων ὄρθρου βαθέως ἐπὶ τὸ μνῆμα ἦλθον φέρουσαι ἃ ἡτοίμασαν ἀρώματα.

John 1:39 -   τὴν ἡμέραν ἐκείνην tells the extent of the time that the two disciples remained with Jesus.

{John 1:39} λέγει αὐτοῖς, Ἔρχεσθε καὶ ὄψεσθε. ἦλθαν οὖν καὶ εἶδαν ποῦ μένει καὶ παρ' αὐτῷ ἔμειναν τὴν ἡμέραν ἐκείνην· ὥρα ἦν ὡς δεκάτη.

John 2:12 -   How long did Jesus and His party remain in Capernaum? "Not many days" (οὐ πολλὰς ἡμέρας).

{John 2:12} Μετὰ τοῦτο κατέβη εἰς Καφαρναοὺμ αὐτὸς καὶ ἡ μήτηρ αὐτοῦ καὶ οἱ ἀδελφοὶ [αὐτοῦ] καὶ οἱ μαθηταὶ αὐτοῦ καὶ ἐκεῖ ἔμειναν οὐ πολλὰς ἡμέρας.

John 6:19 -   σταδίους (masc.), or στάδια (neut.) as some manuscripts read, limits the verbal action of ἐληλακότες in an adverbial way by telling how far they had rowed.

{John 6:19} ἐληλακότες οὖν ὡς σταδίους εἴκοσι πέντε ἢ τριάκοντα θεωροῦσιν τὸν Ἰησοῦν περιπατοῦντα ἐπὶ τῆς θαλάσσης καὶ ἐγγὺς τοῦ πλοίου γινόμενον, καὶ ἐφοβήθησαν.

4.2 Manner - an accusative so used is often construed as an adverb rather than a noun.

Rom 3:24 -   δωρεάν tells how the justification takes place. It happens "freely" insofar as man is concerned.

{Rom 3:24} δικαιούμενοι δωρεὰν τῇ αὐτοῦ χάριτι διὰ τῆς ἀπολυτρώσεως τῆς ἐν Χριστῷ Ἰησοῦ·

4.3 Reference - the action of the verb may be limited by being applied in a certain realm. Sometimes called "accusative of general reference."

Rom 15:17 - In τὰ πρὸς τὸν θεόν the article τὰ is accusative. It identifies the realm in which Paul has a ground for boasting as that of "the things pertaining to God."

{Rom 15:17} ἔχω οὖν [τὴν] καύχησιν ἐν Χριστῷ Ἰησοῦ <u>τὰ πρὸς τὸν θεόν·</u>

Rom 15:22 - "in many things" or "with reference to many things" (τὰ πολλά) specifies the area in which Paul was hindered.

{Rom 15:22} Διὸ καὶ ἐνεκοπτόμην τὰ πολλὰ τοῦ ἐλθεῖν πρὸς ὑμᾶς·

---

1 Thess 1:7 - ὑμᾶς limits the action of γενέσθαι adverbially by telling *who* became: "so that becoming an example with reference to you." More smoothly, "so that you became an example."

{1 Thess 1:7} ὥστε <u>γενέσθαι ὑμᾶς</u> τύπον πᾶσιν τοῖς πιστεύουσιν ἐν τῇ Μακεδονίᾳ καὶ ἐν τῇ Ἀχαΐᾳ.

3.3 COGNATE ACCUSATIVE - places special emphasis on the verbal idea by repeating the same root idea in the object.

John 5:32 - ἥν (relative pronoun) has μαρτυρία as its antecedent. In its relative clause it is the direct object of μαρτυρεῖ. Hence, in effect it means he "*testifies a testimony* concerning me."

{John 5:32} ἄλλος ἐστὶν ὁ μαρτυρῶν περὶ ἐμοῦ, καὶ οἶδα ὅτι ἀληθής ἐστιν ἡ <u>μαρτυρία ἥν μαρτυρεῖ</u> περὶ ἐμοῦ.

John 7:24 - κρίσιν (direct object) and κρίνετε are from the same root idea, giving a double reference to the judgmental process.

{John 7:24} μὴ κρίνετε κατ᾽ ὄψιν, ἀλλὰ τὴν δικαίαν <u>κρίσιν κρίνετε.</u>

John 17:26 - To "love Me (ἠγάπησάς με) with a love (ἀγάπη)" is another instance where the accusative limits the verb to its own idea.

{John 17:26} καὶ ἐγνώρισα αὐτοῖς τὸ ὄνομά σου καὶ γνωρίσω, ἵνα ἡ <u>ἀγάπη</u> ἣν <u>ἠγάπησάς</u> <u>με</u> ἐν αὐτοῖς ᾖ κἀγὼ ἐν αὐτοῖς.

3.4 DOUBLE ACCUSATIVE - the nature of the verbal idea or of the context requires two objects to limit the verbal idea completely.

John 2:16 - τὸν οἶκον is a direct object and οἶκον is a predicate object in apposition with it.

{John 2:16} καὶ τοῖς τὰς περιστερὰς πωλοῦσιν εἶπεν, Ἄρατε ταῦτα ἐντεῦθεν, μὴ ποιεῖτε <u>τὸν οἶκον</u> τοῦ πατρός μου <u>οἶκον</u> ἐμπορίου.

John 5:11 - με is a direct object with ὑγιῆ as a predicate adjective modifying it.

{John 5:11} ὁ δὲ ἀπεκρίθη αὐτοῖς, Ὁ ποιήσας <u>με</u> <u>ὑγιῆ</u> ἐκεῖνός μοι εἶπεν, Ἆρον τὸν κράβαττόν σου καὶ περιπάτει.

John 9:22 - αὐτόν is a direct object and Χριστόν is a predicate object which further limits "confesses Him."

{John 9:22} ταῦτα εἶπαν οἱ γονεῖς αὐτοῦ ὅτι ἐφοβοῦντο τοὺς Ἰουδαίους· ἤδη γὰρ συνετέθειντο οἱ Ἰουδαῖοι ἵνα ἐάν τις <u>αὐτὸν</u> ὁμολογήσῃ <u>Χριστόν</u>, ἀποσυνάγωγος γένηται.

John 10:33 - σεαυτόν and θεόν are direct and predicate objects, respectively.

{John 10:33} ἀπεκρίθησαν αὐτῷ οἱ Ἰουδαῖοι, Περὶ καλοῦ ἔργου οὐ λιθάζομέν σε ἀλλὰ περὶ βλασφημίας, καὶ ὅτι σὺ ἄνθρωπος ὢν ποιεῖς <u>σεαυτὸν</u> <u>θεόν</u>.

John 10:35 - ἐκείνους and θεοὺς are another example of direct and predicate objects.

{John 10:35} εἰ ἐκείνους εἶπεν θεοὺς πρὸς οὓς ὁ λόγος τοῦ θεοῦ ἐγένετο, καὶ οὐ δύναται λυθῆναι ἡ γραφή,

---

John 14:26 -   ὑμᾶς (both occurrences) is a personal direct object and πάντα (both occurrences) is an impersonal direct object.

{John 14:26} ὁ δὲ παράκλητος, τὸ πνεῦμα τὸ ἅγιον, ὃ πέμψει ὁ πατὴρ ἐν τῷ ὀνόματί μου, ἐκεῖνος ὑμᾶς διδάξει πάντα καὶ ὑπομνήσει ὑμᾶς πάντα ἃ εἶπον ὑμῖν [ἐγώ].

3.5 ACCUSATIVE ABSOLUTE (rare in the N. T.) - no grammatical relation to the rest of the sentence.

Acts 26:3 -   γνώστην ὄντα σε, "you being an expert." The accusative pronoun σε refers back to the vocative βασιλεῦ Ἀγρίππα in Acts 26:2. Hence, it has no grammatical relation to the rest of the sentence.

{Acts 26:3} μάλιστα γνώστην ὄντα σε πάντων τῶν κατὰ Ἰουδαίους ἐθῶν τε καὶ ζητημάτων, διὸ δέομαι μακροθύμως ἀκοῦσαί μου.

3.6 ACCUSATIVE with OATHS - also called "accusative of adjuration."

1 Thess 5:27 - One object specifies the persons being placed under oath (ὑμᾶς) and the other (τὸν κύριον) indicates the one on whom the oath is based.

{1 Thess 5:27} Ἐνορκίζω ὑμᾶς τὸν κύριον ἀναγνωσθῆναι τὴν ἐπιστολὴν πᾶσιν τοῖς ἀδελφοῖς.

1.4 COMPARISON OF THE ADJECTIVE (D. & M., 120–21)

Mark 9:42–43 - A positive adjective (καλόν) with μᾶλλον in v. 42 is equivalent to "better." In v. 43 it is a positive adjective (καλόν) with ἤ that results in "better . . . than." (A positive adjective or adverb is one in its simple form without comparison or degree.)

{Mark 9:42} Καὶ ὃς ἂν σκανδαλίσῃ ἕνα τῶν μικρῶν τούτων τῶν πιστευόντων [εἰς ἐμέ], καλόν ἐστιν αὐτῷ μᾶλλον εἰ περίκειται μύλος ὀνικὸς περὶ τὸν τράχηλον αὐτοῦ καὶ βέβληται εἰς τὴν θάλασσαν.

{Mark 9:43} Καὶ ἐὰν σκανδαλίζῃ σε ἡ χείρ σου, ἀπόκοψον αὐτήν· καλόν ἐστίν σε κυλλὸν εἰσελθεῖν εἰς τὴν ζωὴν ἢ τὰς δύο χεῖρας ἔχοντα ἀπελθεῖν εἰς τὴν γέενναν, εἰς τὸ πῦρ τὸ ἄσβεστον.

Luke 13:2 -   ἁμαρτωλοί is a positive adjective followed by a prepositional phrase introduced by παρά.

{Luke 13:2} καὶ ἀποκριθεὶς εἶπεν αὐτοῖς, Δοκεῖτε ὅτι οἱ Γαλιλαῖοι οὗτοι ἁμαρτωλοὶ παρὰ πάντας τοὺς Γαλιλαίους ἐγένοντο, ὅτι ταῦτα πεπόνθασιν;

John 3:19 -   μᾶλλον is a comparative adjective (or adverb) which is followed by ἤ. Note the two possible senses: "the darkness more than the light" or "the darkness rather than the light." The context makes the latter possibility more attractive.

{John 3:19} αὕτη δέ ἐστιν ἡ κρίσις ὅτι τὸ φῶς ἐλήλυθεν εἰς τὸν κόσμον καὶ ἠγάπησαν οἱ ἄνθρωποι μᾶλλον τὸ σκότος ἢ τὸ φῶς· ἦν γὰρ αὐτῶν πονηρὰ τὰ ἔργα.

John 4:1 -   comparative adjective πλείονας and ἤ. Jesus was making and baptizing "more" disciples "than" John (was making and baptizing).

{John 4:1} Ὡς οὖν ἔγνω ὁ Ἰησοῦς ὅτι ἤκουσαν οἱ Φαρισαῖοι ὅτι Ἰησοῦς πλείονας μαθητὰς ποιεῖ καὶ βαπτίζει ἢ Ἰωάννης

John 4:12 -   μείζων, a comparative adjective, followed by the ablative τοῦ πατρός. "Greater than our father Jacob."

{John 4:12} μὴ σὺ <u>μείζων</u> εἶ <u>τοῦ πατρὸς</u> ἡμῶν Ἰακώβ, ὃς ἔδωκεν ἡμῖν τὸ φρέαρ καὶ αὐτὸς ἐξ αὐτοῦ ἔπιεν καὶ οἱ υἱοὶ αὐτοῦ καὶ τὰ θρέμματα αὐτοῦ;

_____
_____
_____

John 21:15 -   a comparative adjective, "more" (πλέον), and an ablative, "these" (τούτων).

{John 21:15} Ὅτε οὖν ἠρίστησαν λέγει τῷ Σίμωνι Πέτρῳ ὁ Ἰησοῦς, Σίμων Ἰωάννου, ἀγαπᾷς με <u>πλέον</u> <u>τούτων</u>; λέγει αὐτῷ, Ναὶ κύριε, σὺ οἶδας ὅτι φιλῶ σε. λέγει αὐτῷ, Βόσκε τὰ ἀρνία μου.

_____
_____
_____

1 John 3:20 -   μείζων (comparative adjective) . . . τῆς καρδίας (ablative). God is "greater than our heart."

{1 John 3:20} ὅτι ἐὰν καταγινώσκῃ ἡμῶν ἡ καρδία, ὅτι <u>μείζων</u> ἐστὶν ὁ θεὸς τῆς <u>καρδίας</u> ἡμῶν καὶ γινώσκει πάντα.

_____
_____

1.5 PRONOUNS (D. & M., 122–35)

2.1 PERSONAL PRONOUNS

John 1:42 -   Σύ and σύ (both occurrences) is the personal pronoun; designating second person singular.

{John 1:42} ἤγαγεν αὐτὸν πρὸς τὸν Ἰησοῦν. ἐμβλέψας αὐτῷ ὁ Ἰησοῦς εἶπεν, <u>Σὺ</u> εἶ Σίμων ὁ υἱὸς Ἰωάννου, <u>σὺ</u> κληθήσῃ Κηφᾶς, ὃ ἑρμηνεύεται Πέτρος.

_____
_____
_____

John 4:22 -   ὑμεῖς (second person plural) and ἡμεῖς (first person plural) are personal pronouns.

{John 4:22} <u>ὑμεῖς</u> προσκυνεῖτε ὃ οὐκ οἴδατε· <u>ἡμεῖς</u> προσκυνοῦμεν ὃ οἴδαμεν, ὅτι ἡ σωτηρία ἐκ τῶν Ἰουδαίων ἐστίν.

_____
_____

John 5:8 -   σου (second person singular) is a personal pronoun in the genitive case
                  used to show possession.

{John 5:8} λέγει αὐτῷ ὁ Ἰησοῦς, Ἔγειρε ἆρον τὸν κράβαττόν <u>σου</u> καὶ περιπάτει.

John 17:4 -   σε (second person singular) is a direct object in the accusative case, and
                  μοι (first person singular) is an indirect object in the dative case.

{John 17:4} ἐγώ <u>σε</u> ἐδόξασα ἐπὶ τῆς γῆς τὸ ἔργον τελειώσας ὃ δέδωκάς <u>μοι</u> ἵνα ποιήσω·

2.2 RELATIVE PRONOUNS - has as its antecedent a substantive and introduces a clause
which in some way describes that substantive.

3.1 Attraction absent - relative pronoun agrees with its antecedent in gender and number,
but its case is determined by the relative's function in its own clause.

John 2:22 -   ὅν agrees with τῷ λόγῳ in gender (masc.) and number (singular), but its
                  case is accusative, not dative as with τῷ λόγῳ, because ὅν serves as the
                  direct object of εἶπεν in the relative clause.

{John 2:22} ὅτε οὖν ἠγέρθη ἐκ νεκρῶν, ἐμνήσθησαν οἱ μαθηταὶ αὐτοῦ ὅτι τοῦτο ἔλεγεν,
καὶ ἐπίστευσαν τῇ γραφῇ καὶ <u>τῷ λόγῳ</u> <u>ὃν</u> <u>εἶπεν</u> ὁ Ἰησοῦς.

John 4:5 -   ὃ agrees with its antecedent τοῦ χωρίου in gender (neut.) and number
                  (sing.), but not in case. The relative pronoun is accusative, not genitive,
                  because it is the direct object of ἔδωκεν.

{John 4:5} ἔρχεται οὖν εἰς πόλιν τῆς Σαμαρείας λεγομένην Συχὰρ πλησίον <u>τοῦ χωρίου</u> <u>ὃ</u>
<u>ἔδωκεν</u> Ἰακὼβ [τῷ] Ἰωσὴφ τῷ υἱῷ αὐτοῦ·

3.2 Direct attraction - relative pronoun attracted to the case of its antecedent.

John 15:20 -   οὗ agrees with its antecedent τοῦ λόγου not only in gender (masc.) and
                  number (sing.), but also in case (genitive), because the relative has been
                  attracted to the case of its antecedent.

{John 15:20} μνημονεύετε τοῦ λόγου οὗ ἐγὼ εἶπον ὑμῖν, Οὐκ ἔστιν δοῦλος μείζων τοῦ κυρίου αὐτοῦ. εἰ ἐμὲ ἐδίωξαν, καὶ ὑμᾶς διώξουσιν· εἰ τὸν λόγον μου ἐτήρησαν, καὶ τὸν ὑμέτερον τηρήσουσιν.

1 Cor 6:19 -   Paul wrote οὗ instead of ὅν, even though the relative is the direct object of ἔχετε which normally takes an accusative object. The pronoun is attracted to the genitive case of its antecedent τοῦ . . . ἁγίου πνεύματός.

{1 Cor 6:19} ἢ οὐκ οἴδατε ὅτι τὸ σῶμα ὑμῶν ναὸς τοῦ ἐν ὑμῖν ἁγίου πνεύματός ἐστιν οὗ ἔχετε ἀπὸ θεοῦ, καὶ οὐκ ἐστὲ ἑαυτῶν;

3.3 Indirect attraction - antecedent attracted to case of relative pronoun.

Mark 12:10 -   Λίθον is accusative even though it is in apposition with the nominative subject οὗτος. Indirect attraction finds the antecedent attracted to the case of the relative pronoun, ὅν, in this verse.

{Mark 12:10} οὐδὲ τὴν γραφὴν ταύτην ἀνέγνωτε, Λίθον ὃν ἀπεδοκίμασαν οἱ οἰκοδομοῦντες, οὗτος ἐγενήθη εἰς κεφαλὴν γωνίας·

1 Cor 10:16 -   τὸν ἄρτον is the antecedent of ὅν and is accusative in agreement with it, even though it is in apposition with the subject of the sentence (the subject is in the verb ἐστίν).

{1 Cor 10:16} τὸ ποτήριον τῆς εὐλογίας ὃ εὐλογοῦμεν, οὐχὶ κοινωνία ἐστὶν τοῦ αἵματος τοῦ Χριστοῦ; τὸν ἄρτον ὃν κλῶμεν, οὐχὶ κοινωνία τοῦ σώματος τοῦ Χριστοῦ ἐστιν;

2.3 DEMONSTRATIVE PRONOUNS

Immediate Demonstrative:
Rom 7:10 -   αὕτη has as its antecedent the relatively near concept of "the commandment" (ἡ ἐντολή).

{Rom 7:10} ἐγὼ δὲ ἀπέθανον καὶ εὑρέθη μοι ἡ ἐντολὴ ἡ εἰς ζωήν, αὕτη εἰς θάνατον·

Remote Demonstrative:

John 1:8 -   ἐκεῖνος points to John in 1:6 as its antecedent, conceiving of him as
                  relatively distant.

{John 1:8} οὐκ ἦν <u>ἐκεῖνος</u> τὸ φῶς, ἀλλ' ἵνα μαρτυρήσῃ περὶ τοῦ φωτός.

John 13:26 -   Ἐκεῖνός has Judas the son of Simon Iscariot (about to be named at the end
                  of v. 26, Σίμωνος Ἰσκαριώτου) as its antecedent. He is relatively distant in
                  thought.

{John 13:26} ἀποκρίνεται [ὁ] Ἰησοῦς, <u>Ἐκεῖνός</u> ἐστιν ᾧ ἐγὼ βάψω τὸ ψωμίον καὶ δώσω
αὐτῷ. βάψας οὖν τὸ ψωμίον [λαμβάνει καὶ] δίδωσιν Ἰούδᾳ <u>Σίμωνος Ἰσκαριώτου</u>.

Both Immediate and Remote Demonstratives:

John 5:19 -   ταῦτα, "these things," points out what the Father does and speaks of them
                  as being relatively near in thought. In the clause just before, ἐκεῖνος,
                  points to Him who is relatively distant in thought.

{John 5:19} Ἀπεκρίνατο οὖν ὁ Ἰησοῦς καὶ ἔλεγεν αὐτοῖς, Ἀμὴν ἀμὴν λέγω ὑμῖν, οὐ
δύναται ὁ υἱὸς ποιεῖν ἀφ' ἑαυτοῦ οὐδὲν ἐὰν μή τι βλέπῃ τὸν πατέρα ποιοῦντα· ἃ γὰρ ἂν <u>ἐκεῖνος</u>
ποιῇ, <u>ταῦτα</u> καὶ ὁ υἱὸς ὁμοίως ποιεῖ.

2.4 INTENSIVE PRONOUNS

The intensive pronoun is αὐτός. Αὐτός is always by definition an intensive pronoun and never
anything else. It may be *used* to function as another type of pronoun, but it is always an intensive
pronoun.

3.1 USED INTENSIVELY

John 4:42 -   αὐτοί intensifies the subject of ἀκηκόαμεν: "we ourselves have heard."

{John 4:42} τῇ τε γυναικὶ ἔλεγον ὅτι Οὐκέτι διὰ τὴν σὴν λαλιὰν πιστεύομεν, <u>αὐτοὶ</u> γὰρ
<u>ἀκηκόαμεν</u> καὶ οἴδαμεν ὅτι οὗτός ἐστιν ἀληθῶς ὁ σωτὴρ τοῦ κόσμου.

Rom 10:12 -   ὁ . . . αὐτὸς κύριος is "the same Lord." He and no other is "over all."
               (αὐτόν at the end of v. 12 is the intensive pronoun used as a personal
               pronoun.)

{Rom 10:12} οὐ γάρ ἐστιν διαστολὴ Ἰουδαίου τε καὶ Ἕλληνος, ὁ γὰρ <u>αὐτὸς κύριος</u>
πάντων, πλουτῶν εἰς πάντας τοὺς ἐπικαλουμένους <u>αὐτόν</u>·

3.2 USED as PERSONAL and POSSESSIVE PRONOUNS

John 2:11 -   αὐτόν is used as a personal pronoun and αὐτοῦ (both occurrences) is used
               as a possessive pronoun.

{John 2:11} Ταύτην ἐποίησεν ἀρχὴν τῶν σημείων ὁ Ἰησοῦς ἐν Κανὰ τῆς Γαλιλαίας καὶ
ἐφανέρωσεν τὴν δόξαν <u>αὐτοῦ</u>, καὶ ἐπίστευσαν εἰς <u>αὐτὸν</u> οἱ μαθηταὶ <u>αὐτοῦ</u>.

3.3 USED as a DEMONSTRATIVE PRONOUN

Luke 2:38 -   The demonstrative force of αὐτῇ is evident: "at *that* hour."

{Luke 2:38} καὶ <u>αὐτῇ</u> τῇ ὥρᾳ ἐπιστᾶσα ἀνθωμολογεῖτο τῷ θεῷ καὶ ἐλάλει περὶ αὐτοῦ
πᾶσιν τοῖς προσδεχομένοις λύτρωσιν Ἰερουσαλήμ.

2.5 POSSESSIVE PRONOUNS

3.1 FIRST PERSON

John 5:30 -   ἐμή, in agreement with κρίσις in gender, number, and case, means "*My*
               judgment." ἐμόν, in agreement with θέλημα in gender, number, and case,
               means "*My* will." (με at the end of the verse is a personal pronoun.)

{John 5:30} Οὐ δύναμαι ἐγὼ ποιεῖν ἀπ' ἐμαυτοῦ οὐδέν· καθὼς ἀκούω κρίνω, καὶ ἡ
<u>κρίσις</u> ἡ <u>ἐμὴ</u> δικαία ἐστίν, ὅτι οὐ ζητῶ τὸ <u>θέλημα</u> τὸ <u>ἐμὸν</u> ἀλλὰ τὸ θέλημα τοῦ πέμψαντός <u>με</u>.

3.2 SECOND PERSON

John 4:42 -   σήν, in gender, number, and case agreement with λαλιάν, means "*your* speech."

{John 4:42} τῇ τε γυναικὶ ἔλεγον ὅτι Οὐκέτι διὰ τὴν <u>σὴν</u> <u>λαλιὰν</u> πιστεύομεν, αὐτοὶ γὰρ ἀκηκόαμεν καὶ οἴδαμεν ὅτι οὗτός ἐστιν ἀληθῶς ὁ σωτὴρ τοῦ κόσμου.

_____
_____
_____

3.3 FIRST and SECOND PERSON

John 17:10 -   τὰ ἐμά, "the things of me," furnishes an example of the possessive pronoun used substantively while ἐμά, "mine," shows its use as a predicate adjective. Both, of course, are first person. The same illustrations are furnished by σά, "yours," and τὰ σά, "the things of you," in the second person.

{John 17:10} καὶ <u>τὰ ἐμὰ</u> πάντα <u>σά</u> ἐστιν καὶ <u>τὰ σὰ</u> <u>ἐμά,</u> καὶ δεδόξασμαι ἐν αὐτοῖς.

_____

2.6 REFLEXIVE PRONOUNS

3.1 FIRST PERSON SINGULAR

John 14:21 -   With the use of ἐμαυτόν Christ promises, "I will manifest *Myself* to him."

{John 14:21} ὁ ἔχων τὰς ἐντολάς μου καὶ τηρῶν αὐτὰς ἐκεῖνός ἐστιν ὁ ἀγαπῶν με· ὁ δὲ ἀγαπῶν με ἀγαπηθήσεται ὑπὸ τοῦ πατρός μου, κἀγὼ ἀγαπήσω αὐτὸν καὶ ἐμφανίσω αὐτῷ <u>ἐμαυτόν.</u>

_____
_____
_____

3.2 SECOND PERSON SINGULAR

John 8:13 -   The Pharisees' accusation against Christ is, "You testify about *yourself* (σεαυτοῦ).

{John 8:13} εἶπον οὖν αὐτῷ οἱ Φαρισαῖοι, Σὺ περὶ <u>σεαυτοῦ</u> μαρτυρεῖς· ἡ μαρτυρία σου οὐκ ἔστιν ἀληθής.

_____

3.3 THIRD PERSON SINGULAR

John 5:19 -   ἀφ' ἑαυτοῦ is the Son's affirmation that He cannot be the ultimate source of anything that He does. He cannot do it "from Himself," but it must be something He sees the Father doing.

{John 5:19} Ἀπεκρίνατο οὖν ὁ Ἰησοῦς καὶ ἔλεγεν αὐτοῖς, Ἀμὴν ἀμὴν λέγω ὑμῖν, οὐ δύναται ὁ υἱὸς ποιεῖν ἀφ' ἑαυτοῦ οὐδὲν ἐὰν μή τι βλέπῃ τὸν πατέρα ποιοῦντα· ἃ γὰρ ἂν ἐκεῖνος ποιῇ, ταῦτα καὶ ὁ υἱὸς ὁμοίως ποιεῖ.

3.4 PLURAL (for all three persons)

John 19:24 -   **ἑαυτοῖς.** Those involved in Christ's crucifixion "divided His garments among *themselves*." (ἀλλήλους is a reciprocal pronoun: "they said to *one another*.")

{John 19:24} εἶπαν οὖν πρὸς ἀλλήλους, Μὴ σχίσωμεν αὐτόν, ἀλλὰ λάχωμεν περὶ αὐτοῦ τίνος ἔσται· ἵνα ἡ γραφὴ πληρωθῇ [ἡ λέγουσα], Διεμερίσαντο τὰ ἱμάτιά μου ἑαυτοῖς καὶ ἐπὶ τὸν ἱματισμόν μου ἔβαλον κλῆρον. Οἱ μὲν οὖν στρατιῶται ταῦτα ἐποίησαν.

2.7 RECIPROCAL PRONOUNS

Col 3:13 -   ἀλλήλων, "forbearing *one another*," is the usual reciprocal pronoun. ἑαυτοῖς, "forgiving *one another*," is a reflexive pronoun used to show reciprocation.

{Col 3:13} ἀνεχόμενοι ἀλλήλων καὶ χαριζόμενοι ἑαυτοῖς ἐάν τις πρός τινα ἔχῃ μομφήν· καθὼς καὶ ὁ κύριος ἐχαρίσατο ὑμῖν, οὕτως καὶ ὑμεῖς·

---

1 Thess 5:15 - ἀλλήλους, "always pursue good toward *one another*."

{1 Thess 5:15} ὁρᾶτε μή τις κακὸν ἀντὶ κακοῦ τινι ἀποδῷ, ἀλλὰ πάντοτε τὸ ἀγαθὸν διώκετε [καὶ] εἰς ἀλλήλους καὶ εἰς πάντας.

2.8 INTERROGATIVE PRONOUN

John 2:18 -   Τί functions as an adjective while asking a question: "What sign do you show us?"

{John 2:18} ἀπεκρίθησαν οὖν οἱ Ἰουδαῖοι καὶ εἶπαν αὐτῷ, Τί σημεῖον δεικνύεις ἡμῖν ὅτι ταῦτα ποιεῖς;

John 12:34 - τίς asks a question while functioning as a substantive (pred. nom.): "Who is this Son of Man?"

{John 12:34} ἀπεκρίθη οὖν αὐτῷ ὁ ὄχλος, Ἡμεῖς ἠκούσαμεν ἐκ τοῦ νόμου ὅτι ὁ Χριστὸς μένει εἰς τὸν αἰῶνα, καὶ πῶς λέγεις σὺ ὅτι δεῖ ὑψωθῆναι τὸν υἱὸν τοῦ ἀνθρώπου; τίς ἐστιν οὗτος ὁ υἱὸς τοῦ ἀνθρώπου;

2.9 INDEFINITE PRONOUN

John 2:25 -   τις (sometimes written τὶς) is used as a substantive, the subject of μαρτυρήσῃ, "that *anyone* testify. . . ."

{John 2:25} καὶ ὅτι οὐ χρείαν εἶχεν ἵνα τις μαρτυρήσῃ περὶ τοῦ ἀνθρώπου· αὐτὸς γὰρ ἐγίνωσκεν τί ἦν ἐν τῷ ἀνθρώπῳ.

James 1:18 - τινα is used as an adjective modifying ἀπαρχήν: "*a certain* first fruits."

{Jas 1:18} βουληθεὶς ἀπεκύησεν ἡμᾶς λόγῳ ἀληθείας εἰς τὸ εἶναι ἡμᾶς ἀπαρχήν τινα τῶν αὐτοῦ κτισμάτων.

1.6 THE ARTICLE

The Greek article is a pointer. It does not tell why something is pointed to, nor does it point out something as near or far, as does the demonstrative pronoun. It simply points out an object for one reason or another. The task of syntax is to clarify the various reasons why the article may point out something.

2.1 REGULAR USES (D. & M., 135–46)

3.1 Pointing Out Individuals

Matt 13:55 -   τοῦ τέκτονος is one particular carpenter and no other. ὁ . . . υἱός is one son
in particular and not one of his brothers.

{Matt 13:55} οὐχ οὗτός ἐστιν ὁ τοῦ τέκτονος υἱός; οὐχ ἡ μήτηρ αὐτοῦ λέγεται Μαριὰμ
καὶ οἱ ἀδελφοὶ αὐτοῦ Ἰάκωβος καὶ Ἰωσὴφ καὶ Σίμων καὶ Ἰούδας;

_____

_____

_____

1 Cor 5:9 -   τῇ ἐπιστολῇ is one particular epistle, not to be confused with any other.

{1 Cor 5:9} Ἔγραψα ὑμῖν ἐν τῇ ἐπιστολῇ μὴ συναναμίγνυσθαι πόρνοις,

_____

_____

3.2 Pointing Out Something Previously Mentioned

John 4:1011 -   In 4:10 ὕδωρ ζῶν is "such a thing as living water," but in 4:11 τὸ
ὕδωρ τὸ ζῶν is quite particular: "the specific living water that I
spoke about."

{John 4:10} ἀπεκρίθη Ἰησοῦς καὶ εἶπεν αὐτῇ, Εἰ ᾔδεις τὴν δωρεὰν τοῦ θεοῦ καὶ τίς ἐστιν
ὁ λέγων σοι, Δός μοι πεῖν, σὺ ἂν ᾔτησας αὐτὸν καὶ ἔδωκεν ἄν σοι ὕδωρ ζῶν.

_____

_____

{John 4:11} λέγει αὐτῷ [ἡ γυνή], Κύριε, οὔτε ἄντλημα ἔχεις καὶ τὸ φρέαρ ἐστὶν βαθύ·
πόθεν οὖν ἔχεις τὸ ὕδωρ τὸ ζῶν;

_____

_____

John 6:9,11 - In 6:9 πέντε ἄρτους κριθίνους describes "something of the nature as to be
five barley loaves," but in 6:11 τοὺς ἄρτους depicts "the particular loaves
that you just spoke about." Similarly, in 6:9 δύο ὀψάρια is "something of
the quality of two fish," while τῶν ὀψαρίων in 6:11 points at the fish: "the
particular fish that you just mentioned."

{John 6:9} Ἔστιν παιδάριον ὧδε ὃς ἔχει πέντε ἄρτους κριθίνους καὶ δύο ὀψάρια· ἀλλὰ
ταῦτα τί ἐστιν εἰς τοσούτους;

_____

_____

{John 6:11} ἔλαβεν οὖν τοὺς ἄρτους ὁ Ἰησοῦς καὶ εὐχαριστήσας διέδωκεν τοῖς ἀνακειμένοις ὁμοίως καὶ ἐκ τῶν ὀψαρίων ὅσον ἤθελον.

3.3 Pointing Out Abstract Nouns - while the Greek language does not require the use of an article with an abstract quality, sometimes it does use it so as to sharpen the focus upon the abstraction.

Rom 1:18 -   τὴν ἀλήθειαν is the truth defined as what is known about God through His revelation of Himself in nature (Rom 1:19 –21a).

{Rom 1:18} 18 Ἀποκαλύπτεται γὰρ ὀργὴ θεοῦ ἀπ' οὐρανοῦ ἐπὶ πᾶσαν ἀσέβειαν καὶ ἀδικίαν ἀνθρώπων τῶν τὴν ἀλήθειαν ἐν ἀδικίᾳ κατεχόντων,

---

Rom 2:2 -   ἀλήθειαν is something that has the quality of truthfulness. It is fair and equitable. It takes all the facts into full account and renders a balanced judgment. It accords with matters as they are, not as they may only pretend to be. It is in accord with experience, facts, or reality. This is not a specific revelation as in Rom 1:18.

{Rom 2:2} οἴδαμεν δὲ ὅτι τὸ κρίμα τοῦ θεοῦ ἐστιν κατὰ ἀλήθειαν ἐπὶ τοὺς τὰ τοιαῦτα πράσσοντας.

3.4 Pointing Out Proper Names - sometimes the article is used, and sometimes it is not. The presence or absence of the article may or may not be significant.

John 1:1 -   τὸν θεόν is the specific identity of the person of God the Father: "the Word was with God the Father." Θεός alludes to the quality of Deity: "the Word possessed the essence of Deity." In this case, the presence and absence of the article are quite significant.

{John 1:1} Ἐν ἀρχῇ ἦν ὁ λόγος, καὶ ὁ λόγος ἦν πρὸς τὸν θεόν, καὶ θεὸς ἦν ὁ λόγος.

Rom 10:19 -   Ἰσραὴλ as a proper name possesses its own definiteness and needs no article to point το it.

{Rom 10:19} ἀλλὰ λέγω, μὴ Ἰσραὴλ οὐκ ἔγνω; πρῶτος Μωϋσῆς λέγει, Ἐγὼ παραζηλώσω ὑμᾶς ἐπ᾽ οὐκ ἔθνει, ἐπ᾽ ἔθνει ἀσυνέτῳ παροργιῶ ὑμᾶς.

---

1 Cor 10:18 -   τὸν Ἰσραὴλ illustrates the use of the same proper name with the article. For some reason, in Paul's mind he saw the need to point at something that already had its own definiteness. In this case we cannot fathom with certainty what that reason was.

{1 Cor 10:18} βλέπετε τὸν Ἰσραὴλ κατὰ σάρκα· οὐχ οἱ ἐσθίοντες τὰς θυσίας κοινωνοὶ τοῦ θυσιαστηρίου εἰσίν;

3.5 Pointing Out Classes or Groups - groups that have something in common are often, though not always, pointed out by the article as a class.

John 3:19 -   οἱ ἄνθρωποι are men looked upon as a class constituting the entirety of the human race. As a whole, they love darkness rather than light.

{John 3:19} αὕτη δέ ἐστιν ἡ κρίσις ὅτι τὸ φῶς ἐλήλυθεν εἰς τὸν κόσμον καὶ ἠγάπησαν οἱ ἄνθρωποι μᾶλλον τὸ σκότος ἢ τὸ φῶς· ἦν γὰρ αὐτῶν πονηρὰ τὰ ἔργα.

Eph. 5:24 -   αἱ γυναῖκες constitute a class of people who have one thing in common: they are all wives. The same is true for τοῖς ἀνδράσιν: they are all husbands.

{Eph 5:24} ἀλλὰ ὡς ἡ ἐκκλησία ὑποτάσσεται τῷ Χριστῷ, οὕτως καὶ αἱ γυναῖκες τοῖς ἀνδράσιν ἐν παντί.

3.6 Pointing Out Pronouns (including πᾶς) - It is a general, though not invariable, rule that when a pronoun is used adjectivally with a substantive (i.e. to modify a substantive), the article will also be used with the substantive. A special situation exists with various combinations and word orders involving πᾶς.

Rom 1:16 -   πᾶς ὁ with a participle (παντὶ τῷ πιστεύοντι) individualizes what is so designated: "everyone who believes."

{Rom 1:16} Οὐ γὰρ ἐπαισχύνομαι τὸ εὐαγγέλιον, δύναμις γὰρ θεοῦ ἐστιν εἰς σωτηρίαν παντὶ τῷ πιστεύοντι, Ἰουδαίῳ τε πρῶτον καὶ Ἕλληνι.

Rom 8:22 -   πᾶς ὁ with other substantives (πᾶσα ἡ κτίσις) signifies totality as πᾶς may do with an anarthrous noun: "all the creation" or "the whole creation."

{Rom 8:22} οἴδαμεν γὰρ ὅτι πᾶσα ἡ κτίσις συστενάζει καὶ συνωδίνει ἄχρι τοῦ νῦν·

1 Cor 9:22   ὁ πᾶς or οἱ πάντες (τοῖς πᾶσιν) contrasts the whole with the part: "to the whole of mankind" or "to the entire human race," as compared with an individual or a sub-group.

{1 Cor 9:22} ἐγενόμην τοῖς ἀσθενέσιν ἀσθενής, ἵνα τοὺς ἀσθενεῖς κερδήσω· τοῖς πᾶσιν γέγονα πάντα, ἵνα πάντως τινὰς σώσω.

3.7 Pointing Out Other Parts of Speech, Phrases, or Clauses

John 1:29 -   Τῇ points to an adverb ἐπαύριον. Literally, it is "on the tomorrow," or idiomatically, "on the next day."

{John 1:29}   Τῇ ἐπαύριον βλέπει τὸν Ἰησοῦν ἐρχόμενον πρὸς αὐτὸν καὶ λέγει, Ἴδε ὁ ἀμνὸς τοῦ θεοῦ ὁ αἴρων τὴν ἁμαρτίαν τοῦ κόσμου.

Rom 8:26 -   τό points out a whole clause: τί προσευξώμεθα. We do not know "the matter of what we should pray for," as the expression could be rendered.

{Rom 8:26} Ὡσαύτως δὲ καὶ τὸ πνεῦμα συναντιλαμβάνεται τῇ ἀσθενείᾳ ἡμῶν· τὸ γὰρ τί προσευξώμεθα καθὸ δεῖ οὐκ οἴδαμεν, ἀλλὰ αὐτὸ τὸ πνεῦμα ὑπερεντυγχάνει στεναγμοῖς ἀλαλήτοις·

Rom 12:18 -   τὸ ἐξ ὑμῶν, literally "the thing which is from you," has the article pointing at a prepositional phrase.

{Rom 12:18} εἰ δυνατὸν τὸ ἐξ ὑμῶν, μετὰ πάντων ἀνθρώπων εἰρηνεύοντες·

Rom 13:9 - τό pulls together four commandments and points to them as a group: "the commandments, you shall not commit adultery, you shall not murder, you shall not steal, you shall not lust."

{Rom 13:9} τὸ γὰρ **Οὐ** μοιχεύσεις, Οὐ φονεύσεις, Οὐ κλέψεις, Οὐκ ἐπιθυμήσεις, καὶ εἴ τις ἑτέρα ἐντολή, ἐν τῷ λόγῳ τούτῳ ἀνακεφαλαιοῦται [ἐν τῷ] Ἀγαπήσεις τὸν πλησίον σου ὡς σεαυτόν.

---

1 Cor 13:10 - The article in τὸ τέλειον points out an adjective ("the mature") and the one in τὸ ἐκ μέρους points out a prepositional phrase ("that which is from a part").

{1 Cor 13:10} ὅταν δὲ ἔλθῃ τὸ τέλειον, τὸ ἐκ μέρους καταργηθήσεται.

2.2 SPECIAL USES (of the article) (D. & M., 146–53)

These special uses of the article are the kinds of occasions when the function of the article as a pointer is not quite so obvious.

3.1 With substantives connected by καί - the single article before the former (or first) of two (or three or more) substantives has the force of pointing to the whole series as one entity.

Acts 2:23 - τῇ ὡρισμένῃ βουλῇ καὶ προγνώσει, "the appointed purpose and foreknowledge" of God. "Purpose" and "foreknowledge" are two descriptions of the same quality in God's preplanning because both are governed by the same article. The latter noun is a further elaboration of the former. Because of this relationship it can be concluded that the foreknowledge of certain persons by God includes His predetermination of their acceptance by Him.

{Acts 2:23} τοῦτον τῇ ὡρισμένῃ βουλῇ καὶ προγνώσει τοῦ θεοῦ ἔκδοτον διὰ χειρὸς ἀνόμων προσπήξαντες ἀνείλατε,

---

1 Thess 5:12 - τούς governs a series of three participles: κοπιῶντας, προϊσταμένους, and νουθετοῦντας. That these are united by the article shows that the same persons did all three: labor, rule, and admonish. The church's leadership was composed of men who were qualified and active in all three areas. There were not three groups, one composed of laborers, another of rulers, and another of admonishers. The one group (and apparently each one in the group) did all three.

{1 Thess 5:12} Ἐρωτῶμεν δὲ ὑμᾶς, ἀδελφοί, εἰδέναι τοὺς κοπιῶντας ἐν ὑμῖν καὶ προϊσταμένους ὑμῶν ἐν κυρίῳ καὶ νουθετοῦντας ὑμᾶς

3.2 As Pronouns

4.1 Demonstrative

Mark 14:31 - ὁ referring to Peter means "that one." "That one was speaking more exceedingly." The article as a demonstrative pronoun is often found in such a connection with δέ, but this is not the only way it is used.

{Mark 14:31} ὁ δὲ ἐκπερισσῶς ἐλάλει, Ἐὰν δέῃ με συναποθανεῖν σοι, οὐ μή σε ἀπαρνήσομαι. ὡσαύτως δὲ καὶ πάντες ἔλεγον.

---

1 John 2:13 - τὸν ἀπ᾽ ἀρχῆς, "that one who has been from the beginning," uses the article as a demonstrative pronoun pointing to Christ. In the evolution of the language the article developed from a demonstrative pronoun (see D. & M., 136.)

{1 John 2:13} γράφω ὑμῖν, πατέρες, ὅτι ἐγνώκατε τὸν ἀπ᾽ ἀρχῆς. γράφω ὑμῖν, νεανίσκοι, ὅτι νενικήκατε τὸν πονηρόν.

4.2 Alternative

1 Cor 7:7 - ὁ μέν..., ὁ δέ. Each one has his own gift from God, "the one (on one hand) thus, and the other (on the other hand) thus." The "one . . . another" combination names the two alternative groups.

{1 Cor 7:7} θέλω δὲ πάντας ἀνθρώπους εἶναι ὡς καὶ ἐμαυτόν· ἀλλὰ ἕκαστος ἴδιον ἔχει χάρισμα ἐκ θεοῦ, <u>ὁ μὲν</u> οὕτως, <u>ὁ δὲ</u> οὕτως.

Eph. 4:11 -   τοὺς μέν. . . τοὺς δέ . . . τοὺς δέ . . . τοὺς δέ. Gifted men whom Christ has given fall into four categories, which are expressed in the form of four groups: "some as apostles, and others as prophets, and others as evangelists, and others as pastors and teachers."

{Eph 4:11} καὶ αὐτὸς ἔδωκεν <u>τοὺς μὲν</u> ἀποστόλους, <u>τοὺς δὲ</u> προφήτας, <u>τοὺς δὲ</u> εὐαγγελιστάς, <u>τοὺς δὲ</u> ποιμένας καὶ διδασκάλους,

4.3 Possessive

John 3:16 -   τὸν υἱόν must, because of the nature of the sentence, have the sense "His Son." The article has the force of a possessive pronoun.

{John 3:16} Οὕτως γὰρ ἠγάπησεν ὁ θεὸς τὸν κόσμον, ὥστε <u>τὸν υἱὸν</u> τὸν μονογενῆ ἔδωκεν, ἵνα πᾶς ὁ πιστεύων εἰς αὐτὸν μὴ ἀπόληται ἀλλ' ἔχῃ ζωὴν αἰώνιον.

Rom 7:25 -   τῷ . . . νοί and τῇ . . . σαρκί are "my mind" and "my flesh" because of the writer's relationship to them and the meaning of the sentence of which they are a part.

{Rom 7:25} χάρις δὲ τῷ θεῷ διὰ Ἰησοῦ Χριστοῦ τοῦ κυρίου ἡμῶν. ἄρα οὖν αὐτὸς ἐγὼ τῷ μὲν <u>νοΐ</u> δουλεύω νόμῳ θεοῦ <u>τῇ</u> δὲ <u>σαρκὶ</u> νόμῳ ἁμαρτίας.

4.4 Relative - this is another position of the attributive adjective.

John 6:13 -   τῶν κριθίνων is set off separately from τῶν πέντε ἄρτων τῶν. It tells about the loaves "*which* were of barley."

{John 6:13} συνήγαγον οὖν καὶ ἐγέμισαν δώδεκα κοφίνους κλασμάτων ἐκ <u>τῶν πέντε ἄρτων</u> <u>τῶν κριθίνων</u> ἃ ἐπερίσσευσαν τοῖς βεβρωκόσιν.

1 John 2:25 -   τὴν αἰώνιον speaks of the life "*which* is eternal." The article, after a manner of speaking, functions as a relative pronoun.

{1 John 2:25} καὶ αὕτη ἐστὶν ἡ ἐπαγγελία ἣν αὐτὸς ἐπηγγείλατο ἡμῖν, τὴν ζωὴν τὴν αἰώνιον.

___

3.3 With the Subject of a Copulative Sentence (a copulative sentence or clause is one in which the verb εἰμί, ἐγένετο, or something comparable is the main verb).

John 1:14 -   The subject is ὁ λόγος, not σάρξ, because λόγος has the article.

{John 1:14} Καὶ ὁ λόγος σὰρξ ἐγένετο καὶ ἐσκήνωσεν ἐν ἡμῖν, καὶ ἐθεασάμεθα τὴν δόξαν αὐτοῦ, δόξαν ὡς μονογενοῦς παρὰ πατρός, πλήρης χάριτος καὶ ἀληθείας.

___

John 17:17 -   "Truth is Thy Word" is incorrect. "Thy Word is Truth" is correct, because λόγος has the article and is therefore the subject.

{John 17:17} ἁγίασον αὐτοὺς ἐν τῇ ἀληθείᾳ· ὁ λόγος ὁ σὸς ἀλήθειά ἐστιν.

___

1 John 4:16 -   "God is love" is correct, because θεός has the article.

{1 John 4:16} καὶ ἡμεῖς ἐγνώκαμεν καὶ πεπιστεύκαμεν τὴν ἀγάπην ἣν ἔχει ὁ θεὸς ἐν ἡμῖν. Ὁ θεὸς ἀγάπη ἐστίν, καὶ ὁ μένων ἐν τῇ ἀγάπῃ ἐν τῷ θεῷ μένει καὶ ὁ θεὸς ἐν αὐτῷ μένει.

___

2.3 ABSENCE OF THE ARTICLE

Without the article a noun may be definite or indefinite, but the emphasis is normally upon quality or character regardless.

John 1:1 -   θεός, since it is anarthrous, speaks of the quality of Deity.

{John 1:1} Ἐν ἀρχῇ ἦν ὁ λόγος, καὶ ὁ λόγος ἦν πρὸς τὸν θεόν, καὶ θεὸς ἦν ὁ λόγος.

___

1 Cor 14:19 -   With prepositions it is common for the article to be absent without any special significance as to quality. Hence, ἐκκλησίᾳ, emphasizes identity because it is the object of ἐν. The same is true with γλώσσῃ.

{1 Cor 14:19} ἀλλὰ <u>ἐν ἐκκλησίᾳ</u> θέλω πέντε λόγους τῷ νοΐ μου λαλῆσαι, ἵνα καὶ ἄλλους κατηχήσω, ἢ μυρίους λόγους <u>ἐν γλώσσῃ</u>.

---

1 Cor 14:35 - οἴκῳ is definite because of ἐν.

{1 Cor 14:35} εἰ δέ τι μαθεῖν θέλουσιν, <u>ἐν οἴκῳ</u> τοὺς ἰδίους ἄνδρας ἐπερωτάτωσαν· αἰσχρὸν γάρ ἐστιν γυναικὶ λαλεῖν ἐν ἐκκλησίᾳ.

---

1 Thess 1:5 - πνεύματι ἁγίῳ is anarthrous because it is the object of a preposition. It refers to the Holy Spirit. By comparison 1 Thess 4:8 has τὸ πνεῦμα . . . τὸ ἅγιον, since here it is the direct object.

{1 Thess 1:5} ὅτι τὸ εὐαγγέλιον ἡμῶν οὐκ ἐγενήθη εἰς ὑμᾶς ἐν λόγῳ μόνον ἀλλὰ καὶ ἐν δυνάμει καὶ ἐν <u>πνεύματι ἁγίῳ</u> καὶ [ἐν] πληροφορίᾳ πολλῇ, καθὼς οἴδατε οἷοι ἐγενήθημεν [ἐν] ὑμῖν δι' ὑμᾶς.

{1 Thess 4:8} τοιγαροῦν ὁ ἀθετῶν οὐκ ἄνθρωπον ἀθετεῖ ἀλλὰ τὸν θεὸν τὸν [καὶ] διδόντα <u>τὸ πνεῦμα</u> αὐτοῦ <u>τὸ ἅγιον</u> εἰς ὑμᾶς.

1.7 TRANSITIVENESS AND VOICE (D. & M., 154–64)

2.1 ACTIVE VOICE

3.1 TRANSITIVENESS - a verb which requires a direct object to complete its meaning is a transitive verb.

Rev 10:7 -   εὐηγγέλισεν has τοὺς . . . δούλους τοὺς προφήτας. as its direct object. "He evangelized" (or "He preached as good news to") requires "His . . . servants the prophets" to complete its meaning. It is therefore transitive.

{Rev 10:7} ἀλλ᾽ ἐν ταῖς ἡμέραις τῆς φωνῆς τοῦ ἑβδόμου ἀγγέλου, ὅταν μέλλῃ σαλπίζειν, καὶ ἐτελέσθη τὸ μυστήριον τοῦ θεοῦ, ὡς <u>εὐηγγέλισεν</u> <u>τοὺς</u> ἑαυτοῦ <u>δούλους τοὺς προφήτας</u>.

_____

_____

_____

3.2 INTRANSITIVENESS - the verbal idea which requires no object to complete its meaning is that of an intransitive verb.

Rev 14:6 -   εὐαγγελίσαι in this verse has no direct object. The verbal idea does not require an object to complete its meaning and is therefore intransitive.

{Rev 14:6} Καὶ εἶδον ἄλλον ἄγγελον πετόμενον ἐν μεσουρανήματι, ἔχοντα εὐαγγέλιον αἰώνιον <u>εὐαγγελίσαι</u> ἐπὶ τοὺς καθημένους ἐπὶ τῆς γῆς καὶ ἐπὶ πᾶν ἔθνος καὶ φυλὴν καὶ γλῶσσαν καὶ λαόν,

_____

_____

_____

3.3 CAUSATIVE - sometimes the subject causes an action and is not involved directly in the results of an action.

John 19:1 -   ἐμαστίγωσεν does not mean that Pilate personally carried out the scourging of Jesus. The nature of his position and of the circumstances indicates that he "had him scourged."

{John 19:1} Τότε οὖν ἔλαβεν ὁ Πιλᾶτος τὸν Ἰησοῦν καὶ <u>ἐμαστίγωσεν</u>.

_____

_____

2.2 MIDDLE VOICE

With a middle voice verb the subject is presented as acting and participating in the action in some additional way.

3.1 DIRECT - the additional participation by the subject may be by way of receiving the action.

1 Cor 6:11 -   ἀπελούσασθε means either "you washed yourselves" or else "you had yourselves washed." It probably means the latter in light of the two passive verbs paralleling it. In either case, however, it is a direct use of the middle voice.

{1 Cor 6:11} καὶ ταῦτά τινες ἦτε· ἀλλὰ <u>ἀπελούσασθε</u>, ἀλλὰ ἡγιάσθητε, ἀλλὰ ἐδικαιώθητε ἐν τῷ ὀνόματι τοῦ κυρίου Ἰησοῦ Χριστοῦ καὶ ἐν τῷ πνεύματι τοῦ θεοῦ ἡμῶν.

3.2 INDIRECT - the additional participation by the subject may be by way of added emphasis on the subject as the actor.

Rom 3:25 -   προέθετο ὁ θεός means, "God on His part set forth." The middle voice of the verb focuses upon God as the agent. When He set forth Christ as a "propitiatory," He did so of His own volition and initiative. He was not prompted to do so by any outside cause.

{Rom 3:25} ὃν <u>προέθετο ὁ θεὸς</u> ἱλαστήριον διὰ [τῆς] πίστεως ἐν τῷ αὐτοῦ αἵματι εἰς ἔνδειξιν τῆς δικαιοσύνης αὐτοῦ διὰ τὴν πάρεσιν τῶν προγεγονότων ἁμαρτημάτων

3.3 PERMISSIVE - the additional participation by the subject comes by way of contextual indications that permission of some type is entailed in the subject's acting.

1 Cor 6:7 -   ἀδικεῖσθε and ἀποστερεῖσθε are instances of the permissive middle voice. "Why not rather permit yourselves to be wronged? Why not rather permit yourselves to be defrauded?" Allowing these injustices without seeking revenge would have been a much better course because of the damage otherwise done to the church testimony.

{1 Cor 6:7} ἤδη μὲν [οὖν] ὅλως ἥττημα ὑμῖν ἐστιν ὅτι κρίματα ἔχετε μεθ᾽ ἑαυτῶν. διὰ τί οὐχὶ μᾶλλον <u>ἀδικεῖσθε</u>; διὰ τί οὐχὶ μᾶλλον <u>ἀποστερεῖσθε</u>;

3.4 RECIPROCAL - the additional participation by the subject is found in an exchange of action by a plurality of agents.

John 9:22 -   συνετέθειντο. A reflexive type of action, "they had agreed with themselves," offers little by way of coherence, but reciprocation, "they had agreed with each other," is quite meaningful in the context.

{John 9:22} ταῦτα εἶπαν οἱ γονεῖς αὐτοῦ ὅτι ἐφοβοῦντο τοὺς Ἰουδαίους· ἤδη γὰρ <u>συνετέθειντο</u> οἱ Ἰουδαῖοι ἵνα ἐάν τις αὐτὸν ὁμολογήσῃ Χριστόν, ἀποσυνάγωγος γένηται.

2.3 PASSIVE VOICE

3.1 TRANSITIVE PASSIVE - certain verbs, even though they are in the passive voice, may require objects to complete their meaning.

Rom 3:2 -   ἐπιστεύθησαν has "they" (referring to the Jews or those of the circumcision, 3:1) as its subject and τὰ λόγια as its direct object. "They were entrusted with the oracles of God."

{Rom 3:2} πολὺ κατὰ πάντα τρόπον. πρῶτον μὲν [γὰρ] ὅτι ἐπιστεύθησαν τὰ λόγια τοῦ θεοῦ.

3.2 CONSTRUCTIONS FOR EXPRESSING AGENCY - the Greek writer or speaker had a variety of options in expressing agency with the passive voice.

Matt 1:22 -   διά followed by the genitive case expresses intermediate agency, and ὑπό with the ablative gives direct agency or the ultimate agent for an action. "The Lord" was the original source of Isa 7:14, but "the prophet" was the intermediate agent through whom it was spoken.

{Matt 1:22} Τοῦτο δὲ ὅλον γέγονεν ἵνα πληρωθῇ τὸ ῥηθὲν ὑπὸ κυρίου διὰ τοῦ προφήτου λέγοντος,

Matt 4:1 -   ὑπό with the ablative is the most frequent means of expressing agency in the NT. "The Spirit" was the original agent who produced Jesus' leading into the wilderness.

{Matt 4:1} Τότε ὁ Ἰησοῦς ἀνήχθη εἰς τὴν ἔρημον ὑπὸ τοῦ πνεύματος πειρασθῆναι ὑπὸ τοῦ διαβόλου.

Mark 5:4 -   πέδαις and ἁλύσεσιν are illustrations of the instrumental case without a preposition to express the means by which an action is carried out. He was often bound by (means of) fetters and chains.

{Mark 5:4} διὰ τὸ αὐτὸν πολλάκις πέδαις καὶ ἁλύσεσιν δεδέσθαι καὶ διεσπάσθαι ὑπ' αὐτοῦ τὰς ἁλύσεις καὶ τὰς πέδας συντετρῖφθαι, καὶ οὐδεὶς ἴσχυεν αὐτὸν δαμάσαι·

Luke 1:45 -   παρά with the ablative is sometimes used to express agency: "the things spoken to her *by the Lord*."

{Luke 1:45} καὶ μακαρία ἡ πιστεύσασα ὅτι ἔσται τελείωσις τοῖς λελαλημένοις αὐτῇ <u>παρὰ</u> κυρίου.

John 1:6 -   παρὰ θεοῦ may be taken as expressing agency with the passive verb ἀπεσταλμένος.

{John 1:6} Ἐγένετο ἄνθρωπος, <u>ἀπεσταλμένος παρὰ θεοῦ</u>, ὄνομα αὐτῷ Ἰωάννης·

Rom 5:1 -   ἐκ with the ablative at times expresses means (or agency). To state that faith is the means of justification is a summary of the conclusion reached in Rom 3:21–4:25.

{Rom 5:1} Δικαιωθέντες οὖν <u>ἐκ</u> πίστεως εἰρήνην ἔχομεν πρὸς τὸν θεὸν διὰ τοῦ κυρίου ἡμῶν Ἰησοῦ Χριστοῦ

Col 1:16 -   ἐν with the instrumental case may express agency. Αὐτῷ, referring to Christ, is the agent who created all things.

{Col 1:16} ὅτι <u>ἐν αὐτῷ</u> ἐκτίσθη τὰ πάντα ἐν τοῖς οὐρανοῖς καὶ ἐπὶ τῆς γῆς, τὰ ὁρατὰ καὶ τὰ ἀόρατα, εἴτε θρόνοι εἴτε κυριότητες εἴτε ἀρχαὶ εἴτε ἐξουσίαι· τὰ πάντα δι᾿ αὐτοῦ καὶ εἰς αὐτὸν ἔκτισται·

James 1:13 -   Ἀπό with the ablative is used on rare occasions to depict an agent who is considered quite remote from the action of the passive verb. It is forbidden to think of God as being even remotely involved as an agent in temptation.

{James 1:13} μηδεὶς πειραζόμενος λεγέτω ὅτι <u>Ἀπὸ</u> θεοῦ πειράζομαι· ὁ γὰρ θεὸς ἀπείραστός ἐστιν κακῶν, πειράζει δὲ αὐτὸς οὐδένα.

1.8 MOOD (D. & M., 165–76)

2.1 INDICATIVE MOOD

3.1 DECLARATIVE AND INTERROGATIVE

John 11:26–27 - Verse 27 gives a declarative statement from Martha (Ναὶ κύριε, κ.τ.λ.). πιστεύεις τοῦτο; (v. 26b) is interrogative, however, because it asks a question.

{John 11:26} καὶ πᾶς ὁ ζῶν καὶ πιστεύων εἰς ἐμὲ οὐ μὴ ἀποθάνῃ εἰς τὸν αἰῶνα. πιστεύεις τοῦτο;

_____

_____

{John 11:27} λέγει αὐτῷ, Ναὶ κύριε, ἐγὼ πεπίστευκα ὅτι σὺ εἶ ὁ Χριστὸς ὁ υἱὸς τοῦ θεοῦ ὁ εἰς τὸν κόσμον ἐρχόμενος.

_____

_____

3.2 COHORTATIVE

1 Pet 1:16 -   ἔσεσθε is a future indicative to express a command. It appeals to the will and is therefore cohortative.

{1 Pet 1:16} διότι γέγραπται [ὅτι] Ἅγιοι ἔσεσθε, ὅτι ἐγὼ ἅγιός [εἰμι].

_____

3.3 POTENTIAL

John 15:22 -   εἴχοσαν as a part of the apodosis of a second class (contrary to fact) _conditional_ sentence views an action as potential, but not actual. Had matters been otherwise, they would not have had sin, but as the facts stand, they did have it.

{John 15:22} εἰ μὴ ἦλθον καὶ ἐλάλησα αὐτοῖς, ἁμαρτίαν οὐκ εἴχοσαν· νῦν δὲ πρόφασιν οὐκ ἔχουσιν περὶ τῆς ἁμαρτίας αὐτῶν.

_____

Rom 9:3 -   Because of a strong _impulse_ Paul wished to come as close as he could to actuality because of his deep burden for his people, but he had to leave the statement in the potential lest he be guilty of blasphemy. Ηὐχόμην (imperfect indicative) says, "I was at the point of wishing that I myself were *anathema*."

{Rom 9:3} <u>ηὐχόμην</u> γὰρ ἀνάθεμα εἶναι αὐτὸς ἐγὼ ἀπὸ τοῦ Χριστοῦ ὑπὲρ τῶν ἀδελφῶν μου τῶν συγγενῶν μου κατὰ σάρκα,

---
---

1 Cor 4:8 -   ὄφελόν (aorist indicative) indicates an *obligation* (or wish). The nature of the verbal idea necessitates potentiality.

{1 Cor 4:8} ἤδη κεκορεσμένοι ἐστέ, ἤδη ἐπλουτήσατε, χωρὶς ἡμῶν ἐβασιλεύσατε· καὶ <u>ὄφελόν</u> γε ἐβασιλεύσατε, ἵνα καὶ ἡμεῖς ὑμῖν συμβασιλεύσωμεν.

---

1 Cor 5:10 -   ὠφείλετε (imperfect indicative) states the readers' *obligation* to go out of the world if they would abstain from contact with all impure persons.

{1 Cor 5:10} οὐ πάντως τοῖς πόρνοις τοῦ κόσμου τούτου ἢ τοῖς πλεονέκταις καὶ ἅρπαξιν ἢ εἰδωλολάτραις, ἐπεὶ <u>ὠφείλετε</u> ἄρα ἐκ τοῦ κόσμου ἐξελθεῖν.

2.2 SUBJUNCTIVE MOOD

3.1 HORTATORY

John 11:7 -   Ἄγωμεν is Christ's word of exhortation to His disciples to join Him in going into Judea again.

{John 11:7} ἔπειτα μετὰ τοῦτο λέγει τοῖς μαθηταῖς, <u>Ἄγωμεν</u> εἰς τὴν Ἰουδαίαν πάλιν

3.2 PROHIBITION

Matt 1:20 -   μὴ φοβηθῇς is the angel's prohibition, telling Joseph not to fear taking Mary as his wife.

{Matt 1:20} ταῦτα δὲ αὐτοῦ ἐνθυμηθέντος ἰδοὺ ἄγγελος κυρίου κατ' ὄναρ ἐφάνη αὐτῷ λέγων, Ἰωσὴφ υἱὸς Δαυίδ, <u>μὴ φοβηθῇς</u> παραλαβεῖν Μαριὰμ τὴν γυναῖκά σου· τὸ γὰρ ἐν αὐτῇ γεννηθὲν ἐκ πνεύματός ἐστιν ἁγίου.

3.3 DELIBERATION

Mark 12:14 -   δῶμεν (both occurrences) asks a deliberative question (a question that does not anticipate an answer, but is put forth to stimulate consideration). "Should we pay taxes to Caesar, or should we stop paying taxes to Caesar?"

{Mark 12:14} καὶ ἐλθόντες λέγουσιν αὐτῷ, Διδάσκαλε, οἴδαμεν ὅτι ἀληθὴς εἶ καὶ οὐ μέλει σοι περὶ οὐδενός· οὐ γὰρ βλέπεις εἰς πρόσωπον ἀνθρώπων, ἀλλ᾽ ἐπ᾽ ἀληθείας τὴν ὁδὸν τοῦ θεοῦ διδάσκεις· ἔξεστιν δοῦναι κῆνσον Καίσαρι ἢ οὔ; <u>δῶμεν</u> ἢ <u>μὴ δῶμεν</u>;

John 6:28 -   ποιῶμεν is not a request for instructions that the questioners intended to follow. Rather it asks, "Supposing you were right, what would be your proposals as to what should be done if one wanted to do the works of God?"

{John 6:28} εἶπον οὖν πρὸς αὐτόν, Τί <u>ποιῶμεν</u> ἵνα ἐργαζώμεθα τὰ ἔργα τοῦ θεοῦ;

3.4 POTENTIALITY

John 3:16 -   ἀπόληται and ἔχῃ in a subordinate clause introduced by ἵνα are potential subjunctives. They are not actual, only purposed.

{John 3:16} Οὕτως γὰρ ἠγάπησεν ὁ θεὸς τὸν κόσμον, ὥστε τὸν υἱὸν τὸν μονογενῆ ἔδωκεν, <u>ἵνα</u> πᾶς ὁ πιστεύων εἰς αὐτὸν μὴ <u>ἀπόληται</u> ἀλλ᾽ <u>ἔχῃ</u> ζωὴν αἰώνιον.

John 5:43-   ἔλθῃ in a subordinate clause introduced by ἐάν is a potential subjunctive. It is not assured to be actual, but is conditional.

{John 5:43} ἐγὼ ἐλήλυθα ἐν τῷ ὀνόματι τοῦ πατρός μου, καὶ οὐ λαμβάνετέ με· <u>ἐὰν</u> ἄλλος <u>ἔλθῃ</u> ἐν τῷ ὀνόματι τῷ ἰδίῳ, ἐκεῖνον λήμψεσθε.

John 7:17 -   θέλῃ is a potential subjunctive in a subordinate clause introduced ἐάν.

{John 7:17} ἐάν τις <u>θέλῃ</u> τὸ θέλημα αὐτοῦ ποιεῖν, γνώσεται περὶ τῆς διδαχῆς πότερον ἐκ τοῦ θεοῦ ἐστιν ἢ ἐγὼ ἀπ᾽ ἐμαυτοῦ λαλῶ.

2.3 OPTATIVE MOOD

3.1 VOLUNTATIVE

Rom 6:2 -   μὴ γένοιτο is used fifteen times in the N. T. to express a strong negative wish: "May it not happen!"

{Rom 6:2} <u>μὴ γένοιτο</u>. οἵτινες ἀπεθάνομεν τῇ ἁμαρτίᾳ, πῶς ἔτι ζήσομεν ἐν αὐτῇ;

1 Thess 3:12 - πλεονάσαι and περισσεύσαι express a prayerful wish that the Lord will multiply and cause the readers to abound in love.

{1 Thess 3:12} ὑμᾶς δὲ ὁ κύριος <u>πλεονάσαι</u> καὶ <u>περισσεύσαι</u> τῇ ἀγάπῃ εἰς ἀλλήλους καὶ εἰς πάντας καθάπερ καὶ ἡμεῖς εἰς ὑμᾶς,

3.2 POTENTIAL

Acts 8:31 - δυναίμην with ἄν speaks of an ability that is only potential, until someone leads the eunuch into a correct understanding of Isaiah's prophecy.

{Acts 8:31} ὁ δὲ εἶπεν, Πῶς γὰρ <u>ἂν</u> <u>δυναίμην</u> ἐὰν μή τις ὁδηγήσει με; παρεκάλεσέν τε τὸν Φίλιππον ἀναβάντα καθίσαι σὺν αὐτῷ.

3.3 DELIBERATIVE

Luke 3:15 -   εἴη is the verb of an indirect deliberative question. The direct deliberative question from which the indirect is derived would probably be expressed with a subjunctive verb.

{Luke 3:15} Προσδοκῶντος δὲ τοῦ λαοῦ καὶ διαλογιζομένων πάντων ἐν ταῖς καρδίαις αὐτῶν περὶ τοῦ Ἰωάννου, μήποτε αὐτὸς <u>εἴη</u> ὁ Χριστός,

2.4 IMPERATIVE MOOD

3.1 COMMAND

Matt 5:44 -   ἀγαπᾶτε and προσεύχεσθε are Christ's correction of the scribal tradition about hating one's enemies. He commands love and prayer for them instead.

{Matt 5:44} ἐγὼ δὲ λέγω ὑμῖν, <u>ἀγαπᾶτε</u> τοὺς ἐχθροὺς ὑμῶν καὶ <u>προσεύχεσθε</u> ὑπὲρ τῶν διωκόντων ὑμᾶς,

---

3.2 PROHIBITION

Matt 7:1 -   Μὴ κρίνετε prohibits continuance of the censorious judgment of which the scribes and Pharisees were guilty.

{Matt 7:1} <u>Μὴ κρίνετε</u>, ἵνα μὴ κριθῆτε·, ἵνα μὴ κριθῆτε·

John 6:20 -   μὴ φοβεῖσθε calls for an end of the disciples' fear when Jesus comes to them walking on the water.

{John 6:20} ὁ δὲ λέγει αὐτοῖς, Ἐγώ εἰμι· <u>μὴ φοβεῖσθε</u>.

3.3 ENTREATY

Mark 9:22 -   βοήθησον is the father's urgent (aorist tense) plea for Jesus to help him and his son.

{Mark 9:22} καὶ πολλάκις καὶ εἰς πῦρ αὐτὸν ἔβαλεν καὶ εἰς ὕδατα ἵνα ἀπολέσῃ αὐτόν· ἀλλ᾽ εἴ τι δύνῃ, <u>βοήθησον</u> ἡμῖν σπλαγχνισθεὶς ἐφ᾽ ἡμᾶς.

John 17:11 -   τήρησον is Christ's earnest petition to His Father that the ones whom the Father had given Him should be kept safe and secure.

{John 17:11} καὶ οὐκέτι εἰμὶ ἐν τῷ κόσμῳ, καὶ αὐτοὶ ἐν τῷ κόσμῳ εἰσίν, κἀγὼ πρὸς σὲ ἔρχομαι. Πάτερ ἅγιε, <u>τήρησον</u> αὐτοὺς ἐν τῷ ὀνόματί σου ᾧ δέδωκάς μοι, ἵνα ὦσιν ἓν καθὼς ἡμεῖς.

_____

_____

_____

3.4 PERMISSION

Matt 10:13 - ἐλθάτω and ἐπιστραφήτω do not command, prohibit, or entreat. Rather they instruct as to what is to be permitted.

{Matt 10:13} καὶ ἐὰν μὲν ᾖ ἡ οἰκία ἀξία, <u>ἐλθάτω</u> ἡ εἰρήνη ὑμῶν ἐπ' αὐτήν, ἐὰν δὲ μὴ ᾖ ἀξία, ἡ εἰρήνη ὑμῶν πρὸς ὑμᾶς <u>ἐπιστραφήτω</u>.

_____

_____

_____

1 Cor 7:15 - χωριζέσθω does not command the unbelieving spouse to depart, but conveys the notion of *allowing* him to do so in the given situation if he is so inclined.

{1 Cor 7:15} εἰ δὲ ὁ ἄπιστος χωρίζεται, <u>χωριζέσθω</u>· οὐ δεδούλωται ὁ ἀδελφὸς ἢ ἡ ἀδελφὴ ἐν τοῖς τοιούτοις· ἐν δὲ εἰρήνῃ κέκληκεν ὑμᾶς ὁ θεός.

_____

_____

_____

1.9 TENSE

2.1 THE PRESENT TENSE (D. & M., 176–86)

3.1 PROGRESSIVE

4.1 Descriptive - description of action currently in progress

John 5:7 - ἔρχομαι is used to describe action while it is going on: "in the time during which I am coming." Likewise καταβαίνει depicts a progressive action simultaneous with it: "another is in the process of going down."

{John 5:7} ἀπεκρίθη αὐτῷ ὁ ἀσθενῶν, Κύριε, ἄνθρωπον οὐκ ἔχω ἵνα ὅταν ταραχθῇ τὸ ὕδωρ βάλῃ με εἰς τὴν κολυμβήθραν· ἐν ᾧ δὲ <u>ἔρχομαι</u> ἐγώ, ἄλλος πρὸ ἐμοῦ <u>καταβαίνει</u>.

_____

_____

_____

1 John 2:8 -   "Darkness is in the process of passing away (παράγεται) and the true light
                is already shining (φαίνει)."

{1 John 2:8} πάλιν ἐντολὴν καινὴν γράφω ὑμῖν, ὅ ἐστιν ἀληθὲς ἐν αὐτῷ καὶ ἐν ὑμῖν, ὅτι ἡ
σκοτία <u>παράγεται</u> καὶ τὸ φῶς τὸ ἀληθινὸν ἤδη <u>φαίνει</u>.

4.2 Existing Results - present results of something that has happened in the past

John 11:28 -   πάρεστιν, He is present, having arrived at a previous time. φωνεῖ. He
                called at an earlier time and the unanswered call still remains.

{John 11:28} Καὶ τοῦτο εἰποῦσα ἀπῆλθεν καὶ ἐφώνησεν Μαριὰμ τὴν ἀδελφὴν αὐτῆς
λάθρᾳ εἰποῦσα, Ὁ διδάσκαλος <u>πάρεστιν</u> καὶ <u>φωνεῖ</u> σε.

4.3 Duration - something begun in the past and continuing into the present

John 5:6 -   ἔχει. The man had been ill for a long time and was still ill.

{John 5:6} τοῦτον ἰδὼν ὁ Ἰησοῦς κατακείμενον καὶ γνοὺς ὅτι πολὺν ἤδη χρόνον <u>ἔχει</u>,
λέγει αὐτῷ, Θέλεις ὑγιὴς γενέσθαι;

3.2 CUSTOMARY - a recurring, routine happening that regularly occurs under a given
set of circumstances. Might be called "gnomic."

Matt 7:17 -   ποιεῖ (both occurrences). It is consistently true that a good tree bears
                beautiful fruit and a rotten tree bears bad fruit.

{Matt 7:17} οὕτως πᾶν δένδρον ἀγαθὸν καρποὺς καλοὺς <u>ποιεῖ</u>, τὸ δὲ σαπρὸν δένδρον
καρποὺς πονηροὺς <u>ποιεῖ</u>.

---

1 Cor 5:6 -   ζυμοῖ. It is axiomatic that a small amount of leaven always leavens the
                whole of the lump of which it is a part.

{1 Cor 5:6} Οὐ καλὸν τὸ καύχημα ὑμῶν. οὐκ οἴδατε ὅτι μικρὰ ζύμη ὅλον τὸ φύραμα
<u>ζυμοῖ</u>;

3.3 ITERATIVE - an action that is repeated from time to time.

1 Cor 10:16 - Blessing the cup (εὐλογοῦμεν) and breaking the bread (κλῶμεν) were
               carried out on a weekly basis.

{1 Cor 10:16} - τὸ ποτήριον τῆς εὐλογίας ὃ <u>εὐλογοῦμεν</u>, οὐχὶ κοινωνία ἐστὶν τοῦ αἵματος
τοῦ Χριστοῦ; τὸν ἄρτον ὃν <u>κλῶμεν</u>, οὐχὶ κοινωνία τοῦ σώματος τοῦ Χριστοῦ ἐστιν;

1 Cor 11:29 - Unless one discerns the body, he eats (ἐσθίει) and drinks (πίνει) judgment
               for himself repeatedly, each time he participates in the Lord's Supper.

{1 Cor 11:29} ὁ γὰρ ἐσθίων καὶ πίνων κρίμα ἑαυτῷ <u>ἐσθίει</u> καὶ <u>πίνει</u> μὴ διακρίνων τὸ
σῶμα.

3.4 AORISTIC - durative action disappears from the present tense.

Matt 5:22 -   λέγω refers to one statement, not a continuing discourse.

{Matt 5:22} ἐγὼ δὲ <u>λέγω</u> ὑμῖν ὅτι πᾶς ὁ ὀργιζόμενος τῷ ἀδελφῷ αὐτοῦ ἔνοχος ἔσται τῇ
κρίσει· ὃς δ' ἂν εἴπῃ τῷ ἀδελφῷ αὐτοῦ, Ῥακά, ἔνοχος ἔσται τῷ συνεδρίῳ· ὃς δ' ἂν εἴπῃ, Μωρέ,
ἔνοχος ἔσται εἰς τὴν γέενναν τοῦ πυρός

John 16:21 -   τίκτῃ speaks of the event of birth. The nature of the verbal idea requires
               that it be a single happening, not a continuing process. Since the time of
               ἔχει coincides with the birth, it too must be punctilear.

{John 16:21} ἡ γυνὴ ὅταν <u>τίκτῃ</u> λύπην <u>ἔχει</u>, ὅτι ἦλθεν ἡ ὥρα αὐτῆς· ὅταν δὲ γεννήσῃ τὸ
παιδίον, οὐκέτι μνημονεύει τῆς θλίψεως διὰ τὴν χαρὰν ὅτι ἐγεννήθη ἄνθρωπος εἰς τὸν κόσμον.

3.5 FUTURISTIC - the event is future, but the process which will culminate in its
happening is already underway.

John 14:3 -   The nature of the verbal idea of ἔρχομαι together with the context throws
               the action into the future (note παραλήμψομαι). "I am on my way and will
               come."

{John 14:3} καὶ ἐὰν πορευθῶ καὶ ἑτοιμάσω τόπον ὑμῖν, πάλιν <u>ἔρχομαι</u> καὶ <u>παραλήμψομαι</u> ὑμᾶς πρὸς ἐμαυτόν, ἵνα ὅπου εἰμὶ ἐγὼ καὶ ὑμεῖς ἦτε.

1 Cor 3:13 -   ἀποκαλύπτεται becomes futuristic by being parallel with two future tense verbs (δηλώσει and δοκιμάσει).

{1 Cor 3:13} ἑκάστου τὸ ἔργον φανερὸν γενήσεται, ἡ γὰρ ἡμέρα <u>δηλώσει</u>, ὅτι ἐν πυρὶ <u>ἀποκαλύπτεται</u>· καὶ ἑκάστου τὸ ἔργον ὁποῖόν ἐστιν τὸ πῦρ [αὐτὸ] <u>δοκιμάσει</u>.

3.6 HISTORICAL - a past event is pictured in the speaker's (or writer's) mind as being present.

Mark 12:13 -   ἀποστέλλουσιν describes a past sending, but Mark regards it as going on as he writes. This has the effect of transferring his readers to the scene of the past event.

{Mark 12:13} Καὶ <u>ἀποστέλλουσιν</u> πρὸς αὐτόν τινας τῶν Φαρισαίων καὶ τῶν Ἡρῳδιανῶν ἵνα αὐτὸν ἀγρεύσωσιν λόγῳ.

Mark 12:18 -   ἔρχονται in parallel with the imperfect ἐπηρώτων is obviously historical. "They come and were asking."

{Mark 12:18} Καὶ <u>ἔρχονται</u> Σαδδουκαῖοι πρὸς αὐτόν, οἵτινες λέγουσιν ἀνάστασιν μὴ εἶναι, καὶ <u>ἐπηρώτων</u> αὐτὸν λέγοντες,

3.7 TENDENTIAL - also called "conative." Indicates effort, not necessarily successful.

John 10:32 -   λιθάζετε. They intended or tried to stone Christ, but He eluded them (John 10:39) before they could do so.

{John 10:32} ἀπεκρίθη αὐτοῖς ὁ Ἰησοῦς, Πολλὰ ἔργα καλὰ ἔδειξα ὑμῖν ἐκ τοῦ πατρός· διὰ ποῖον αὐτῶν ἔργον ἐμὲ <u>λιθάζετε</u>;

John 13:6 -	νίπτεις. Jesus was trying (or beginning) to wash Peter's feet, and Peter did not want Him to do it. The subsequent context shows that the effort was eventually successful.

{John 13:6} ἔρχεται οὖν πρὸς Σίμωνα Πέτρον· λέγει αὐτῷ, Κύριε, σύ μου <u>νίπτεις</u> τοὺς πόδας;

3.8 STATIC - very close to the customary present, except the idea of routineness is missing.

John 7:52 -	The speaker declares that a state exists in which no prophet arises out of Galilee (οὐκ ἐγείρεται).

{John 7:52} ἀπεκρίθησαν καὶ εἶπαν αὐτῷ, Μὴ καὶ σὺ ἐκ τῆς Γαλιλαίας εἶ; ἐραύνησον καὶ ἴδε ὅτι ἐκ τῆς Γαλιλαίας προφήτης <u>οὐκ ἐγείρεται</u>.

2.2 IMPERFECT TENSE (D. & M., 186–91)

3.1 PROGRESSIVE - a past tense corresponding to the progressive present

4.1 Descriptive

John 19:3 -	ἤρχοντο. The soldiers were coming to him. They are pictured in the process of their movement toward Him. The graphic description of how they were hitting Him is also given (ἐδίδοσαν).

{John 19:3} καὶ <u>ἤρχοντο</u> πρὸς αὐτὸν καὶ ἔλεγον, Χαῖρε ὁ βασιλεὺς τῶν Ἰουδαίων· καὶ <u>ἐδίδοσαν</u> αὐτῷ ῥαπίσματα.

4.2 Duration

1 John 2:7 -	εἴχετε. They had had the old commandment prior to receiving the new commandment.

{1 John 2:7} Ἀγαπητοί, οὐκ ἐντολὴν καινὴν γράφω ὑμῖν ἀλλ᾽ ἐντολὴν παλαιὰν ἣν <u>εἴχετε</u> ἀπ᾽ ἀρχῆς· ἡ ἐντολὴ ἡ παλαιά ἐστιν ὁ λόγος ὃν ἠκούσατε.

3.2 CUSTOMARY

1 Cor 10:4 -   ἔπινον. The children of Israel under Moses' leadership were accustomed to drinking from the spiritual rock which followed them.

{1 Cor 10:4} καὶ πάντες τὸ αὐτὸ πνευματικὸν ἔπιον πόμα· ἔπινον γὰρ ἐκ πνευματικῆς ἀκολουθούσης πέτρας, ἡ πέτρα δὲ ἦν ὁ Χριστός.

3.3 ITERATIVE

John 3:22 -   The nature of the action in ἐβάπτιζεν requires that the baptism was done from time to time and not continuously.

{John 3:22} Μετὰ ταῦτα ἦλθεν ὁ Ἰησοῦς καὶ οἱ μαθηταὶ αὐτοῦ εἰς τὴν Ἰουδαίαν γῆν καὶ ἐκεῖ διέτριβεν μετ' αὐτῶν καὶ ἐβάπτιζεν.

John 5:18 -   The Jewish leaders would not accuse Jesus of breaking the Sabbath more than once a week. Hence, ἔλυεν says, "He kept breaking" the Sabbath each time one occurred.

{John 5:18} διὰ τοῦτο οὖν μᾶλλον ἐζήτουν αὐτὸν οἱ Ἰουδαῖοι ἀποκτεῖναι, ὅτι οὐ μόνον ἔλυεν τὸ σάββατον, ἀλλὰ καὶ πατέρα ἴδιον ἔλεγεν τὸν θεὸν ἴσον ἑαυτὸν ποιῶν τῷ θεῷ.

3.4 TENDENTIAL - considered the same as the "inceptive" imperfect by some grammatical authorities.

Matt 3:14 -   διεκώλυεν. John was trying to hinder Christ from being baptized, but unsuccessfully, as subsequent verses show.

{Matt 3:14} ὁ δὲ Ἰωάννης διεκώλυεν αὐτὸν λέγων, Ἐγὼ χρείαν ἔχω ὑπὸ σοῦ βαπτισθῆναι, καὶ σὺ ἔρχῃ πρός με;

Luke 1:59 -   Elizabeth's relatives attempted to name (ἐκάλουν) her new-born baby after the father Zecharias, but Elizabeth would not permit them to do so.

{Luke 1:59} Καὶ ἐγένετο ἐν τῇ ἡμέρᾳ τῇ ὀγδόῃ ἦλθον περιτεμεῖν τὸ παιδίον καὶ <u>ἐκάλουν</u> αὐτὸ ἐπὶ τῷ ὀνόματι τοῦ πατρὸς αὐτοῦ Ζαχαρίαν.

3.5 VOLUNTATIVE

Rom 9:3 -   ηὐχόμην (also a potential indicative) says that Paul was at the point of wishing himself accursed, but never actually did so.

{Rom 9:3} <u>ηὐχόμην</u> γὰρ ἀνάθεμα εἶναι αὐτὸς ἐγὼ ἀπὸ τοῦ Χριστοῦ ὑπὲρ τῶν ἀδελφῶν μου τῶν συγγενῶν μου κατὰ σάρκα,

Gal 4:20 -   Paul was on the verge of wishing (ἤθελον) to be present with them and to change his voice. This expresses how deeply concerned he was over his readers, i.e., to the point that he was almost ready to try an entirely different approach with them.

{Gal 4:20} <u>ἤθελον</u> δὲ παρεῖναι πρὸς ὑμᾶς ἄρτι καὶ ἀλλάξαι τὴν φωνήν μου, ὅτι ἀποροῦμαι ἐν ὑμῖν.

3.6 INCEPTIVE - considered the same as the "tendential" imperfect by some grammatical authorities.

Matt 5:2 -   In this introduction to the Sermon on the Mount, it is noted that Jesus "began teaching" (ἐδίδασκεν).

{Matt 5:2} καὶ ἀνοίξας τὸ στόμα αὐτοῦ <u>ἐδίδασκεν</u> αὐτοὺς λέγων,

Mark 14:72 -   ἔκλαιεν. Upon recollection of Jesus' prediction Peter "started to cry."

{Mark 14:72} καὶ εὐθὺς ἐκ δευτέρου ἀλέκτωρ ἐφώνησεν. καὶ ἀνεμνήσθη ὁ Πέτρος τὸ ῥῆμα ὡς εἶπεν αὐτῷ ὁ Ἰησοῦς ὅτι Πρὶν ἀλέκτορα φωνῆσαι δὶς τρίς με ἀπαρνήσῃ· καὶ ἐπιβαλὼν <u>ἔκλαιεν</u>.

2.3 FUTURE TENSE (D. & M., 191–93)

3.1 PREDICTIVE - limited to those uses of the future that designate single occurrences.

Matt 1:21 -   The acts of begetting (τέξεται) and naming (καλέσεις) are single events to take place in the future, each at its own time.

{Matt 1:21} <u>τέξεται</u> δὲ υἱόν, καὶ <u>καλέσεις</u> τὸ ὄνομα αὐτοῦ Ἰησοῦν· αὐτὸς γὰρ σώσει τὸν λαὸν αὐτοῦ ἀπὸ τῶν ἁμαρτιῶν αὐτῶν.

John 8:32 -   Both γνώσεσθε and ἐλευθερώσει are instantaneous. At the moment they come to know the truth, they will also be liberated.

{John 8:32} καὶ <u>γνώσεσθε</u> τὴν ἀλήθειαν, καὶ ἡ ἀλήθεια <u>ἐλευθερώσει</u> ὑμᾶς.

3.2 PROGRESSIVE - sometimes the verbal notion and/or the context require continuous action in the future.

John 12:32 -   ἑλκύσω speaks of Christ's drawing all people to Himself over a long period of time.

{John 12:32} κἀγὼ ἐὰν ὑψωθῶ ἐκ τῆς γῆς, πάντας <u>ἑλκύσω</u> πρὸς ἐμαυτόν.

Rom 6:2 -   Though it also may be considered a deliberative future, the ζήσομεν is taken by some to be progressive because it covers a continuing human experience.

{Rom 6:2} μὴ γένοιτο. οἵτινες ἀπεθάνομεν τῇ ἁμαρτίᾳ, πῶς ἔτι <u>ζήσομεν</u> ἐν αὐτῇ;

Phil 1:18 -   Contextually it is clear that χαρήσομαι means, "I will go on rejoicing."

{Phil 1:18} τί γάρ; πλὴν ὅτι παντὶ τρόπῳ, εἴτε προφάσει εἴτε ἀληθείᾳ, Χριστὸς καταγγέλλεται, καὶ ἐν τούτῳ χαίρω. ἀλλὰ καὶ <u>χαρήσομαι</u>,

---

3.3 IMPERATIVE

Matt 5:43 - "You *shall* love (Ἀγαπήσεις) your neighbor" is equivalent to "love your neighbor."

{Matt 5:43} Ἠκούσατε ὅτι ἐρρέθη, <u>Ἀγαπήσεις</u> τὸν πλησίον σου καὶ μισήσεις τὸν ἐχθρόν σου.

Matt 5:48 - "You shall be (ἔσεσθε) perfect" is tantamount to a command to be perfect.

{Matt 5:48} <u>Ἔσεσθε</u> οὖν ὑμεῖς τέλειοι ὡς ὁ πατὴρ ὑμῶν ὁ οὐράνιος τέλειός ἐστιν.

3.4 DELIBERATIVE - Deliberative questions are not designed to learn facts, but rather seek to ascertain whether a certain course of action is possible, desirable, or necessary.

Rom 3:6 - "How will God judge (κρινεῖ) the world" if the previously stated condition implied in ἐπεί is true. The implied answer is, "He cannot." But it is the foregone conclusion that He will, so the supposition of ἐπεί, i.e. that God is unrighteous for inflicting wrath, must be false.

{Rom 3:6} μὴ γένοιτο· <u>ἐπεὶ</u> πῶς <u>κρινεῖ</u> ὁ θεὸς τὸν κόσμον;

3.5 GNOMIC - (see customary present and gnomic aorist)

Rom 5:7 - ἀποθανεῖται. It is axiomatic that scarcely anyone would die for a righteous person.

{Rom 5:7} μόλις γὰρ ὑπὲρ δικαίου τις <u>ἀποθανεῖται</u>· ὑπὲρ γὰρ τοῦ ἀγαθοῦ τάχα τις καὶ τολμᾷ ἀποθανεῖν·

Rom 7:3 - It goes without saying that a woman is termed (χρηματίσει) "an adulteress" if she marries another man while her husband is alive.

{Rom 7:3} ἄρα οὖν ζῶντος τοῦ ἀνδρὸς μοιχαλὶς <u>χρηματίσει</u> ἐὰν γένηται ἀνδρὶ ἑτέρῳ· ἐὰν δὲ ἀποθάνῃ ὁ ἀνήρ, ἐλευθέρα ἐστὶν ἀπὸ τοῦ νόμου, τοῦ μὴ εἶναι αὐτὴν μοιχαλίδα γενομένην ἀνδρὶ ἑτέρῳ.

2.4 AORIST TENSE (D. & M., 193–200)

3.1 CONSTATIVE - views actions in their totality, whether it be momentary, extended, or somewhere between. This is the broadest category of usage for the aorist tense.

John 2:20 -   οἰκοδομήθη views an extended action of forty-six years in its entirety as a single unit.

{John 2:20} εἶπαν οὖν οἱ Ἰουδαῖοι, Τεσσεράκοντα καὶ ἓξ ἔτεσιν οἰκοδομήθη ὁ ναὸς οὗτος, καὶ σὺ ἐν τρισὶν ἡμέραις ἐγερεῖς αὐτόν;

_____

_____

Rom 5:12 -   ἥμαρτον refers to the consequences of the single act of Adam's disobedience, even though committed by "all." In this case the action is a momentary one.

{Rom 5:12} Διὰ τοῦτο ὥσπερ δι' ἑνὸς ἀνθρώπου ἡ ἁμαρτία εἰς τὸν κόσμον εἰσῆλθεν καὶ διὰ τῆς ἁμαρτίας ὁ θάνατος, καὶ οὕτως εἰς πάντας ἀνθρώπους ὁ θάνατος διῆλθεν, ἐφ' ᾧ πάντες ἥμαρτον·

_____

_____

_____

Rev 20:4 -   ἐβασίλευσαν views 1000 years of reigning as one happening.

{Rev 20:4} Καὶ εἶδον θρόνους καὶ ἐκάθισαν ἐπ' αὐτοὺς καὶ κρίμα ἐδόθη αὐτοῖς, καὶ τὰς ψυχὰς τῶν πεπελεκισμένων διὰ τὴν μαρτυρίαν Ἰησοῦ καὶ διὰ τὸν λόγον τοῦ θεοῦ καὶ οἵτινες οὐ προσεκύνησαν τὸ θηρίον οὐδὲ τὴν εἰκόνα αὐτοῦ καὶ οὐκ ἔλαβον τὸ χάραγμα ἐπὶ τὸ μέτωπον καὶ ἐπὶ τὴν χεῖρα αὐτῶν. καὶ ἔζησαν καὶ ἐβασίλευσαν μετὰ τοῦ Χριστοῦ χίλια ἔτη.

_____

_____

_____

3.2 INGRESSIVE - principal attention is given to the beginning of an action.

John 11:35 -   ἐδάκρυσεν. Since Jesus was not weeping prior to this moment, this aorist must mean, "started to weep."

{John 11:35} ἐδάκρυσεν ὁ Ἰησοῦς.

_____

_____

Rom 14:9 -   ἔζησεν in such a situation as this must mean "came to life." The same is true in Rev 2:8; 13:14; 20:5. This ingressive aorist describes resurrection from the dead.

{Rom 14:9} εἰς τοῦτο γὰρ Χριστὸς ἀπέθανεν καὶ ἔζησεν, ἵνα καὶ νεκρῶν καὶ ζώντων κυριεύσῃ.

---

1 Cor 4:8 -   ἐπλουτήσατε means, "you have become rich." Stative verbs are often ingressive when used in the aorist tense.

{1 Cor 4:8} ἤδη κεκορεσμένοι ἐστέ, ἤδη ἐπλουτήσατε, χωρὶς ἡμῶν ἐβασιλεύσατε· καὶ ὄφελόν γε ἐβασιλεύσατε, ἵνα καὶ ἡμεῖς ὑμῖν συμβασιλεύσωμεν.

3.3 CULMINATIVE - views an action from the standpoint of its completion. There is no reference to existing results, however.

Matt 7:28 -   The verbal idea of ἐτέλεσεν lends itself to the culminative emphasis: "Jesus completed these words."

{Matt 7:28} Καὶ ἐγένετο ὅτε ἐτέλεσεν ὁ Ἰησοῦς τοὺς λόγους τούτους, ἐξεπλήσσοντο οἱ ὄχλοι ἐπὶ τῇ διδαχῇ αὐτοῦ·

Mark 7:35 -   The nature of the situation shows that the loosing (ἐλύθη) broke the bond completely. Afterward the man was speaking "rightly," whereas before he spoke but with difficulty (v. 32).

{Mark 7:35} καὶ [εὐθέως] ἠνοίγησαν αὐτοῦ αἱ ἀκοαί, καὶ ἐλύθη ὁ δεσμὸς τῆς γλώσσης αὐτοῦ καὶ ἐλάλει ὀρθῶς.

Phil 4:11 -   ἔμαθον. Of necessity Paul had learned the lesson completely. Otherwise, contentment under all kinds of circumstances would have been impossible.

{Phil 4:11} οὐχ ὅτι καθ᾽ ὑστέρησιν λέγω, ἐγὼ γὰρ ἔμαθον ἐν οἷς εἰμι αὐτάρκης εἶναι.

3.4 GNOMIC - an action generally accepted as an axiomatic truth. Its recurrence is so certain that it is spoken of in the aorist tense even though it continues in the present and will continue in the future.

Matt 13:44 -   ἔκρυψεν. It is characteristic of human nature under these circumstances that a man will hide a treasure. So the Lord here utilizes a gnomic aorist.

{Matt 13:44} Ὁμοία ἐστὶν ἡ βασιλεία τῶν οὐρανῶν θησαυρῷ κεκρυμμένῳ ἐν τῷ ἀγρῷ, ὃν εὑρὼν ἄνθρωπος ἔκρυψεν, καὶ ἀπὸ τῆς χαρᾶς αὐτοῦ ὑπάγει καὶ πωλεῖ πάντα ὅσα ἔχει καὶ ἀγοράζει τὸν ἀγρὸν ἐκεῖνον.

_____

_____

_____

1 Pet 1:24 -   ἐξηράνθη and ἐξέπεσεν. It is in accord with observable happenings that the grass always dries up and its flower always withers. These happenings are so regular that they are axiomatic.

{1 Pet 1:24} διότι πᾶσα σὰρξ ὡς χόρτος καὶ πᾶσα δόξα αὐτῆς ὡς ἄνθος χόρτου· ἐξηράνθη ὁ όρτος καὶ τὸ ἄνθος ἐξέπεσεν·

_____

_____

3.5 EPISTOLARY - here the writer projects himself forward to reflect the viewpoint of the readers.

1 Cor 5:11 -   νῦν shows that Paul has reference to what he is currently writing. Hence, ἔγραψα is aorist because when the readers received the letter, the writing would lie in past time.

{1 Cor 5:11} νῦν δὲ ἔγραψα ὑμῖν μὴ συναναμίγνυσθαι ἐάν τις ἀδελφὸς ὀνομαζόμενος ᾖ πόρνος ἢ πλεονέκτης ἢ εἰδωλολάτρης ἢ λοίδορος ἢ μέθυσος ἢ ἅρπαξ, τῷ τοιούτῳ μηδὲ συνεσθίειν.

_____

_____

_____

Eph 6:22 -   ἔπεμψα refers to the sending of Tychicus in conjunction with this very epistle. By the time of his arrival with this epistle, however, the sending will be a past happening. The writer views the act from the viewpoint of his readers.

{Eph 6:22} ὃν ἔπεμψα πρὸς ὑμᾶς εἰς αὐτὸ τοῦτο, ἵνα γνῶτε τὰ περὶ ἡμῶν καὶ παρακαλέσῃ τὰς καρδίας ὑμῶν.

3.6 DRAMATIC - present action is expressed in the aorist to give it emphasis, to make it more climactic and dramatic.

John 12:27 - ἦλθον. At the moment He spoke, Jesus was coming to the hour. He says it as though He had already arrived, however, because of the all-important significance of His going to the cross.

{John 12:27} Νῦν ἡ ψυχή μου τετάρακται, καὶ τί εἴπω; Πάτερ, σῶσόν με ἐκ τῆς ὥρας ταύτης; ἀλλὰ διὰ τοῦτο ἦλθον εἰς τὴν ὥραν ταύτην.

3.7 PROPHETIC - corresponding to the Hebrew perfect tense, this use predicts a future happening with an aorist because of the absolute certainty of its fulfillment. This usage of the aorist is limited to contexts where there is a Semitic influence on the linguistic pattern.

Luke 1:51 - ἐποίησεν and διεσκόρπισεν are prophetic of what the Lord will do in the future through the child to be born to the virgin Mary. Obviously He had not accomplished these things at the time Mary uttered these words.

{Luke 1:51} Ἐποίησεν κράτος ἐν βραχίονι αὐτοῦ, διεσκόρπισεν ὑπερηφάνους διανοίᾳ καρδίας αὐτῶν·

2.5 PERFECT TENSE (D. & M., 200–205)

3.1 INTENSIVE - attention is focused upon the continuing results of a completed process.

John 1:15 - κέκραγεν is parallel to μαρτυρεῖ. John's continuing cry is viewed as the result of an initial completed proclamation. Its continuance is comparable to the durative action of μαρτυρεῖ.

{John 1:15} Ἰωάννης μαρτυρεῖ περὶ αὐτοῦ καὶ κέκραγεν λέγων, Οὗτος ἦν ὃν εἶπον, Ὁ ὀπίσω μου ἐρχόμενος ἔμπροσθέν μου γέγονεν, ὅτι πρῶτός μου ἦν.

---

1 Cor 7:14 -   ἡγίασται (both occurrences) means, "stands sanctified." It is an ongoing condition growing out of an initial completed sanctification.

{1 Cor 7:14} ἡγίασται γὰρ ὁ ἀνὴρ ὁ ἄπιστος ἐν τῇ γυναικὶ καὶ ἡγίασται ἡ γυνὴ ἡ ἄπιστος ἐν τῷ ἀδελφῷ· ἐπεὶ ἄρα τὰ τέκνα ὑμῶν ἀκάθαρτά ἐστιν, νῦν δὲ ἅγιά ἐστιν.

_____

_____

Rev 3:20 -   ἵστημι in the perfect tense has a present meaning. This happens because this verb in the perfect is always intensive. "I have taken My stand and remain standing." With the perfect of this verb the focus is always on the existing result.

{Rev 3:20} ἰδοὺ ἕστηκα ἐπὶ τὴν θύραν καὶ κρούω· ἐάν τις ἀκούσῃ τῆς φωνῆς μου καὶ ἀνοίξῃ τὴν θύραν, [καὶ] εἰσελεύσομαι πρὸς αὐτὸν καὶ δειπνήσω μετ᾽ αὐτοῦ καὶ αὐτὸς μετ᾽ ἐμοῦ.

_____

_____

3.2 CONSUMMATIVE - special emphasis falls upon the completion of a process. Existing results are not excluded, but they are not the principal thing in view.

Matt 3:2 -   ἤγγικεν. The kingdom of heaven has drawn near. It has come to a point of nearness (and remains there).

{Matt 3:2} [καὶ] λέγων, Μετανοεῖτε· ἤγγικεν γὰρ ἡ βασιλεία τῶν οὐρανῶν.

_____

_____

John 17:6 -   They have completed the process of keeping (τετήρηκαν) your word (and remain in the state of doing so).

{John 17:6} Ἐφανέρωσά σου τὸ ὄνομα τοῖς ἀνθρώποις οὓς ἔδωκάς μοι ἐκ τοῦ κόσμου. σοὶ ἦσαν κἀμοὶ αὐτοὺς ἔδωκας καὶ τὸν λόγον σου τετήρηκαν.

_____

_____

3.3 ITERATIVE - the completed process is not continuous, but repeated at different times.

John 1:18 -   ἑώρακεν. "No one has ever seen" carries with it the connotation "from time to time no one has ever seen." Hence, this verb refers to repeated action.

{John 1:18} θεὸν οὐδεὶς ἑώρακεν πώποτε· μονογενὴς θεὸς ὁ ὢν εἰς τὸν κόλπον τοῦ πατρὸς ἐκεῖνος ἐξηγήσατο.

3.4 DRAMATIC - a more vivid way of designating an action. This is a special use of the intensive perfect.

James 1:24 -   ἀπελήλυθεν. This is part of a vivid illustration of what the average person does when he looks into a mirror.

{Jas 1:24} κατενόησεν γὰρ ἑαυτὸν καὶ ἀπελήλυθεν καὶ εὐθέως ἐπελάθετο ὁποῖος ἦν.

2.6 PLUPERFECT TENSE (D. & M., 205–06)

3.1 INTENSIVE - same as the intensive perfect except the point of reference is a time in the past instead of the present.

John 1:31 -   ᾔδειν is translated as an imperfect because the verb οἶδα is always intensive.

{John 1:31} κἀγὼ οὐκ ᾔδειν αὐτόν, ἀλλ' ἵνα φανερωθῇ τῷ Ἰσραὴλ διὰ τοῦτο ἦλθον ἐγὼ ἐν ὕδατι βαπτίζων.

John 1:35 -   εἱστήκει is intensive and therefore imperfect in meaning. These are results continuing in the past time. This verb is always intensive in the perfect and pluperfect tenses.

{John 1:35} Τῇ ἐπαύριον πάλιν εἱστήκει ὁ Ἰωάννης καὶ ἐκ τῶν μαθητῶν αὐτοῦ δύο

3.2 CONSUMMATIVE - same as the consummative perfect except the completion came prior to some reference point in the past.

John 4:8 -   ἀπεληλύθεισαν. His disciples had gone into the city prior to the time Jesus began His conversation with the woman.

{John 4:8} οἱ γὰρ μαθηταὶ αὐτοῦ ἀπεληλύθεισαν εἰς τὴν πόλιν ἵνα τροφὰς ἀγοράσωσιν.

John 9:22 -   συνετέθειντο. The Jews had agreed with one another before the blind
                man's parents said these things.

{John 9:22} ταῦτα εἶπαν οἱ γονεῖς αὐτοῦ ὅτι ἐφοβοῦντο τοὺς Ἰουδαίους· ἤδη γὰρ
συνετέθειντο οἱ Ἰουδαῖοι ἵνα ἐάν τις αὐτὸν ὁμολογήσῃ Χριστόν, ἀποσυνάγωγος γένηται.

2.7 INTERPRETATION OF TENSE (D. & M., 206–08)

3.1 Rom 6:12–13 - Use the basic connotation of the tense, the context, and the idea of the
verb to determine the particular tense usage.

{Rom 6:12} Μὴ οὖν βασιλευέτω ἡ ἁμαρτία ἐν τῷ θνητῷ ὑμῶν σώματι εἰς τὸ ὑπακούειν
ταῖς ἐπιθυμίαις αὐτοῦ,

{Rom 6:13} μηδὲ παριστάνετε τὰ μέλη ὑμῶν ὅπλα ἀδικίας τῇ ἁμαρτίᾳ, ἀλλὰ
παραστήσατε ἑαυτοὺς τῷ θεῷ ὡσεὶ ἐκ νεκρῶν ζῶντας καὶ τὰ μέλη ὑμῶν ὅπλα δικαιοσύνης τῷ
θεῷ. **14** ἁμαρτία γὰρ ὑμῶν οὐ κυριεύσει· οὐ γάρ ἐστε ὑπὸ νόμον ἀλλὰ ὑπὸ χάριν.

(1)   The *tense* of βασιλευέτω and παριστάνετε is present. The durative nature of the
        tense function shows that sin was reigning and that they were presenting their
        members as instruments of sin. The prohibition tells them to cease doing so. By
        contrast the tense of παραστήσατε is aorist. The positive command views an
        action as a single unit. It is not an extended single unit, because Paul would have
        continued the present tense to express this idea. Hence, it is a momentary act of
        presenting oneself to God that is commanded.

(2)   The *context* has spoken of single momentary acts (e.g. ἀπεθάνομεν, 6:2) and of
        continuing actions (e.g., λογίζεσθε, 6:11). It is therefore not a meaningless
        phenomenon that the present and aorist tenses are contrasted in 6:12–13 (notice
        also ἐπιμένωμεν in 6:1 and ἁμαρτήσωμεν in 6:15).

(3)   The *verbal idea* of βασιλευέτω lends itself to the notion of a process in the present
        time as does παρίστημι. In the aorist, however, βασιλεύω might have been
        construed "begin to reign," an ingressive aorist, as it often is. So Paul limits the
        positive command to παρίστημι.

It is thus conclusive that the two verbs expressing prohibition are progressive presents of
description and that the aorist of the positive command is a constative of the punctilear type.

3.2 Rom 12:1–2 - Tense connotation, context, and idea of verb meaning determine tense usage.

{Rom 12:1} Παρακαλῶ οὖν ὑμᾶς, ἀδελφοί, διὰ τῶν οἰκτιρμῶν τοῦ θεοῦ <u>παραστῆσαι</u> τὰ σώματα ὑμῶν θυσίαν ζῶσαν ἁγίαν εὐάρεστον τῷ θεῷ, τὴν λογικὴν λατρείαν ὑμῶν·

{Rom 12:2} καὶ μὴ <u>συσχηματίζεσθε</u> τῷ αἰῶνι τούτῳ, ἀλλὰ <u>μεταμορφοῦσθε</u> τῇ ἀνακαινώσει τοῦ νοὸς εἰς τὸ δοκιμάζειν ὑμᾶς τί τὸ θέλημα τοῦ θεοῦ, τὸ ἀγαθὸν καὶ εὐάρεστον καὶ τέλειον.

---

(1)   The *tense* of παραστῆσαι is aorist. In contrast, συσχηματίζεσθε and μεταμορφοῦσθε are present tenses. This contrast presents a situation similar to 6:12–13. The presentation takes place at one point. The command to stop being conformed means the cessation of something in progress, and the transforming is to continue on.

(2)   *Context*. This exhortation and these commands are the desired response, by way of general reaction, to nine chapters of instruction about the provisions of God's grace and mercy. They precede specific instructions as to more detailed matters of Christian conduct. The repetition of the aorist tense of παρίστημι is more than accidental. Similarities between this section and 6:12–13 of this epistle make it necessary to conclude that this too is a momentary act as it was in the earlier portion.

(3)   The *verbal idea* of παρίστημι coincides with seeing a decisive act in the aorist tense. Conforming and transforming also lend themselves well to the process notion where ongoing action is in view. Therefore, the aorist here is again a constative of the punctilear type, and the presents are descriptive progressives once again.

1.10 THE INFINITIVE (D.& M., 208–20)

2:1 VERBAL USES

3:1 PURPOSE - expresses the intention of a finite verb with which it is used.

Matt 2:2 -   προσκυνῆσαι designates the aim of ἤλθομεν. "We have come with this purpose: to worship Him."

{Matt 2:2} λέγοντες, Ποῦ ἐστιν ὁ τεχθεὶς βασιλεὺς τῶν Ἰουδαίων; εἴδομεν γὰρ αὐτοῦ τὸν ἀστέρα ἐν τῇ ἀνατολῇ καὶ <u>ἤλθομεν προσκυνῆσαι</u> αὐτῷ.

Matt 5:17 - καταλῦσαι (both occurrences) and πληρῶσαι identify the purposes of ἦλθον (both occurrences). Jesus twice denies that He came with the purpose of destroying the law and claims that the purpose of His coming was to fulfill it.

{Matt 5:17} Μὴ νομίσητε ὅτι ἦλθον <u>καταλῦσαι</u> τὸν νόμον ἢ τοὺς προφήτας· οὐκ <u>ἦλθον</u> καταλῦσαι ἀλλὰ <u>πληρῶσαι</u>.

Rom 1:20 - εἶναι expresses the purpose of the evident nature of God's invisible attributes ("things"). They are clearly seen with the goal of taking away every excuse from rebellious mankind. God did it so that no man anywhere can say, "I didn't know about God."

{Rom 1:20} τὰ γὰρ ἀόρατα αὐτοῦ ἀπὸ κτίσεως κόσμου τοῖς ποιήμασιν νοούμενα καθορᾶται, ἥ τε ἀΐδιος αὐτοῦ δύναμις καὶ θειότης, εἰς τὸ <u>εἶναι</u> αὐτοὺς ἀναπολογήτους,

3.2 RESULT - expresses the outcome of the action of a finite verb which the infinitive accompanies.

Rom 7:3 - The result of her being free from the law is that she is (εἶναι not an adulteress if she marries another husband).

{Rom 7:3} ἄρα οὖν ζῶντος τοῦ ἀνδρὸς μοιχαλὶς χρηματίσει ἐὰν γένηται ἀνδρὶ ἑτέρῳ· ἐὰν δὲ ἀποθάνῃ ὁ ἀνήρ, ἐλευθέρα ἐστὶν ἀπὸ τοῦ νόμου, τοῦ μὴ <u>εἶναι</u> αὐτὴν μοιχαλίδα γενομένην ἀνδρὶ ἑτέρῳ.

3.3 TIME - time is relative, not absolute. It is normally related to the time of the main verb.

4.1 John 1:48 (antecedent time) - Πρό shows that Jesus saw Nathaniel before Philip called him. The time of the finite action takes place prior to the time of the infinitival action.

{John 1:48} λέγει αὐτῷ Ναθαναήλ, Πόθεν με γινώσκεις; ἀπεκρίθη Ἰησοῦς καὶ εἶπεν αὐτῷ, <u>Πρὸ</u> τοῦ σε Φίλιππον φωνῆσαι ὄντα ὑπὸ τὴν συκῆν εἶδόν σε.

4.2 Luke 1:8 (simultaneous or contemporaneous time) - ἐν shows that Zacharias was selected by lot during the time he was serving as priest. The finite action takes place at the same time as the infinitival action.

{Luke 1:8} Ἐγένετο δὲ <u>ἐν</u> τῷ ἱερατεύειν αὐτὸν ἐν τῇ τάξει τῆς ἐφημερίας αὐτοῦ ἔναντι τοῦ θεοῦ,

4.3 Luke 12:5 (subsequent time) - μετά shows that the authority to cast into Gehenna is in force after one dies. The finite action takes place subsequent to the infinitival action.

{Luke 12:5} ὑποδείξω δὲ ὑμῖν τίνα φοβηθῆτε· φοβήθητε τὸν <u>μετὰ</u> τὸ ἀποκτεῖναι ἔχοντα ἐξουσίαν ἐμβαλεῖν εἰς τὴν γέενναν. ναὶ λέγω ὑμῖν, τοῦτον φοβήθητε.

3.4 CAUSE - the infinitival action states the cause of which the finite action is the result.

John 2:24 -   The cause is stated by γινώσκειν and the effect by ἐπίστευεν.

{John 2:24} Ἰησοῦς οὐκ <u>ἐπίστευεν</u> αὐτὸν αὐτοῖς διὰ τὸ αὐτὸν <u>γινώσκειν</u> πάντας

Phil 1:7 -   The cause of Paul's feeling for the Philippian believers was that he had (ἔχειν) them in his heart.

{Phil 1:7} καθώς ἐστιν δίκαιον ἐμοὶ τοῦτο φρονεῖν ὑπὲρ πάντων ὑμῶν διὰ τὸ <u>ἔχειν</u> με ἐν τῇ καρδίᾳ ὑμᾶς, ἔν τε τοῖς δεσμοῖς μου καὶ ἐν τῇ ἀπολογίᾳ καὶ βεβαιώσει τοῦ εὐαγγελίου συγκοινωνούς μου τῆς χάριτος πάντας ὑμᾶς ὄντας.

3.5 COMMAND - strong contextual indications show that a command is intended.

Rom 12:15 -   χαίρειν and κλαίειν are commands to rejoice and weep. The imperatives of v. 14 set the stage for this understanding.

{Rom 12:15} χαίρειν μετὰ χαιρόντων, κλαίειν μετὰ κλαιόντων.

2.2 SUBSTANTIVAL USES

3.1 SUBJECT - used as the subject of a clause.

Phil 1:21 -   τὸ ζῆν and τὸ ἀποθανεῖν are subjects while Χριστός and κέρδος are predicate nominatives.

{Phil 1:21} ἐμοὶ γὰρ τὸ ζῆν Χριστὸς καὶ τὸ ἀποθανεῖν κέρδος.

3.2 OBJECT - used as the object of a verb.

Phil 2:6 -   ἡγήσατο has a double accusative as its object. Τὸ εἶναι is the direct object and ἁρπαγμὸν is the predicate object.

{Phil 2:6} ὃς ἐν μορφῇ θεοῦ ὑπάρχων οὐχ ἁρπαγμὸν ἡγήσατο τὸ εἶναι ἴσα θεῷ,

3.3 INDIRECT OBJECT - close to the verbal use which expresses purpose, but here purpose is either non-existent or very weak.

Mark 6:31 -   φαγεῖν tells that with reference to which they did not have opportunity.

{Mark 6:31} καὶ λέγει αὐτοῖς, Δεῦτε ὑμεῖς αὐτοὶ κατ᾽ ἰδίαν εἰς ἔρημον τόπον καὶ ἀναπαύσασθε ὀλίγον. ἦσαν γὰρ οἱ ἐρχόμενοι καὶ οἱ ὑπάγοντες πολλοί, καὶ οὐδὲ φαγεῖν εὐκαίρουν.

3.4 APPOSITION - a further explanation of another substantive.

1 Thess 4:3 -   ἀπέχεσθαι is a further definition of ὁ ἁγιασμὸς.

{1 Thess 4:3} οἴδατε γὰρ τίνας παραγγελίας ἐδώκαμεν ὑμῖν διὰ τοῦ κυρίου Ἰησοῦ. 3 τοῦτο γάρ ἐστιν θέλημα τοῦ θεοῦ, ὁ ἁγιασμὸς ὑμῶν, ἀπέχεσθαι ὑμᾶς ἀπὸ τῆς πορνείας,

3.5 MODIFIER - certain kinds of nouns and adjectives often expect something additional to complete their meanings.

Rom 13:11 -   ὥρα needs some qualification to tell which hour. The infinitive ἐγερθῆναι modifies it by stating it is the one at which you are to be awakened from sleep.

{Rom 13:11} Καὶ τοῦτο εἰδότες τὸν καιρόν, ὅτι <u>ὥρα</u> ἤδη ὑμᾶς ἐξ ὕπνου <u>ἐγερθῆναι</u>, νῦν γὰρ ἐγγύτερον ἡμῶν ἡ σωτηρία ἢ ὅτε ἐπιστεύσαμεν.

1.11 THE PARTICIPLE (D. & M., 220–33)

2.1 ADJECTIVAL USES - usually indicated by an article with the participle.

John 1:16 -   Ὁ . . . ἐρχόμενος. In this verse the participle functions as a substantive.

{John 1:16} Οὗτος ἦν ὃν εἶπον, <u>Ὁ</u> ὀπίσω μου <u>ἐρχόμενος</u> ἔμπροσθέν μου γέγονεν, ὅτι πρῶτός μου ἦν.

2.2 ADVERBIAL USES

3.1 TELIC (or PURPOSE) - expresses the aim of the action of the finite verb.

Matt 27:49 -   σώσων gives the purpose of Elijah's coming (ἔρχεται).

{Matt 27:49} οἱ δὲ λοιποὶ ἔλεγον, Ἄφες ἴδωμεν εἰ <u>ἔρχεται</u> Ἡλίας <u>σώσων</u> αὐτόν.

3.2 TEMPORAL - expresses an action occurring at a given time in relation to the time of the finite verb.

John 16:8 -   ἐλθὼν is best rendered, "when He comes," or perhaps "after He comes." The former is simultaneous time, and the latter antecedent time (see section 2.3 below). Every adverbial participle relates in a relative way to the time of the main verb (cf. 2.3 below), but this category classifies only those where time is the principal emphasis of the relationship.

{John 16:8} καὶ <u>ἐλθὼν</u> ἐκεῖνος ἐλέγξει τὸν κόσμον περὶ ἁμαρτίας καὶ περὶ δικαιοσύνης καὶ περὶ κρίσεως·

1 Pet 5:10 - παθόντας is temporal as shown by its use with the temporal adverb ὀλίγον. The participle points to a time antecedent to that of the main verbs καταρτίσει, στηρίξει, σθενώσει, θεμελιώσει.

{1 Pet 5:10} Ὁ δὲ θεὸς πάσης χάριτος, ὁ καλέσας ὑμᾶς εἰς τὴν αἰώνιον αὐτοῦ δόξαν ἐν Χριστῷ [Ἰησοῦ], <u>ὀλίγον</u> <u>παθόντας</u> αὐτὸς <u>καταρτίσει, στηρίξει, σθενώσει, θεμελιώσει.</u>

3.3 CAUSAL - the participle expresses the cause of which the main verb is the effect.

Matt 4:2 - It was because of His fasting (νηστεύσας) that Jesus was hungry (ἐπείνασεν).

{Matt 4:2} αὶ <u>νηστεύσας</u> ἡμέρας τεσσεράκοντα καὶ νύκτας τεσσεράκοντα, ὕστερον <u>ἐπείνασεν</u>.

Rom 5:1 - The cause is justification (Δικαιωθέντες) by faith. The result is having (ἔχομεν) peace with God.

{Rom 5:1} <u>Δικαιωθέντες</u> οὖν ἐκ πίστεως εἰρήνην <u>ἔχομεν</u> πρὸς τὸν θεὸν διὰ τοῦ κυρίου ἡμῶν Ἰησοῦ Χριστοῦ

3.4 CONDITIONAL - the participle states the supposition or condition (the protasis) and the finite verb gives the statement based on the supposition (the apodosis).

Rom 2:27 - What is by nature uncircumcision, if it keeps the law (τὸν νόμον τελοῦσα), will judge the Jewish person who is a transgressor of law.

{Rom 2:27} καὶ κρινεῖ ἡ ἐκ φύσεως ἀκροβυστία <u>τὸν νόμον τελοῦσα</u> σὲ τὸν διὰ γράμματος καὶ περιτομῆς παραβάτην νόμου.

Heb 2:3 -The supposition is, "if we neglect (ἀμελήσαντες) so great a salvation." The question (rhetorical) which functions as the apodosis is, "how shall we escape?"

{Heb 2:3} πῶς ἡμεῖς ἐκφευξόμεθα τηλικαύτης <u>ἀμελήσαντες</u> σωτηρίας, ἥτις ἀρχὴν λαβοῦσα λαλεῖσθαι διὰ τοῦ κυρίου ὑπὸ τῶν ἀκουσάντων εἰς ἡμᾶς ἐβεβαιώθη,

3.5 CONCESSIVE - the participle states the concession ("though" or "although"). The main verb states the action that attains reality in spite of the concession.

Rom 1:21 -   γνόντες. "Although they knew" God, they did not glorify Him as God and were not thankful.

{Rom 1:21} διότι <u>γνόντες</u> τὸν θεὸν οὐχ ὡς θεὸν ἐδόξασαν ἢ ηὐχαρίστησαν, ἀλλ' ἐματαιώθησαν ἐν τοῖς διαλογισμοῖς αὐτῶν καὶ ἐσκοτίσθη ἡ ἀσύνετος αὐτῶν καρδία.

1 Cor 9:19 -   ὤν. "Though I am" free from all, I have enslaved myself to all.

{1 Cor 9:19} Ἐλεύθερος γὰρ <u>ὢν</u> ἐκ πάντων πᾶσιν ἐμαυτὸν ἐδούλωσα, ἵνα τοὺς πλείονας κερδήσω·

3.6 INSTRUMENTAL - The participle is the instrument which the main verb uses to carry out its action.

Matt 6:27 -   Who can add "by being anxious" (μεριμνῶν)

{Matt 6:27} τίς δὲ ἐξ ὑμῶν <u>μεριμνῶν</u> δύναται προσθεῖναι ἐπὶ τὴν ἡλικίαν αὐτοῦ πῆχυν ἕνα;

3.7 MODAL - the manner, as compared to the means or instrument, does not qualify the finite verb quite so strongly.

Matt 3:1 -   κηρύσσων was not the means by which John appeared. It depicts a characteristic action of his appearance.

{Matt 3:1} Ἐν δὲ ταῖς ἡμέραις ἐκείναις παραγίνεται Ἰωάννης ὁ βαπτιστὴς <u>κηρύσσων</u> ἐν τῇ ἐρήμῳ τῆς Ἰουδαίας

3.8 COMPLEMENTARY - the finite verb has its meaning completed by the participle.

Col 1:9 -   προσευχόμενοι and αἰτούμενοι define the the cessation (παυόμεθα).

{Col 1:9} Διὰ τοῦτο καὶ ἡμεῖς, ἀφ᾽ ἧς ἡμέρας ἠκούσαμεν, οὐ παυόμεθα ὑπὲρ ὑμῶν προσευχόμενοι καὶ αἰτούμενοι, ἵνα πληρωθῆτε τὴν ἐπίγνωσιν τοῦ θελήματος αὐτοῦ ἐν πάσῃ σοφίᾳ καὶ συνέσει πνευματικῇ,

_____
_____
_____

3.9 CIRCUMSTANTIAL - an additional circumstance is added by the participle.

Matt 19:22 -   The young man heard (ἀκούσας) and went away grieving. The hearing
               was the added detail. (λυπούμενος is a modal participle.)

{Matt 19:22} ἀκούσας δὲ ὁ νεανίσκος τὸν λόγον ἀπῆλθεν λυπούμενος· ἦν γὰρ ἔχων κτήματα πολλά.

_____
_____

3.10 IMPERATIVAL - contextual indications show that a command is intended.

Rom 12:16 -   φρονοῦντες (both occurrences) and συναπαγόμενοι require certain courses
               of action from the readers. A verb in the imperative mood in the same
               verse (γίνεσθε) is a clue to detecting this.

{Rom 12:16} τὸ αὐτὸ εἰς ἀλλήλους φρονοῦντες, μὴ τὰ ὑψηλὰ φρονοῦντες ἀλλὰ τοῖς ταπεινοῖς συναπαγόμενοι. μὴ γίνεσθε φρόνιμοι παρ᾽ ἑαυτοῖς.

_____
_____

2.3 RELATIVE TIME OF THE PARTICIPLE - time is in relation to that of the finite verb. Every adverbial use of the participle entails relative time.

3.1 ANTECEDENT TIME - participial action takes place prior to the time of the main verb action.

Matt 4:2 -   (see causal participle illustration above in section 2.2 for this verse) The
               fasting (νηστεύσας) preceded the hunger.

{Matt 4:2} καὶ νηστεύσας ἡμέρας τεσσεράκοντα καὶ νύκτας τεσσεράκοντα, ὕστερον ἐπείνασεν.

_____
_____

3.2 SIMULTANEOUS TIME - participial and main verb action are contemporaneous.

Matt 16:28 -   The coming (ἐρχόμενον) and the seeing (ἴδωσιν) coincide with each other temporally.

{Matt 16:28} ἀμὴν λέγω ὑμῖν ὅτι εἰσίν τινες τῶν ὧδε ἑστώτων οἵτινες οὐ μὴ γεύσωνται θανάτου ἕως ἂν <u>ἴδωσιν</u> τὸν υἱὸν τοῦ ἀνθρώπου <u>ἐρχόμενον</u> ἐν τῇ βασιλείᾳ αὐτοῦ.

_____
_____

_____

3.3 SUBSEQUENT TIME - participial action follows the finite verb action. Subsequent action is never expressed by the aorist participle in the N. T.

Matt 27:49 -   The saving (σώσων) follows the coming (ἔρχεται). This is a future participle.

{Matt 27:49} οἱ δὲ λοιποὶ ἔλεγον, Ἄφες ἴδωμεν εἰ <u>ἔρχεται</u> Ἠλίας <u>σώσων</u> αὐτόν.

_____

_____

2.4 PERIPHRASTIC TENSES

3.1 PERIPHRASTIC PRESENT - present tense of εἰμί and a present participle. Durative action is more pronounced than with the simple present tense.

John 1:41 -   ἐστιν μεθερμηνευόμενον, which "is being interpreted."

{John 1:41} εὑρίσκει οὗτος πρῶτον τὸν ἀδελφὸν τὸν ἴδιον Σίμωνα καὶ λέγει αὐτῷ, Εὑρήκαμεν τὸν Μεσσίαν, ὅ <u>ἐστιν μεθερμηνευόμενον</u> Χριστός·

_____

_____

3.2 PERIPHRASTIC IMPERFECT - imperfect tense of εἰμί and a present participle. Durative action is more pronounced than with the simple imperfect tense.

Matt 7:29 -   ἦν . . . διδάσκων, "He was teaching" continually.

{Matt 7:29} <u>ἦν</u> γὰρ <u>διδάσκων</u> αὐτοὺς ὡς ἐξουσίαν ἔχων καὶ οὐχ ὡς οἱ γραμματεῖς αὐτῶν.

_____

_____

Luke 24:32 -   καιομένη ἦν, their hearts "were burning" continually.

{Luke 24:32} καὶ εἶπαν πρὸς ἀλλήλους, Οὐχὶ ἡ καρδία ἡμῶν <u>καιομένη ἦν</u> [ἐν ἡμῖν] ὡς ἐλάλει ἡμῖν ἐν τῇ ὁδῷ, ὡς διήνοιγεν ἡμῖν τὰς γραφάς;

_____
_____
_____

3.3 PERIPHRASTIC FUTURE - future tense of εἰμί and a present participle. The action is clearly durative.

1 Cor 14:9 -   ἔσεσθε . . . λαλοῦντες, "you will be speaking into the air."

{1 Cor 14:9} οὕτως καὶ ὑμεῖς διὰ τῆς γλώσσης ἐὰν μὴ εὔσημον λόγον δῶτε, πῶς γνωσθήσεται τὸ λαλούμενον; <u>ἔσεσθε</u> γὰρ εἰς ἀέρα <u>λαλοῦντες</u>.

_____
_____

3.4 PERIPHRASTIC PERFECT - present tense of εἰμί and a perfect participle. Usually intensive, placing emphasis on continuing results.

John 2:17 -   γεγραμμένον ἐστίν, "it stood (or stands) written."

{John 2:17} Ἐμνήσθησαν οἱ μαθηταὶ αὐτοῦ ὅτι <u>γεγραμμένον ἐστίν</u>, Ὁ ζῆλος τοῦ οἴκου σου καταφάγεταί με.

_____
_____

3.5 PERIPHRASTIC PLUPERFECT - imperfect tense of εἰμί and a perfect participle. Usually intensive, placing emphasis on continuing results.

Luke 15:24 -   ἦν ἀπολωλὼς, "he was lost" (he had been lost with the continuing result that he was lost).

{Luke 15:24} ὅτι οὗτος ὁ υἱός μου νεκρὸς ἦν καὶ ἀνέζησεν, <u>ἦν ἀπολωλὼς</u> καὶ εὑρέθη. καὶ ἤρξαντο εὐφραίνεσθαι.

_____
_____

3.6 PERIPHRASTIC FUTURE PERFECT - future tense of εἰμί and a perfect participle. Usually intensive, placing emphasis on continuing results.

Matt 16:19 -   ἔσται δεδεμένον, "will be bound." A consummative meaning would be, "will have been bound." The same tense meaning applies to ἔσται λελυμένον.

{Matt 16:19} δώσω σοι τὰς κλεῖδας τῆς βασιλείας τῶν οὐρανῶν, καὶ ὃ ἐὰν δήσῃς ἐπὶ τῆς γῆς ἔσται δεδεμένον ἐν τοῖς οὐρανοῖς, καὶ ὃ ἐὰν λύσῃς ἐπὶ τῆς γῆς ἔσται λελυμένον ἐν τοῖς οὐρανοῖς.

_____
_____
_____

(c) *Historical and cultural setting.* It is vital in the process of syntactical exegesis to examine the historical and cultural setting of the passage under investigation. In many cases this is an important factor in determining the correct interpretation.

A notable instance of this importance is in Matt 5:32. The issue has to do with the exception to the "no divorce" principle laid down by Christ. This passage along with a similar one in Matt 19:9 is the principal source of widespread opinion that Christ allowed for divorce (and remarriage) on the grounds of adultery.

A number of factors are involved in understanding this complex statement, but the present discussion will be limited to historical matters. The Lord made His statement against the backdrop of a twofold Jewish tradition. One school of Rabbinic tradition, that of Hillel, allowed for divorce on very trivial grounds. It was in a discussion of this philosophy that the Matthew 19:9 statement of Christ was made. Quite obviously He rejected a viewpoint that looked at the marriage bond so lightly.

A second school of Jewish thought, the school of Shammai, was more strict in its interpretation of the Law. These allowed for divorce only on one ground: the sin of adultery. Nothing short of adultery justified it, but adultery did justify it in the eyes of these Rabbis.

To interpret Christ's "exception clause" in Matt 5:32 to be permissive of divorce is to bring Him into agreement with this stricter interpretation of His contemporaries. A searching question in such a case must be asked: how does this agreement fit with the context of the Sermon on the Mount of which the statement is a part?

The Sermon on the Mount has its pivotal thought expressed in Matthew 5:20. It was an evaluation of "the righteousness of the scribes and Pharisees" in the light of that required for entrance into the kingdom of heaven. Needless to say, theirs fell far short. The fifth chapter, in fact, contains a series of six antitheses, in each case the contrast being between the traditional interpretation of the Law and the correct interpretation given by Christ. For example, His teachings about murder (5:21–24) and adultery (5:27–28) were far above the level of the highest Jewish teaching.

But if one's interpretation of the "exception clause" in 5:32 makes it into an adequate ground for divorce, then Christ does not differ at all from one group of His contemporaries on this issue. The antithesis between verses 31 and 32 is thereby rendered non-existent. Such a conclusion is totally unacceptable, because it is completely out of keeping with the surrounding context.

The only conclusion in the light of historical and cultural background and context is to understand that Jesus allowed no grounds for divorce and to explain the "exception clause" as having to do with something other than the marriage union itself, e.g. an act committed prior to the consummation of the marriage union during the betrothal period.

(d) *Word order*. The word order used by a writer is often a key to the emphasis he wishes to convey. In the NT the order will usually be verb, subject, object, supplementary participle, etc. An emphasis on any part of the sentence will cause it to be brought forward. For example, τῇ Ἐλισάβετ, an indirect object, is placed before the verb in Luke 1:57 because Luke wanted to emphasize that it was to Elizabeth that the time to bring forth had been fulfilled. Another means for emphasis is separating words that belong together. In Rom 1:11 τι, χάρισμα, and πνευματικόν belong together as their case endings show: "some spiritual gift." But the three words are separated from each other, τι being first (before the verb) and πνευματικόν being last in the clause. Of course, τι has emphasis because it is first, but so does πνευματικόν even though it is last, because it is separate from the other words of the expression.

(e) *Figures of speech*. Figures of speech involving multiple words abound in the NT. Two consecutive arguments "from the greater to the lesser" are found in Rom 5:9, 10. In verse 9 Paul reasons, if God did the greater thing for us in justifying us through Christ's blood, He will surely ("much more") do the lesser one by saving us from the wrath. In verse 10 he continues, if while we were enemies of God we were reconciled (the greater thing) through the death of God's Son, we will surely be saved by His life. Such rhetorical figures as these are numerous.

(f) *Other typical categories* for consideration under syntactical exegesis are thought patterns of the authors, context, elliptical constructions, idiomatic phrases, and other interpretive matters of a more general nature.

c. *Synthesis and Outline*.

(1) *Synthesis*. Following the step of syntactical exegesis, it is necessary to merge the data accumulated into a single written description. This is done in the writing of a "synthesis" of the passage or book being studied. Until this point, there has been a gathering of many facts regarding the text; this is desirable and necessary, but the procedure is not complete at this point. It remains to combine all this information into a meaningful form, meaningful both to the interpreter and to those whom he seeks to benefit through his research. This involves a "synthesis" or a "putting together" (συν plus τίθημι) of his material in a way such as will make it most fruitful to the understanding of both the interpreter and those who may read his work. By way of describing the compiling of a synthesis, perhaps an enumeration of its characteristics will be most advantageous:

(a) The synthesis will expand what the author is saying in the words of the exegete. Its aim will also be to capture the thought of the author which, though not expressed, may be implied in the terminology chosen or grammatical constructions utilized. When the thought has been learned, it should be reproduced in English in as expressive a form as possible. For instance, if Paul uses a hyperbole in one of his letters, the synthesis would not note the presence of this figure of speech by name, but would adopt some English equivalent such as "the effect was so great that it would seem . . ." or some such expression.

(b) The synthesis will bring out the principal emphases of the passage, as they have come to light in the steps of Lexical and Syntactical Exegesis. It will bring out the connections between one part of the text and the next, and thus will trace the "argument" of the book as it progresses. The logical development of the author's thoughts will be set forth in such a fashion as to be very conspicuous.

(c) The synthesis will incorporate as much material as possible within the limits of practicality. The description should be continuous, without major digressions, but into its continuity should be woven as much fruit of earlier study as is possible. The descriptive effect of the synthesis will be enhanced by the inclusion of much exegetical data.

(d) Information utilized in the synthesis will be derived from the notes on Lexical Exegesis, those on Syntactical Exegesis, and the Greek text. The reason for using the Greek text is the need to incorporate the routine items of the text which have not been dealt with thus far in the procedure.

(e) The synthesis will be written entirely in the third person in order to facilitate the incorporation of as much material as possible. The use of the first and second persons limits unnecessarily the amount of material that can be utilized effectively.

(f) Marginal notations in the format of the synthesis shall include chapter and verse notations and notations of the structural divisions. These will greatly facilitate the organization of the material for outline purposes at a later stage. Some system of outlining procedure can be adopted to note the structural divisions which have come to light (i.e., "A. . . . B. . . ." or "1B . . . 2B. . . .").

(g) The synthesis will contain no Greek words or technical grammatical terminology. Instead it will use the information resulting from a knowledge of what these words and this terminology mean.

(h) The synthesis will be composed in a running narrative style. It will be organized into paragraphs, though the paragraph divisions are not considered binding for purposes of outlining. In some instances outlining of the material will cause the interpreter to re-evaluate and change a previous conclusion regarding a paragraph division.

(i) In the case of a problem that has been left unresolved up to this point, the synthesis will include all alternatives, one in the continuing text of the narrative and the others in parenthesis immediately following.

For illustrative purposes, a synthesis of 1 Thess 1:4–5 will be reproduced at this point. It should be emphasized that this is not *the* synthesis of the verses, because there is room for great variation. Individual preferences as to modes of description are inevitable, but certain exegetical data of the text should be reflected in one way or another in any synthesis. A sample portion of a synthesis is as follows:

1:4   In describing the thanksgiving further, the writer lists, last of all, its cause.

C. A knowledge of the election of his readers was what brought about an expression of gratitude to God. At this point in the enumeration the writer cannot refrain from expressing strong attachment to his readers. They belonged to the same spiritual family as he, a relationship closer than that of his own natural family and race. Moreover, he found greater reason for loving them in that they, like himself, were objects of God's love.

pr.   / The substance of what he knew about them centered in the events surrounding their conversion to Christ. He had been there and had witnessed their decisions as well as the subsequent transformation of their lives. (or, The substance of his knowledge about the readers carried back to eternity past when God according to His sovereign choice had chosen them out of the midst of lost humanity. Consequently, at the time of the missionaries' visit to the city the results of the choice became evident as the listeners responded positively to the invitation of the gospel.)

1:5 pr.   / In amplification of what constituted the election of the readers, the writer
1.   now goes on to detail the circumstances of the historical call. (or, Prompted by a desire to explain how the missionaries knew about the sovereign choice of the readers by God, the writer now gives specific occurrences which show how the choice became evident.) There are two parts in the description thus introduced. The former of these deals with the bringing of the gospel by the missionaries. To be sure, the gospel was what accomplished changes in the lives of the listeners. This comprehensive message, which included not only the basic plan of salvation, but also various other facets of Christian doctrine, was conveyed by human instruments and it is upon the subjective experience of the human instruments that the writer focuses at this point. Though their ministry was a spoken one, it was not this alone, because on their part they sensed unusual power, such as could have been experienced only in the realm where the Holy Spirit prevails. On the basis of this inner awareness as they preached, they were completely convinced as to the effectiveness of their message in the listeners' lives. In order to re-enforce the previous statement about the inner state of the missionaries, the writer appeals to his readers' knowledge. Should anyone arise to question the propriety of their motives, the readers have their own recollection of the quality of life produced in the missionaries by the Holy Spirit. Under the influence of the Spirit's ministry through them, they assumed a character which would rule out the possibility of their ministering in any sense from selfish motives. Such was the outward evidence of what the Spirit's domination meant to them inwardly.

(2) *Outline*. After writing a synthesis, the final step in this stage of exegesis is the formulation of an outline of the passage or book under consideration. This outline should be based upon the synthesis which has been produced, and should carry the same emphases and organization as contained therein. This is called an "interpretive" outline.

Two other types of outlines will be pointed out and illustrated before the interpretive type is described and illustrated. This is done for the sake of contrast. The other two are inadequate reflectors of exegetical study of a book (or passage) and are therefore less desirable.

(a) *Homiletical Outline*. First of all, there is the *homiletical* type of outline. A homiletical outline, of course, is one that is easily remembered, one that makes a quick impression in public presentation because of the clever words used, the alliteration, the progression of thought, the familiarity of concepts, or some such device. The homiletical is one that communicates very effectively with an audience. Many times a homiletical outline will follow the chapter divisions of a book exactly, while sacrificing something from the standpoint of accuracy, just to stay with the chapter divisions. This happens because the chapter divisions are easily remembered. It happens that the homiletical outline cited below is not of this type. An outline can ignore the chapter divisions, and still be a homiletical type.

There are five main points of this sample outline. Only enough detail is given to illustrate the nature of a homiletical outline.

I. Introduction (1:1–10). The introduction is, of course, the groundwork for Paul's presentation of the main content of the letter. It is suggested that the first chapter is introductory.

II. The Reception of the Gospel--Faith, the past (2:1–12). In 2:1–12 it is suggested that the apostle Paul is dealing with the way in which the Thessalonians received the gospel, and, of course, their reception of the gospel was on the basis of faith. Undoubtedly the reception of the gospel is mentioned in 2:1–12, but is this the main emphasis of the section? This is the test of a good outline, i.e. its accuracy in reflecting the writer's emphasis from section to section.

One aspect that is added to this first point is that he deals with the past in this portion. Compared with the points to follow, this also will facilitate memorization.

III. The Fruit of the Gospel--Love, the present (2:13–4:12). In this section the writer does mention Christian works. Sometimes they are his own, sometimes those of his readers, other times those which he is encouraging his readers to perform. And works, or the fruit of the gospel, do deal with the present, resulting in a "past-present" sequence for the first two major sections.

IV. The Anticipation of the Gospel--Hope, the future (4:13–5:11). This portion does deal with the future. And so here results a nice three-point outline for the main body of the book: past, present, future; faith, works, hope; reception, fruit and anticipation.

V. The Conclusion (5:12–28).
This type of popular outline or something like it could be exemplified from many sources. It depends largely on the expositor's ability to contrive combinations that people are familiar with and that will be easily fixed in their minds.

The three-volume work by Zodhiates on James is in point here. *The Work of Faith* is the first volume. It covers the first section of James. *The Labor of Love* is the second volume, covering the middle section, and *The Patience of Hope* is the third volume. There are probably very few passages or books of the New Testament that could not be outlined along the line of faith, love and hope. But the question is, is this an accurate portrayal of the author's emphasis? For 1 Thessalonians the answer must be negative.

(b) *Descriptive Outline.* An opposite extreme from a homiletical outline is a descriptive one. Here one is attempting to be very analytical. This outline describes without regard for being communicative, without a view to be being systematic, without a view to organization or anything of the sort.

I. Introduction (1:1).

II. Historical and Personal (1:2–3:13). One could give this same title to the early chapters of Galatians. Yet "historical and personal" does describe what is here. Paul talks about himself, talks about his own personal needs, and so forth. Yet it is not interpretive enough to distinguish this section from portions of Scripture elsewhere.

    A. The Effect of the Gospel at Thessalonica (1:2–10). This is accurate. The apostle talks about what effect the gospel had at Thessalonica upon himself and upon his listeners.

    B. The Missionary's Retrospect of His Labors There (2:1–16). This heading describes what Paul does in the section, but it makes no attempt at interpreting, analyzing or organizing what is there. It simply tells, in a sort of noncommittal fashion, what the nature of the discussion is, without analyzing why he did it, the way he did it, or anything of the sort. It describes in a very superficial way.

    C. His Care For, and Desire to Be With, the Converts (2:17–3:10). Once again, this describes, but makes no attempt to explain why the section is in the book. Why did he put it in here? Why or what was his motivation? What relationship does this bear to earlier verses in chapter two, or to later verses in chapter three?

    D. His prayer for Them (3:11–13). And once again there is a description of the prayer without an attempt to relate it to the broad section. Why does he write out a prayer that he had prayed, and so forth?

III. Doctrinal and Hortatory (4:1–5:24). Once again this is accurate, but you could say the same thing about Galatians 3–6. It describes what is there in Galatians as well as what is here in 1 Thessalonians.

    A. Exhortations to the Converts to "Maintain Good Works" (4:1–12). This is accurate, but what are the good works? Why exhort Christians who are doing so well? No attempt at analyzing the category of good works is made.

    B. Teaching concerning the Coming of the Lord (4:13–5:11). In a general way, that is what this section talks about, although 5:1–11 talks about the coming of the day of the Lord more than it does about the coming of the Lord Himself. There is a relationship between these two, of course.

    C. Further Exhortations to the Converts (5:12–22). This heading describes, but it certainly does not interpret anything. How are these further exhortations different from the former exhortations? Why did the apostle separate them from the former exhortations?

D. *And Prayer for Them (5:23–24)*.

IV. Conclusion. This, then, is a descriptive outline. It describes what is there. It does not interpret. It is not particularly adapted to communicating. It is suggested that between these two extremes, between the homiletical outline and the descriptive outline, there is a happy medium.

(c) *Interpretive Outline*. This third type of outline is what may be described as an *interpretive* outline because it seeks to reflect as accurately as possible the interpretation of the text which is dictated by the Grammatico-historical method followed in the exegetical process.
    An example of this type will be furnished in order to give an idea of some of the characteristics of such an outline.

I. The Thanksgiving for the Thessalonians (1:1–10). This says more than just "Introduction." It gives the nature of the first chapter, which grammatically is built around εὐχαριστοῦμεν (1:2).

II. Defense of the Apostolic Conduct (2:1–3:13). This interprets. It interprets Paul's motives for including so lengthy a section dealing with personal matters. It interprets his motives as being called for by the attacks against his person, the insinuations about his motivation in preaching the gospel, and so forth.

A. Their Actions (2:1–16).
B. *Their Absence (2:17–3:13)*. Notice that an outline can be accurate as well as communicative. It takes a little more searching to find the right word or the right phrase to do this, but it can be done. It is possible to be in line with the emphasis of the Greek and, at the same time, utilize a reasonable amount of homiletical skill.

III. The Exhortation to the Thessalonians (4:1–5:28).

A. Personal Life (4:1–12). This is much better than just "exhortations" which might be confused with the "further exhortations" later on. Those here deal with the personal life. "Personal life" looks at these and says what the emphasis is at this point, as distinguished from what the emphasis is in section "C" below.

B. The Coming of Christ (4:13–5:11). This is a broad category. More detail is required in a finalized outline. Furthermore, there is room for variation under categories that are broadly stated.

C. The Assembly Life (5:12–28). Here is an area of exhortation dealing with the group as distinguished from individuals (cf. "A" above).

D. *Resolving of Difficulties*. The fourth major step in the Grammatico-historical Method of Exegesis is to solve the problems of interpretation which are encountered at the earlier stages of study. They have been listed in skeletal form as parts of Lexical Exegesis and Syntactical Exegesis, without conclusions, of course. At this point in the process it is appropriate to take these difficulties and subject them to careful scrutiny with a view toward arriving at satisfactory conclusions for them all.

Four types of data are needed for solving each problem:

(1) A clear statement of what the problem is. Sometimes it will be impossible at the earlier stages of investigation to grasp the problem sufficiently to formulate such a statement. If so, the problem statement should be revised to reflect accurately just what the difficulty is.

(2) A clear statement of all alternatives that have been offered as solutions to the problem. It is best to formulate these only after a good bit of study has gone into the problem at hand.

(3) A listing and discussion of all points of evidence which support each of the alternative solutions.

(4) A listing and discussion of all points of evidence which oppose each of the alternative solutions.

A thorough search of all the resources for Lexical and Syntactical Exegesis is necessary once again if the interpreter is to arrive at the correct solution.

With all the data before him, the interpreter is ready to weigh the relative strengths of the various arguments and to come to a conclusion. Through all of this he will also find he has come to a better understanding of other details of the passage.

E. *Re-evaluation.* After he resolves all difficulties of his book or passage, the interpreter is ready for the final step of interpretation. He must re-evaluate his earlier findings. He has two reasons for doing so:

(1) The first is more obvious. He has reached conclusions regarding problematic issues. These conclusions must be incorporated into the final form of his synthesis, i.e. the wrong alternatives must be eliminated. Also his conclusions may necessitate reworking some of his Lexical and Syntactical Exegesis.

(2) The second reason stems from the way an interpreter's knowledge of his passage grows with each step of the process. In researching Syntactical Exegesis, for example, he inevitably learns matters of Lexical Exegesis that escaped him earlier. The same is true with the Synthesis and Outline and with the Resolving of Difficulties. By listing these additional data as he progresses, he can incorporate them into the appropriate places when he re-evaluates, if of course, he has not done so sooner.

The step of Re-evaluation concludes the process of the Grammatico-historical Method of Exegesis.

INDEX OF PASSAGES CITED

Reference	Page	Reference	Page	Reference	Page
John 1:35	131	John 4:42	79	John 14:3	119
John 1:37	85	John 4:42	95	John 14:21	47
John 1:39	86	John 4:42	96	John 14:21	96
John 1:41	141	John 5:6	118	John 14:26	89
John 1:42	142	John 5:7	117	John 15:20	93
John 1:48	91	John 5:8	92	John 15:22	112
	134	John 5:11	88	John 15:26–27	37
John 2:1	82	John 5:18	122	John 16:8	137
John 2:3	75	John 5:19	94	John 16:21	119
John 2:11	95	John 5:19	97	John 16:27	47
John 2:12	86	John 5:20	46	John 17:1	68
John 2:16	88	John 5:20	47	John 17:4	92
John 2:17	73	John 5:30	95	John 17:6	130
John 2:17	141	John 5:32	88	John 17:10	96
John 2:18	98	John 5:43	114	John 17:11	116
John 2:20	53	John 6:9	99	John 17:17	106
John 2:20	84	John 6:11	99	John 17:21	68
John 2:20	125	John 6:13	105	John 17:26	88
John 2:21	73	John 6:19	87	John 18:39	80
John 2:22	92	John 6:20	116	John 19:1	108
John 2:24	134	John 6:28	114	John 19:3	121
John 2:25	98	John 6:41	50	John 19:24	97
John 3:1	65	John 6:45	77	John 20:2	47
John 3:1	65	John 7:13	73	John 20:19	82
John 3:1	79	John 7:17	114	John 20:30–31	19
John 3:1	80	John 7:24	88	John 21:2	70
John 3:2	65	John 7:38	66	John 21:8	81
John 3:6	49	John 7:38	69	John 21:15–17	47
John 3:16	105	John 7:52	121	John 21:15	70
John 3:16	114	John 8:13	96	John 21:15	91
John 3:19	90	John 8:32	123		
John 3:19	101	John 9:22	89	Acts	
John 3:22	122	John 9:22	109		
John 3:26	79	John 9:22	131	Acts 1:6	43
John 3:29	84	John 10:8	75	Acts 2:23	103
John 3:35	46	John 10:32	120	Acts 2:33	58
John 3:35	47	John 10:33	89	Acts 8:31	115
John 3:36	80	John 10:35	89	Acts 10:8	11
John 4:1	91	John 10:39	120	Acts 15:12	11
John 4:5	92	John 11:7	113	Acts 15:14	11
John 4:8	131	John 11:13	74	Acts 21:19	11
John 4:9	75	John 11:26–27	112	Acts 22:16	56
John 4:9	78	John 11:28	118	Acts 26:3	89
John 4:9	75	John 11:35	126		
John 4:10–11	99	John 12:27	128	Romans	
John 4:10	72	John 12:32	124		
John 4:10	78	John 12:34	98	Rom 1:3–4	49
John 4:12	77	John 13:6	120	Rom 1:7	77
John 4:12	91	John 13:13	66	Rom 1:11	143
John 4:21	81	John 13:23	47	Rom 1:16	101
John 4:22	92	John 13:26	95	Rom 1:17	51

Printed in Great Britain
by Amazon